National Cinema and Beyond

STUDIES IN IRISH FILM SERIES

1 *National Cinema and Beyond*
Kevin Rockett, Trinity College, Dublin
& John Hill, University of Ulster, editors

NATIONAL CINEMA AND BEYOND

Studies in Irish Film 1

Kevin Rockett & John Hill
EDITORS

FOUR COURTS PRESS

Set in 10.5 on 12.5 Ehrhardt for
FOUR COURTS PRESS LTD
7 Malpas Street, Dublin 8, Ireland
e-mail: info@four-courts-press.ie
http://www.four-courts-press.ie
and in North America by
FOUR COURTS PRESS
c/o ISBS, 920 N.E. 58th Street, Suite 300, Portland, OR 97213.

ISBN 1–85182–873–7 hbk
ISBN 1–85182–874–5 pbk

Printed in England by
Antony Rowe Ltd, Chippenham, Wilts.

Contents

Acknowledgments

Special thanks to the Higher Education Authority North South Programme for Collaborative Research for providing financial assistance for this publication. Thanks also to Emer Rockett, who initially identified the need for the Postgraduate Film Research Seminar; to Robert Porter at the University of Ulster for assistance with the preparation of the manuscript; to Carol Kyle and Sally Quinn at the University of Ulster for secretarial support; to Janet McCabe and Paula Quigley at Trinity College, Dublin and Martin McLoone and Paul Willemen at the University of Ulster for chairing sessions at the Seminar; the School of Drama, Trinity College, Dublin; the Faculty of Arts (Letters), TCD; the Visiting Professors Fund, TCD; Institute of International Integration Studies, TCD; and the Vice-Chancellor's Research Fund, UUC.

Introduction

JOHN HILL & KEVIN ROCKETT

Film Studies, more particularly Media Studies, emerged as a degree subject in the late 1970s at the University of Ulster at Coleraine, and in the Republic of Ireland in the early 1980s at Dublin City University (though colleges such as the National College of Art and Design, Dublin offered film studies courses from the late 1970s). Film Studies as a specialist activity was not established until 1992 when University College Dublin introduced an MA in Film Studies, while Dublin City University introduced an MA in Film and Television Studies. In 2003, Trinity College Dublin established the first undergraduate degree programme in Film Studies in the Republic of Ireland. Additionally, many of the colleges which have developed as Institutes of Technology, most especially the National Film School at Dun Laoghaire Institute of Art, Design and Technology, offer specialist undergraduate film-making degree courses, though digital video production courses are more common in such colleges. The National Film School has also introduced an MA in Scriptwriting as has the National University of Ireland, Galway, which, like University College, Cork, also offers inter-departmental film courses. Queen's University, Belfast, has also developed an undergraduate film studies course in recent years. Other institutions where the academic and practical are offered include Dublin Institute of Technology and Colaiste Dulaigh, Dublin, though there are many other venues for training. This healthy institutional environment for both the academic study of cinema and for the training of film-makers and industry technicians would appear to suggest that film education and training in Ireland is in good shape. This is not entirely the case, however, particularly in relation to published research.

Until the 1980s, film scholarship focusing on the history of Irish cinema as well as on the representation of the Irish in film was virtually non-existent. Certainly, there had been work by a few amateur historians/archivists and collectors of cinema memorabilia but little attempt had been made to chronicle systematically Irish film history or analyse critically film representations of the Irish. It was this gap that *Cinema and Ireland* (London, 1987), written by these two authors and Luke Gibbons, partly sought to fill. This has encouraged further work on Irish cinema and recent studies such as Martin McLoone's *Irish Film: The Emergence of a Contemporary Cinema* (London, 2000) and Lance Pettitt's *Screening Ireland* (Manchester, 2000) have successfully built upon the concerns of the earlier book and expanded its focus. A number of other publications, such as Cork University Press' 'Ireland into Film' series, have also encouraged critical discussions of Irish films (albeit within the confines of a traditional focus on adaptations of literary and dramatic works). More popular writing on film, often industry-related, has been sustained by *Film Ireland* and the now-defunct *Film West*. However, it is only recently that a more academic journal, the annual *Film and Film Culture* (published by Waterford Institute of Technology) has appeared. However, while the academic study of Irish cinema has clearly grown, and produced work of some distinction, the study of Irish film remains under-developed by comparison with other European cinemas and still lacks a solid infrastructure of original research.

This is partly to do with the fragile position occupied by postgraduate research study into Irish film. While there has been a growth of undergraduate and Master's courses in film and other media within Ireland, this has not been matched by a similar growth of activity at doctoral level. The first PhD on Irish cinema was awarded as recently as 1989 and since then there have been relatively few completed research degrees in this area. The reasons for this are complex and include general factors such as the attraction of the Irish jobs market in the 1990s and the comparatively poor rewards of a career in academia. However, it also has to do with the specific academic standing of Film Studies in Ireland and the profile of research into Irish film, in comparison with other areas of Irish culture (especially drama and literature).

It was in response to these concerns that the Irish Postgraduate Film Research Seminar was conceived. The ambition was to provide a supportive environment for postgraduate researchers in film to come together to exchange ideas and discuss methodological issues. In this way, it was also hoped that the event would assist the training and career advancement of young film scholars and help raise the profile of Irish Film Studies more generally. The Seminar held its inaugural event at Trinity College Dublin on 10–11 April 2003. Invitations were issued to current and recent postgraduates in Ireland and elsewhere (if working on an Irish topic). In all, nineteen papers by students from Ireland, North and South, Scotland, France, Italy, and the USA were presented. Revised and edited versions of twelve of these are published here. (Two papers from research students at the University of Ulster are not included as they have already been accepted by academic journals.) We also include Tom Gunning's opening address to the conference. The event is planned to alternate between Trinity College and the University of Ulster at Coleraine, and the second conference was held in April 2004 at the Portrush campus, the proceedings of which will be published in 2005.

The Irish Postgraduate Film Research Seminar, as well as postgraduate film studies in Ireland more generally, received an important boost when Film Studies at the School of Drama, Trinity College and the School of Media and Performing Arts, University of Ulster, Coleraine (our host departments) were awarded substantial support in 2003 by the Higher Education Authority under its North South Programme for Collaborative Research. The HEA is not only providing resources during 2003–6 for the continuation of the Seminar but also the publication of its proceedings and the holding of specialist film methodology workshops. It is also funding three full-time postgraduate film research students – two of whom are based at Trinity College, and one at Ulster. This award has provided a timely impetus to postgraduate Film Studies at both institutions and, more generally, demonstrated a commitment at a national level to the discipline within Ireland.

HISTORY

In supporting Irish postgraduate research, it has been an ambition of the Seminar to support and encourage original historical research and new approaches to the study and analysis of Irish film. The work that is presented here may be seen to fall into these categories. Much of it involves research on Irish film history while other work involves the investigation of Irish – and other national – films through novel critical perspectives. The first section is devoted to essays on Irish film history. It is appropriate that the distinguished film scholar Tom Gunning leads off this section. He has pioneered an approach to film history that has involved the critical rescue of neglected film traditions and the re-conceptualization of their significance.

In 'Waking and faking: Ireland and cinema astray', Gunning continues his argument that early cinema began not with a desire to tell stories, nor with a pedagogic or political purpose, but rather with a 'poetics', or 'vocabulary of illusions and transformations'. He also emphasizes how the history of cinema, including the histories of national cinemas, must be understood in terms of their international scope and function. This, he argues, is particularly true of Irish cinema which he identifies as a 'diasporic cinema' that 'spread around the world with Irish immigration, enriching especially the cinema industries of Great Britain and Hollywood'. In a suggestive – and possibly provocative – conclusion, he suggests how the 'trickery' of early cinema and the Irish diasporic imagination may be seen to coalesce in Hollis Frampton's experimental film *Murphy's Wake*.

Although Gunning identifies how a 'cinema of attractions' historically preceded forms of narrative fiction and documentary in film it is, as he suggests, these forms that have played a key role in sustaining national cinemas, and the national imaginaries manifest through them. A central concern of Irish film history has therefore been the exploration of the ways in which Irish drama and documentary have historically sustained, and later challenged, myths of Irish nationhood. A number of articles pursue this theme across different periods. In 'Filming the story of Ireland: the yoking together of historical drama and contemporary newsreel in silent Irish films', Denis Condon shows how films such as *Ireland a Nation* (1914–20) and *In the Days of St Patrick/Aimsir Padraig* (1920) contributed to the formation of an Irish national imaginary at a critical stage of the struggle for national liberation. By employing a composite aesthetic, combining historical drama and contemporary newsreel, Condon suggests how these films fashioned images of the nation that corresponded to popular forms of nationalism during this period.

In 'The great escape?: *The Islandman* (1938)', Emilie Pine focuses on a critically neglected film of the 1930s and explores how it addresses contemporary ideological anxieties. In particular, she examines the 'tension between tradition and modernity' to be found in the film as well as Irish culture more generally. Despite the film's apparent indebtedness to nationalist myths of the west of Ireland, Pine argues that the film should not be read as advocating a retreat from modernity but rather a reconciliation of the traditional and the modern, the rural and the urban.

A similar tension between tradition and modernity is also identified by Barry Monahan in his essay on the collaboration between Emmet Dalton, the Abbey Theatre and Ardmore Studios. Based on original research into the written records, Monahan identifies both the interpersonal and broader ideological conflicts responsible for the demise of this project. Thus while Monahan reveals the internal problems confronted by those involved, he also argues that the project faltered due to the unresolved tension between cultural liberalism and conservative nationalism characteristic of the late 1950s and early 1960s.

In the final essay in this section, 'From no wave to national cinema: the cultural landscape of Vivienne Dick's early films (1978–85)', Maeve Connolly challenges the pre-eminence given to feature-length drama and documentary in histories of national cinema, and of Irish cinema in particular. By focusing on the work of the avant-garde film-maker Vivienne Dick, she seeks to reinstate the importance of an understanding of apparently 'marginal' cinemas for an understanding of 'national' cinema histories and the analysis of the cinema's relationship to national identity. Echoing Gunning's interest in an 'Irish diasporic cinema', she traces the trajectory of Dick's work from her involvement in the New York 'no wave' through to her more recent film work in Ireland. For Connolly, Dick's work exists on the 'margins' of both 'avant-garde practice' and 'national cinema', exemplifying a postmodern film practice in which the local and the international, the rural and the urban, the traditional and the modern may be seen to intersect.

FORM AND REPRESENTATION

The second section of the book focuses on more recent films and the formal and representational issues to which these give rise. A number of the essays focus on the 'Troubles' in Northern Ireland and the films that have emerged in the wake of the ceasefires of 1994. Whereas earlier work on 'Troubles' movies has analyzed the ways in which representations of the conflicts in the North have conformed to particular dramatic and ideological patterns, these essays explore the ways in which more recent films have sought to address the traumas of the past and contribute to the 'winning of the peace'. Joseph Moser's essay 'Fighting within the rules: masculinity in the films of Jim Sheridan' explores this theme through a discussion of the representation of masculinity in *The Field* (1990), *In the Name of the Father* (1993) and *The Boxer* (1997). Whereas *The Field* is seen to demonstrate the tragic consequences of a destructive and violent masculinity, Moser argues that *In the Name of the Father* and *The Boxer* provide alternative models of masculinity, in which the apparently weak, and peaceful, are revealed to be the genuinely strong.

In her essay 'Imagining the future: post-Troubles comic fiction', Dervila Layden looks to comedy as the means through which the traumas of the past may be confronted and overcome. Taking *Eureka Street* (1999) and *Wild about Harry* (2000) as her examples, Layden suggests how comedy permits the creation of a utopian space in which old political ideologies are suspended and new forms of sociality become possible. The issue of trauma, and the memory of it, is also central to Margaret O'Neill's discussion of the cinematic representation of one of the most traumatic events in the history of the 'Troubles': 'Bloody Sunday'. Taking Paul Greengrass's *Bloody Sunday* (2002) as her primary focus, O'Neill investigates the links between memory, trauma and narrativization, suggesting how the film may be read as a struggle between two 'ways of knowing': the organised order represented by maps and the traumatic 'crying out' of popular memory.

Although not concerned with the North, Ellen Sweeney's essay on Neil Jordan's *The Butcher Boy* (1997) focuses on similar issues. Like O'Neill, Sweeney argues that the film not only deals with the memory of trauma – in this case the maltreatment and sexual abuse of children in the Irish industrial school system – but that the traces of trauma are themselves embodied in the film's formal strategies and the ways in which the boundaries between the 'inside' and the 'outside' are dissolved. *The Butcher Boy* also figures in Sarah Neely's discussion of the voice-over in recent Irish and Scottish films, one of a number of essays to focus on formal issues. In her essay on *Disco Pigs* (1999) and *Accelerator* (2001), Díog O'Connell employs the narratological method of David Bordwell and Edward Branigan to analyse the differences in approach to character in the two films. In this context, O'Connell argues for a less parochial Irish cinema in favour of one capable of addressing more universal concerns. In 'The musicality of film rhythm', Danijela Kulezic-Wilson argues for the value of the concept of 'rhythm' in understanding the aesthetics of film. Film rhythm (and its 'musicality'), she argues, should be understood in visual as well as aural terms. Using examples from Darren Aronofsky's *Requiem for a Dream* (2000) and Andrei Tarkovsky's *Mirror* (1974), she indicates how the aesthetics of the shot and the cut may in turn be linked to concepts of external and internal rhythm. Kulezic-Wilson is one of a number of researchers located in Ireland working on film topics that are not themselves specifically related to Ireland. This was also so of some other papers presented at the original conference which do not appear in this volume. It is, of course, important for Irish film scholarship that it is not confined to Irish topics just as Irish Film Studies benefits from the researches of those outside of Ireland. Two of the papers, in this regard, grew out of work on Scottish cinema and represent a growth of interest in comparative studies, particularly in the context of the 'Celtic fringe'.

In her essay 'Cultural ventriloquism: the voice-over in film adaptations of contemporary Irish and Scottish literature', Sarah Neely examines the 'prevalent use of the voice-over in Irish and Scottish cinema', arguing that it is not simply the product of literary adaptation but represents a means whereby 'marginalized cultures' may 'subvert the dominant forms of Hollywood'. In his essay, 'Convents or cowboys? Millennial Scottish and Irish film industries and imaginaries in *The Magdalene Sisters*', Jonathan Murray also explores parallels between Scottish and Irish cinema, taking as his focus the Irish-Scottish hybrid *The Magdalene Sisters* (2001). He explicitly addresses an issue running through many of the contributions: the role of national cinema in an era of growing globalization. Murray is sceptical of discourses which seek to defend the 'purity' of national film cultures against external Hollywood influence, or simplistically counterpose European 'art' to Hollywood 'mart' cinema. Rather, he suggests the value of a critical dialogue between Scottish and Irish films and Hollywood, a process which he sees exemplified in the way in which *The Magdalene Sisters* both works with and against Hollywood genre conventions.

CONCLUSION

Although representing work in progress, the papers presented here successfully indicate some of the directions new research on Irish cinema is taking. Historical research continues to be of critical importance, filling the gaps of earlier work and charting the connections between film and other aspects of social life. Clearly, however, there is scope for more work of this kind. There is still, for example, relatively little work done on patterns of cinema-going in Ireland (particularly outside of Dublin) and the reception of both Irish and non-Irish films within Ireland. The history of cinema exhibition and distribution also remains to be written.

Understandably, given the relative ease and low cost of textual analysis, much recent research focuses on contemporary films. Linked to a history of debates concerning the representation of the Irish on screen, this work adds to our understanding of ways in which 'Irishness' continues to function as a key signifier within contemporary cinema. While much of this work inevitably deals with issues of 'national identity', there has also been an increased growth of work on other forms of cultural identification (related to gender, sexuality, ethnicity and region) within Ireland. In this way, the identification of new kinds of questions about Irish cinema has helped to open up new ways of conceptualizing and researching the formal and representational strategies employed by Irish films. At its worst this can simply involve the wheeling out of 'high theory' within a local context; at its best, however, it can involve a genuine dialogue between general theory and local experience which benefits both. As the work of the Irish Postgraduate Film Research Seminar proceeds, it is hoped that it will contribute to the support and development of both new forms of empirical enquiry into the history of Irish cinema as well as theoretically-informed critical reflections upon this history and the films which it has produced.

Part 1: Film History

Waking and faking: Ireland and cinema astray

TOM GUNNING

I appear before you as that living breathing cliché, an Irish-American, returning to the place of his ancestors, with all the tiresome romanticism that position entails (and which I am afraid forms a part of my personality). I come at a time when I feel somewhat uncomfortable with the image my country is now projecting to the world. But I also come to you as a somewhat less frequent visitor: a film scholar who wants to talk about my profession and my field, because in many ways my true home is the cinema and the cinema always begins as an international form.

This is perhaps an untimely reflection in a period in which film studies, particularly in an academic context, seems partly fuelled by the desire on the part of area studies programmes (whether the traditional European languages and culture programmes of, or programmes in Asian and Third World cultures) have discovered cinema as both a key part of national culture and a way of attracting students to courses. It might also seem untimely to proclaim cinema's international nature in a country that has recently fostered a surprisingly powerful national cinema with a strong sense of national identity. But here the friction is more apparent than real. It is widely recognized that the success of a national cinema like Ireland will partly be measured by its success on the international market.

But there are other considerations in the history of cinema than academic programmes or commercial success – at least I hope there are. The cinema I study (and in which I move and breathe and have my being) is not simply what everyone thinks of as the movies: Hollywood, the international circuit of stars, project and glamour. Although I love that aspect of cinema too, I want to talk about alternative traditions of cinema that I feel have relevance to Irish academic institutions beginning to recognize officially the field of cinema studies. I want us to explore the full field of cinema, including the margins of that field which I find often to be as rich and revealing as its more familiar centre.

I know an Irish cinema exists (especially in the last decade), with peaks and furrows in production, with films that have garnered awards and displayed and trained extremely talented technicians and artists. This cinema has always had to struggle in a global climate stacked against the productions of countries with relatively small populations and with languages with a less than global reach. But to me Irish cinema has always also been a diasporic cinema, one that spread around the world with Irish immigration, enriching especially the cinema industries of Great Britain and Hollywood, its principal Goliath-like opponents. But it is not simply the work of hyphenated Irish filmmakers I want to consider tonight. Instead, I want to think about the way that cinema, which began as a marginal form of expression, first attended by a motley crew of working-class patrons who embraced it as somehow something different from official culture, something rough and lively like themselves, maintains a particular relation to the marginal figures of tricksters and travellers, roamers and illusionists.

In my own work as a film historian, with an emphasis I will admit is partly polemic, I have maintained that cinema did not begin with the desire to tell stories, least of all the tales of authority and nationhood that eventually characterized it. Rather, like literature, one could claim that cinema began with a poetics, with a vocabulary of illusions and transformation. If cinema cannot truly claim to begin in the magical spells of bards and prophets, nonetheless it began as a sort of magic trick, and its earliest films conjured astonishment, rather than representing anything we could assign simply to either documentary (with its pedagogical or political purposes) or narrative fiction (with its patterns of conflict and resolution and ideological containment).

It has often been stated that cinema came from two original traditions, often identified with early French filmmakers. Lumière on the one hand, supposedly endowed the cinema with a tradition of realism, while Méliès, on the other, provided cinema with an origin in magic. But, in fact, I see these two original traditions as sharing a similar fascination with the wonders of the moving image, a wonder of display quite different from the narrative cinema that gradually emerged.

In American novelist Frank Norris' 1897 *McTeague* there is a description which inspired me years ago to realize that what may appear as realism to some audiences may also seem to be a manufactured trick, an illusion, especially on first viewing. *McTeague*, of course, later formed the basis of one the narrative masterpieces of American cinema, Erich von Stroheim's 1923 *Greed* (like many of the most searing treatments of American society, the work of an immigrant). But the original novel took place in 1897 when cinema was still a novelty. In this passage Trina and Mac have gone with Trina's mother to the vaudeville theatre to celebrate their engagement. There they see the latest wonder, Edison's projecting kinetoscope, showing as the description makes clear a Lumière-like film, an actuality of urban street-life:

> The kinetoscope fairly took their breaths away.
> 'What will they do next?' observed Trina in amazement. 'Ain't that wonderful Mac?'
> McTeague was awestruck.

'Look at that horse move his head', he cried excitedly, quite carried away. 'Look at the cable car coming – and the man going across the street. See, here comes a truck. Well, I never in all my life! What would Marcus say to this?'

'It's all a drick!' exclaimed Mrs Sieppe with sudden conviction. 'I ain't no fool; dot's nothing but a drick.'

'Well, of course Mama', exclaimed Trina; 'it's –

But Mrs Sieppe put her head in the air. 'I'm too old to be fooled.' She persisted 'It's a drick. Nothing more could be got out of her than this.'[1]

The novel here presciently captures the audience that would embrace cinema in the USA a few years after the novel was written, the immigrant family. The contrast here between Mrs Sieppe's old world, apparently foolish, incomprehension and suspicion, with a younger generation's embrace of the technological novelty with relative sophistication, may seem to predict the Americanization of a generation of immigrants, a process supposedly achieved at least in part through their consumption of the cinema. But we might wonder if Mrs Sieppe's seeing through the cinema, her suspicion that someone might be making a fool of her with this illusion, is entirely silly.

It is more than a simple coincidence that the emergence of the cinema at the end of the nineteenth century intersects with the launching of the Irish Renaissance. The turn of the last century was in many ways not simply a full throttle charge into modernity, but also a sort of recoil, as artists throughout Europe began to temper the enthusiasm for the new and the mechanical with a seeking out of the archaic and the organic. The worldwide turn to folklore and the recording of passing ways of life constitutes more than an anti-modern nostalgia, a reactionary longing for simpler systems. Rather, like the Romantics of the previous turn of the century, artists in each country believed that a modern world somehow might re-awaken the ancient stirrings of myth, bringing the supernatural back to the conscious attention of humanity. This dialectic of the ancient and the modern characterizes both the Irish Renaissance and, in a somewhat more mediated manner, the first decade and reception of cinema.

Thus I would claim that the rediscovery of the fairy faith in Celtic countries had more than antiquarian interest and is oddly not unrelated to the reappearance of fairies, magicians and demons on the movie screens of early cinema. Arthur Conan Doyle, astonished by what he thought was photographic proof of the return of the fairies, and William Butler Yeats, enraptured by the tales of old women, both believed these traces of the old ones contained an energy useful for national revival. However, the cinematic fairies that scam-

1 Frank Norris, *McTeague: a story of San Francisco*, New York: New American Library, 1964: 85–6.

pered about the screen in this era showed no specific national heritage, even if their most genial creators, Georges Méliès and the directors at the Pathé Company, endowed their versions with a decidedly Gallic cast. As Michael Raine has claimed, cinema was international before it was national, just as I have claimed it was poetic and fanciful before it was coherent and narrative.

The image I will somewhat arbitrarily propose for an Irish cinema has less to do with the invocation of the 'troubles' or national oppression, as powerful as those images have been for both Irish and diasporic Irish cinema, and enduringly important for sorting out Ireland's unique role in an era of continuing imperialism. Uncertain as I currently am of my own nation's adventures into narratives of liberation and actions of destruction in other people's countries, I prefer now to invoke a different energy (without denying the need for awakening tomorrow to the grim realities of our current global disasters). Therefore my personal image for a cinema that cannot be chained to discourses of authority invokes a figure from traditional Irish literature who was resurrected in the era of cultural rediscovery that preceded (and also nourished) rebellion: Mad Sweeney, the warrior and poet cursed by a Christian cleric to wander about the land naked, living in the tree-tops, subsisting on water cress, growing feathers like a bird and spouting verses that mingle beauty with paranoia. *Buile Suibhne*, which I know both in Seamus Heaney's beautiful 1984 translation and in Flann O'Brien's retelling in the novel *At Swim-Two-Birds* (1939), was first translated and published in 1913, the year coincidentally in which the first feature films were appearing in many countries.

After being cursed by St Ronan in the midst of the battle of Moira, Sweeney, in Heaney's version, 'was possessed by a dark rending energy'.

> His brain convulsed
> His mind split open.
> Vertigo, hysteria, lurchings
> And launchings came over him,
> He staggered and flapped desperately,
> He was revolted by the thought of known places
> And dreamed strange migrations.

Sweeney's madness, for which Heaney has chosen words that seem intensely modern, involves not only a desire for migration which seems to predict the nomadic fate of much of the Irish population (impelled in their case, as in Sweeney's, by forces beyond their control, by unbearable hardship and oppression), but also recalls the rather universal modern affliction of never being able to stay still which the cinema seemed fashioned to portray and service, the flickering and often jiggling image dancing on the screen.

It was perhaps the cultures existing on the margins, the metropolises in the non-dominant countries, which saw most clearly, and experienced most intensely, the coming of modern urbanization and electrification. Semi-colonial countries observed this new culture of speed and danger with a certain distance and reserve. And cinema provided them with a new art form, mechanical and electrical, that seemed designed to both portray and exemplify the new culture of modernity. Take, for example, this column written by the journalist known as Joao do Rio in Brazil in 1909, entitled 'Hurry Up!:'

> No one takes one's time to do things any more. All the great discoveries of the last twenty years have been designed to speed up daily life. The great symbols of our era, the automobile, our delight, and the phonograph, our torment, collapse distances and preserve voices just to avoid wasting time. In the future, if our planet does not hurry to its finish and end up carried off on the tail of a comet, the man of our era, I declare in a hurry, will be classified as the '*homo cinematographicus*'.
>
> Our modern lives are nothing but a delirious succession of cinematographic images. In a program lasting less than half an hour we present a terrifying and complex spectacle under the all-inclusive title: 'Hurry up!'

Sweeney with his grand leaps all over Ireland, collapsing distances as he flees in fear from human presence, seems a prescient form of this *homo cinematicus*. But like the phonograph and the automobile, the cinema provided speeded-up bits of sensational pleasure, compressing stories into less than half an hour, delivering doses of visual pleasures in a hurry. Within this modern hurly burly, the emerging technological art of the cinema, initially tucked away into peep shows and tiny electric theatres, seemed to give voice to both the promises and anxieties of modernity, without simply repeating the official narratives of progress and dominion. Besides expressing the hectic rush to get things done, the new cinema whispered in hushed back-alley tones of a new availability of pleasures, of sights usually forbidden, but now placed within the reach of the hand that cranked the Mutoscope and the eye glued to its eyepiece. As Joyce had Leopold Bloom muse in the Nausicaa chapter of *Ulysses:*

> Ah yes. Mutoscope pictures in Capel street: for men only. Peeping Tom. Willy's Hat and what the girls did with it. Do they snapshot those girls or is it all a fake?

Both *Peeping Tom* and *Willie's Hat* are titles of actual early films, the first a Pathé film from 1906 and the second a Mutoscope reel by the Biograph company from 1904. What the girls do to Willie's hat is rather anodyne, using it for an exercise of high kicking, which does nonetheless reveal a fair amount of female leg, not to mention demonstrating the girls athletic prowess and lack of respect for Willie. (The same treatment is given as well to the eponymous *The*

Minister's Hat, another Biograph Mutoscope reel, with the hat's reputed ownership giving the disrespectful kick a certain additional spice.) These brief flickering images of erotic promise and physical release exemplify Do Rios' accelerated modern temporality, and these brief, even abbreviated, pleasures captured the mixture of excitement and anxiety that beset the *homo cinematicus*.

But what about Joyce's or Bloom's suspicion, apparently shared by Norris's Mrs Sieppe, that all of this moving imagery might be a fake, nothing but a trick? Joyce seems to tackle the basic trick of the cinema in Bloom's question: 'do they snapshot those girls?' Another innovation of the modern era, appearing in the 1880s, the snapshot, the instantaneous photograph that could freeze action in full flight, producing seemingly absurd images of leapers suspended in mid-jump and mid-air, or naughty ladies in mid-kick, would seem to be the exact opposite of a motion picture in which jumps and kicks proceed from start to finish in full arc. But in fact the snapshot underlies the moving image, and technically formed its necessary antecedent.

Consider the reputed inventors of the motion picture as we known it, the fathers of the cinematograph, the Lumière Freres. The Lumière company began under Papa Lumière as a photographic supply company supplying the new ready-to-use photographic dry plates which replaced the complicated wet collodion plate process in the 1880s and opened photography to a new range of amateurs by simplifying the procedure, while simultaneously radically shortening the exposure time needed to make a photographic image. Thus amateurs using the Lumière plates etiquette bleu could photograph their friends and family, freezing their actions, producing an image both fascinating and more than slightly ridiculous, occasionally a bit erotic.[2]

Snapshots. 'Were they real or were they faked?' people asked. And the answer was not so clear, since for the first time photographs obviously departed from the familiarity of human sight. Snapshots did not fake reality in the way that, say, spirit photographs had, using the technique of superimposition to fake an image. The snapshot was simply the result of the photographic process, only now speeded up so that it was literally quicker than the eye, as well as quicker than the human body. But if they showed something no one could see, was it real? What now were the bases on which the real was to be judged? While the testimony of instruments revealing visual evidence beyond the human senses had gradually been accepted in science beginning in the seventeenth century,[3] these snapshots did not reveal wiggling amoebas or the rings of Saturn, but bits of everyday life, the neighborhood girls kicking the gong

2 For a discussion of the Lumières background in instantaneous photography, see Tom Gunning, 'New thresholds of vision: instantaneous photography and the early cinema of Lumière', in Terry Smith (ed.), *Impossible presence: surface and screen in the photogénie era*, Sidney: Power Publications, 200: 71–100. 3 See Catherine Wilson, *The invisible world: an early modern philosophy and the invention of the microscope*, Princeton: Princeton University Press, 1995.

around. Modern life not only speeded up time, it also froze it, seemed to abolish it, and placed it on display.

But the miracle of suspended motion was not enough for the Lumière brothers. Following the lead of scientists like Etienne-Jules Marey using instantaneous photography to study the body in motion, and like their American competitor, Thomas Edison, the Lumières undertook to capture motion on the fly, create what had until then sounded like an inherent contradiction: 'motion pictures'. But how could snapshots be made to move? How could frozen images be endowed with the appearance of life, animated?

The actual physiological and psychological process of bringing pictures to life, of motion pictures, is based upon a visual illusion. Described by various perceptual and physiological models, 'the persistence of vision', or the 'Phi phenomenon', this perceptual defect sees motion where there isn't any. Lumière's invention, the Cinématographe, only took a succession of still images, in effect a long string of snapshots. However, they were photographed and then projected at such a speed that the human sensorium perceives them as moving. Based on the phenomenon exploited in children's toys since the eighteenth century, Marey, Edison and the Lumières' devices simply added instantaneous photography to such visual toys in order to produce the movies.

As Ingmar Bergman has confessed, the filmmaker exploits a defect of human vision: a capacity for seeing motion that isn't 'really' there. And Bergman immediately adds that as a filmmaker he is always an illusionist, a magician, a trickster. Thus cinema, as part of a long history, marks the site where science and magic intersect. Cinema, understood as part of the centuries old 'great art of light and shadow' displays a truly dialectical and perhaps even contradictory relation to the project of scientific enlightenment. As an optical device, cinema and its visual ancestors derive from the new science of optics that fascinated Descartes and other enlightenment figures, including Christian Huygens, the most likely inventor of the magic lantern at the end of the seventeenth century. However, as Barbara Stafford has shown in her study of eighteenth-century visual devices, *Artful Science*, such devices were designed for two rather contrary, yet dialectically related, purposes. The first was scientific and enlightening. By demonstrating the visual logic behind an optical illusion the savant or philosopher could make scientific demonstration triumphant, dissolving a wondrous illusion into its generative and explicable logic. However, in the hands of a mountebank, these illusions might create nothing but wonder, or, worse yet, might engender superstitious beliefs, especially when presented before a gullible audience.[4]

To a nineteenth-century audience (including Mrs Sieppe, perhaps), cinema appeared within a tradition of visual magic that had become part of popular

4 Barbara Maria Stafford, *Artful science: enlightenment entertainment and the eclipse of visual education*, Cambridge: MIT Press, 1994: 29–103.

entertainment at least since the enlightenment, reaching a technological climax at the end of the nineteenth century.[5] Rarely claiming supernatural powers nineteenth-century magicians more frequently operated within a realm of demystification. Such modern magicians claimed no extra-human aid, yet fervently concealed the secrets behind their illusions. Provoking curiosity and astonishment, they produced illusions that entertained by denying supernatural revelation or miracles, but also avoiding a fully explicated demonstration of their mysterious processes. The pleasure such illusions offered lay in making the audience attend to their own sensuous experience, and asking them to doubt their very eyes, even as they experienced an uncanny sort of seeing.

But this offering of pure illusion sharply contrasts with the use of visual illusion within discourses of authority rather than entertainment. For in investigating the use of tricks and visual illusions in the West we find that tricks are almost always inducted into an ideological context, of either scientific instruction or religious allegory. The scientific tradition sought to reveal the trick or illusion as nothing other than illusion, that is, as not revealing any supernatural powers, while explaining what really caused the apparent miracle. Thus the true target of demystification would be a possible deception of a viewer about true cause and effect. Magic tricks operated like commodity capitalism though an occluding of labour, concealing the actual effective gesture and seeming to produce things 'by magic'. Tricks that undo themselves are thus essential to an enlightenment system that seeks to separate visual illusion from scientific certainty.

The enlightenment interest in 'philosophical toys', those visual devices that demonstrated illusions and the manner in which they were caused (including the various motion devices such as the thaumatrope or phenakistoscope to which the origins of the cinema are frequently traced) were designed, as Barbara Stafford has shown, primarily for the scientific education of the elite young.[6] Science, while rendered entertaining, nonetheless carried the essential lesson that these illusions were explainable. Thus they also inoculated the young against the spectacles of superstition that the *philosophes* associated especially with the Catholic Church.

But, in fact, optical devices had also been used by the Jesuits during the Counter-Reformation as visual allegories, not simply to convince the ignorant of the powers of God and his Church, but to reveal to the learned the conditional nature of knowledge and perception in the fallen world of creation. Thus an anamorphic landscape painting, which could appear either as a craggy mountain or as the face of an old man, bore the caption: 'Your attempts to view me are vain/ If you perceive me, you will not see me anymore.'[7] Sim-

5 See, Erik Barnouw, *The magician and the cinema*, New York: Oxford University Press, 1981. Also see Matthew Paul Solomon, 'Stage magic and the silent cinema: Méliès, Houdini, Browning', unpublished PhD thesis, UCLA, 2001. 6 Stafford, *Artful science*, 58–89. 7 Barbara Maria

ilarly, the extraordinary devices and illusions manufactured by Jesuit theologian Athanasius Kircher through 'Natural Magic' served less to demonstrate scientific principles than to reveal the wondrous and mysterious nature of God's creation.[8] Such visual demonstrations and illusions called perception and knowledge into question. Thus both rational demystifying demonstration and religiously mystic enigmas used optical illusions as means less to deceive the viewer than to cause her to reflect on the limited and fragile nature of human perception. Science or faith could, however, dispel these uncertainties.

We could therefore specify three different receptions, practices and understandings surrounding visual illusions in the modern era. The first tradition, scientific and enlightened, would explain, for instance, the superimposed images of a thaumatrope as illustrating the physiological optics of the eye. The confusion of the images does not exist in reality, but is merely the product of persistence of vision. Thus the illusion itself is dissolved in favour of its explanatory function about the nature of perception. On the other hand, within a tradition dedicated to faith and authority, visual illusion could demonstrate not so much the working of perception as its inherent fallibility, the untrustworthy nature of human senses and consciousness in need of a transcendent faith, beyond what can be seen or even explained, to make sense of the world. But our third option, which we might term the option of entertainment and astonishment, that of the magician-illusionist, invokes neither faith nor science, but wonder. The modern magician would announce that the illusion was not dependent on supernatural forces, and could be explained in terms of natural forces. However, unlike the enlightenment pedagogue, the magician withholds the explanation, delivers no debunking demonstration. Instead, he or she leaves the spectator suspended in their uncertainty, doubting what they have just seen, yet unable to deny or thoroughly explain it away. In this suspense dwells the entertaining pleasure of uncertainty and ambiguity.

Optical illusions form a complex figure, whose power may not primarily lie in the ability to fool someone into taking them for 'reality'. Rather they confound habitual attitudes towards perception, indeed sowing doubts about the nature of reality. These doubts could play a pedagogic role in either rational systems (perception is not to be trusted, but must be buttressed by knowledge of scientific causes and the demonstration for which the scientific method calls) or transcendent systems of belief (mere perception is fallible and only faith in transcendence can make sense of creation). But outside of their appropriation by larger pedagogical systems, such illusions primarily spawn wonder, astonishment and curiosity. Rather than buttressing the power of vision, they

Stafford and Frances Terpak, *Devices of wonder: from the world in a box to images on screen*, Los Angeles: Getty Research Institute, 2000: 250–1. 8 On Kircher and the purposes of natural magic see, Thomas L. Hankins and Robert J. Silverman, *Instruments and the imagination*, Princeton: Princeton University Press, 1995: 32–6.

may call it into question, the essential claim of the conjurer being that 'the hand is quicker than the eye'. Thus the magician, at least since the age of enlightenment, avoids claims of supernatural power, but also refuses to reveal the basis of his trick. The magician's vow (admittedly often violated, but what vows are not?) to never reveal the trick does more than preserve a guild and professional secret. It maintains an attitude of uncertainty and wonder on the spectator's part who must always wrestle with what she saw and what she thinks she saw, with both the uncertainty and the power of perception.

Traditionally, the conjurer and the juggler have been identified, and both have been equally condemned as untrustworthy and potentially evil. Before the nineteenth century, legal, religious and even philosophic institutions condemned the juggler as passionately as the conjurer; sleight of hand apparently generated as much anxiety as (false?) claims of supernatural power. As Stafford points out, manual facility even in the arts was often viewed with suspicion, seen as a tool of deception.[9] I think that within the suspicion of the cinematic that certain critics and viewers have expressed, we find a similar anxiety about an art of vision that is also, as a mechanical art, quicker than the eye, able to make us see things we know are not there. Linking the cinema with the juggler, I want to examine one venerable magic trick that greatly predates, but I think anticipates, the cinema. Consider the combination of manual dexterity and visual illusion which master magician and historian Ricky Jay terms 'blow books', but which I prefer, for reasons that will be obvious, to call by another of their traditional names 'flick books'.[10] Flick books employed notched pages and carefully arranged visual illustrations that a mountebank could manipulate to make images seem to appear, disappear or transform magically. Reginald Scott's sixteenth-century *The Discoverie of Witchcraft* described flick books this way:

> Ye hab they saie a booke, wherof he would make you think first that every leafe was clean white paper: then by virtue of words he would shew your everie leaf to be painted with birds, then with beasts, then with serpents, then with angels etc. [...]

Scott found it nearly impossible to describe this book, its manipulation and effects, in words, saying, 'Best because you will hardlie conceive hereof by this description, you shall (if you be disposed) see or buie for a small value the like booke', giving an address of a book shop where it could be purchased 'for your further instruction'.[11]

The term 'flick book' proleptically evokes early cinema, the 'flickers' or, in contemporary vernacular, 'flicks'. The derivation of the term bifurcates in

9 Stafford, *Artful science*, 79–85. 10 Ibid., 69–70; Stafford and Terpak, *Devices of wonder*, 252–5. 11 Ibid., 252–3.

an interesting manner. Our conjurer's flick book refers to the deft and rapid movement of the hand, the 'flick of a wrist'. The cinema gained its name through an analogously rapid motion of light, originally describing the behaviour of flames or mirror reflections as 'flickering'. The term thus unites the two aspects of optical trickery, the manual skill of juggling and the rapidity of light itself, accenting light's ability not only to reveal, illuminate and enlighten but to conceal, cast shadows, create illusions. The history of early cinema's imbrication with stage magic appears here again; stage magicians like Felicien Trewey, John Stuart Blackton or Georges Méliès adopted the cinema at the end of the nineteenth century as the latest conjurer device, one more nineteenth-century example of the precision machine replacing the skilled hand.

Thus the power of cinema (or one of them, why must its power be restricted to one?), may lie precisely in its lack of certainty, the confusion it sows, its maintenance of a realm of playful rather than total illusion, an uncanny questioning of perception (did I really see that?) rather than religious revelation or scientific certainty. Cinema's early history, its recurring devices and (if we wanted to extend this discussion beyond the period of early cinema) its genres and special effects, display a recurring fascination with the visually uncertain and uncanny, with flickering illusion.

It would probably be pernicious to associate this love of trickery with a national identity since it is a universal trait. But trickery, clever tactics rather than long-term strategies, do typify countries unable and even unwilling to dominate. I would like to end this lecture with a discussion of an Irish-American filmmaker whom I think has rarely been approached in terms of his ethnic heritage. Hollis Frampton is not really a household name, although some of us consider him one of the greatest filmmakers in the history of the American avant-garde. He worked entirely outside the Hollywood system: his artisanal mode of production, his experimental approach to film form and his highly intellectual and yet also wry concept of what cinema could and should be was totally at odds with the dominant Hollywood cinema. He was, in every sense, a filmmaker who operated on the margins, a photographer and writer, a man equally witty in his use of words and images. His models for cinema came less from other films than from his literary mentors: James Joyce, Ezra Pound and Jorge Borges. A consummate (though non-academic) scholar, a subtle theorist, a witty wordsmith, he was also a trickster, one who made movies out of nothing at all, producing films that redefined the nature of cinema by enlarging the margins of its possibility.

Some of Frampton's films are intellectual exercises, such as *Poetic Justice*, which consists entirely of shots of the pages of a film script that describes the image that might fill the screen if it were filmed. Other films invite the viewer to join the filmmaker in a succession of games, such as *Zorns Lemma*, a seemingly endless cycle of words and images based on the Roman alphabet, or *Nostalgia* a film autobiography in which word and image are out of sync resulting in an explosive punch-line of an ending. His *magnum opus*, a film based on Magellan's voyage around the world, which was supposed to be shown every night in a cycle of 360 days, was never finished, but he did complete a number of its pieces.

I think the most glorious of these fragments is the film called *Gloria*. It is also the film in which Frampton reflects on his own heritage, through both his debt to his Irish-American maternal grandmother Elizabeth Catlett Cross and his literary model, Joyce's *Finnegans Wake*. This is a film that hardly seems to be a film at all, in a way similar to the novels of Joyce and Flann O'Brien. But since we are probably less used to films that don't seem like films I will spend a few moments describing this most unlikely and tricky of hyphenated Irish films.

The film consists of a number of elements. First there are two relics from the era of early cinema that book-end the film. Frampton was one of the experimental filmmakers who, inspired partly by Ken Jacobs' *Tom Tom the Piper's Son*, not only rediscovered the delights of early cinema, but also mined the unique collection of paper prints at the Library of Congress and used these forgotten films in his own work. Thus this film includes two early films from this collection, both of them based on the ballads of the Finnegans Wake cycle. The joke of these ballads, and the films based on them, lies in the old saw that an Irishman cannot stay dead, ever at his own wake, if there is drink available. Thus Frampton ends his own film with Biograph's *Murphy's Wake*, a two-shot film from 1903, and begins it with a similar one-shot film whose title I have not yet identified. Both these films stage a parody of the resurrection, as thirsty and apparently dead Irishmen rise from their coffins to partake of the drink offered at their wakes.

When Frampton's film was made its second element was still looking toward a technological future, paralleling Frampton's archaeological research into cinema's origins with his enthusiastic embrace of the computer screen, the element that takes over the greater part of this film. Made during a still fairly primitive stage of computer technology, words alone fill this screen, not images. They seem to simply supply information, a list of nearly random facts (or possibly tall tales) about Frampton's maternal grandmother. Each numbered they appear typed in at the bottom of the screen (the last sign of the author's hand in this new media?), then when complete ascend to the top of the screen and disappear, leaving a blank screen for the next bit of information. These seemingly random facts (for which Frampton proposes two different systems of ordering) in fact offer one of the most carefully written of Frampton's texts, supplying a legendary memoir of his grandmother, as its assembly of little nuggets of information gradually cohere to create a vivid picture of an extraordinary influential and eccentric woman. This is Frampton's computerized memorial, his futuristic wake for his deceased grandmother, which takes on both a ribald sense of humour and a surprisingly affecting sense of mourning, extracting a quality of authentic emotion from the distanced technological form of the computerized words appearing on the screen.

Most of this short film is silent, including the two short silent films and the computerized writing. However, in the penultimate section of the film Frampton adds a sound-track and another visually minimal element, a mottled green screen, which might be that of the computer (which appears with an appropriately black screen at the end as Frampton types out his official *in memoriam*), or might be an element of colour Frampton superimposed over the computer. Over this non-image we hear traditional piping music that seems to correspond exactly with the music that, as penultimate computerized facts tells us, Frampton's grandmother recalled being played at her wedding (which we know from another one of the entries took place in 1909, a few weeks after her thirteenth birthday) in which pipes seemed to quack like ducks. The memory, the previous computer screen told us, was one that she kept 'to the last', the first phrase to invoke her death. The conjunction of this music and this minimal image of a colour field that jiggles just a bit supplies for me an unexpected emotional whollop.

Edison once described his new invention as pictures that danced. 'Dancing pictures' might be a better description than motion pictures. And in this abstract section, without showing us any picture (which is supplied immediately after in the dance which begins *Murphy's Wake*) Frampton and the piping music, remembered for so many decades even after the dancers have died, until, in fact, the rememberer's death, makes a computer screen empty of words or images suddenly dance for us. Do we really see it? Is it all a trick? Today it may seem that cinema as we knew it is dying, that the image projected on the screen is disappearing. But Frampton's film, that celebrates and mourns a woman born in 1896, the year in which cinema first appeared on screens around the world (and in which Mac and Trina went to the movies for the first time), shows us something does survive even after being pronounced dead and already mourned. Like Mad Sweeney it leaps up again, perhaps in a new form and guise, but still possessed of the same anxiety and enthusiasm, the same desire to wander astray, kick up its heels and dance, even in the face of oppression or death.

Filming the story of Ireland: the yoking together of historical drama and contemporary newsreel in silent Irish films[1]

DENIS CONDON

This essay discusses the combination of drama and actuality footage in two feature films produced in Ireland before the foundation of the Irish Free State in 1922. It shows that this mixture of fiction and nonfiction was unusual after feature films achieved international dominance through cinema exhibition in the mid-1910s. The two films on which it focuses are *Ireland a Nation*, first shown in New York in 1914, and *Aimsir Padraig/In the Days of St Patrick* (for brevity, *Aimsir Padraig*), which premièred in Dublin in 1920. It outlines the structural parallels between the films, emphasizing the ways in which selected events in Ireland's past are dramatically re-imagined and shown to have immediate relevance by following them with contemporary newsreel. It argues that the addition of newsreel material to the dramatic portions of these films is not the result of adherence to an outmoded filmic aesthetic but part of a process of conceptualizing the Irish nation that is also present in popular written histories of the late nineteenth and early twentieth centuries.

The earliest filmmaking was dominated internationally by the production of short actuality films but, after 1904, film manufacturing companies made their biggest profits from story films.[2] These short fiction films, however, do not employ strategies that disguise the constructedness of the filmic narrative, such as occurs with the continuity system of classical Hollywood.[3] It was possible, in 1904, for Edwin Porter to cut shots from three earlier Edison actuality films into his *European Rest Cure*, a fictional travel film that also included scenes shot against pasteboard sets of pyramids, Roman ruins, and

1 Research for this essay was made possible by funding from the Irish Research Council for the Humanities and Social Sciences. Thanks are due to those who commented on the paper before and during the seminar: Lisa Kilbride, Frank Condon, Chris Morash, Tom Gunning, and John Hill; and to Kevin Rockett for his extensive comments as the paper was revised for publication. 2 Charles Musser, *The emergence of cinema: the American screen to 1907*, Berkeley, Los Angeles, and London: University of California Press, 1994: 375. 3 See Kristin Thompson, 'The Formulation of the classical style, 1909–28', in David Bordwell, Janet Staiger, and Kristin Thompson, *The Classical Hollywood cinema: film style and mode of production to 1960*, London: Routledge and Kegan Paul, 1985: 175–240. 4 Charles Musser, 'The travel genre in 1903–1904: moving towards fictional narrative,' in Thomas Elsaesser (ed.), *Early cinema: space, frame, narrative*, London: BFI, 1990: 125; Kevin Rockett, *The Irish filmography*, Dublin: Red Mountain

the Blarney Stone.[4] By the middle of the 1910s, however, rapid expansion made multireel feature films exhibited in picture houses the focus of the industry. 'When filmmakers began to relate more complex stories,' argues Eileen Bowser, pointing up the paradoxical importance of artifice to an emerging cinematic realism, '[r]eality began to be demanded for the staged fiction film, [and] anything that dragged the spectator out of that dream was subject to criticism on the grounds of breaking the illusion of reality'.[5] Nonfiction films were, of course, still made in large numbers, but the tendency was to distinguish them clearly from the dramatic feature and to relegate them to supporting positions in the cinema programme.[6]

Films from fundamentally nonnarrative genres generally appeared as part of a programme that was headed by a feature and included a number of other films and/or variety acts. In 1917, when *Ireland a Nation* was first exhibited at Dublin's Rotunda, variety acts did not feature in the city's advertised cinema programmes.[7] Supporting films had displaced them from the well-publicized cinemas, such as the Rotunda, the Grafton, and the Bohemian. The listed attractions at the Rotunda in the week before *Ireland a Nation* opened, for example, were topped by *The Yellow Fang*, 'A New Triangle Drama in 5 Acts, dealing with a Mysterious Chinese Crime, featuring Tully Marshall'. The programme also featured two two-reel Keystone comedies, *His Bread and Butter* and *A Love Riot*, as well as the *Pathé Gazette* newsreel.[8]

While the cinematic programme headed by a drama that featured an international star was the emerging norm for the cinema of the late 1910s, experiments in the combination of nonfiction and dramatic film continued. An example of a hybrid actuality-fiction feature of the mid1910s is the five-reel *From Dusk to Dawn* (1913, USA). Telling the story of the romance and struggle against capitalist exploitation of a foundry worker and a laundress, it combined scenes shot in the studio with shots of real working-class demonstrations. 'One of the first multireel docudramas ever made', writes Steven J. Ross, '*Dusk* used documentary footage as integral parts of its plot and not simply as colorful background'.[9] *From Dusk to Dawn* strives to produce a

Media, 1996: 239. 5 Eileen Bowser, *The transformation of cinema: 1907–1915*, Berkeley, Los Angeles, and London: University of California Press, 1994: 55. 6 Of recent work on the cinema programme, Andrew Higson (ed.), *Young and innocent? The cinema in Britain, 1896–1930*, Exeter: University of Exeter Press, 2002. This contains a section on some of the supporting elements of the cinematic programme, 'A Full Supporting Programme: Serials, Cinemagazines, Interest Films, Travelogues and Travel Films, and Film Music in the 1910s and 1920s'. 7 Variety and film still mixed at the Empire, Theatre Royal, and Tivoli variety theatres and would continue to do so at such venues well into the mid twentieth century, with wide fluctuations in the frequency of showings and the balance between live acts and film. The cinema programme did not banish variety completely from the dedicated picture houses; the Rotunda advertised its shows for a time after April 1918 under the banner of the Rotunda Pictures and Varieties. 8 *Irish Times*, 1 January 1917: 6. 9 Steven J. Ross, *Working-class*

generic synthesis and this distinguishes it from the two films considered here, which are content to yoke actualities and drama together without an attempt at integration.

The synthesis of actuality and drama footage was attempted in at least one well-publicized film shown in Dublin in 1917.[10] In the travelogue drama *Lost in the Eternal City*, Rome 'is lavishly portrayed [*sic*] in the story of a little girl who gets lost, and obligingly looks for her father in all the pet scenes of the city'.[11] The drama that frames the travelogue is complicated by the fact that father and daughter are sundered by the machinations of 'a jealous woman and her equally unscrupulous though misguided lover' and are reunited by the actions of 'the good Angel of the story, the beautiful and talented Madam Valli'.[12] Reviewers of the film's first run at the Theatre Royal, Dublin in March 1917 agree that the sights of Rome are of at least as much interest as the drama, but they are divided on their assessments of the effectiveness of the fictive elements. The *Irish Times* reviewer suggested that drama and travelogue are successfully integrated, contending that '[t]he finding of the child is interwoven with a love story which has interesting developments before it is brought to a satisfactory conclusion'.[13] The writer for the *Freeman's Journal*, however, argues that '[i]t would have been better to have given frankly a series of Roman pictures without the story. The child jumps about from one quarter of the city to another – from the Pigeon House to the Park, so to speak – with incredible rapidity'.[14] The film was distributed by the General Film Supply's Norman Whitten, the producer of the 1917–1920 *Irish Events* newsreel and future director of *Aimsir Padraig*. In relation to the timing of the release of *Aimsir Padraig*, it is significant that *Lost in the Eternal City* was considered 'suitable for exhibition during Lent' and that it was shown at the Theatre Royal with the General Film Supply's 1913 *Irish National Pilgrimage to Lourdes*, targeting an audience that went to see religious films during the religious festivals.[15] Like *From Dusk to Dawn*, the structure of this film is distinct from that of *Ireland a Nation* and *Aimsir Padraig* in that its drama and actualities are integrated, however clumsily, into the narrative.

Hollywood: silent film and the shaping of class in America, Princeton: Princeton University Press, 1998: 97. **10** In relation to the films shot by the Kalem Company in Ireland in the early 1910s, there is some work on the shots of landscape motivated not by narrative but by the desire to provide spectators with 'scenics'; see Kevin Rockett, Luke Gibbons, and John Hill, *Cinema and Ireland*, London: Croom Helm, 1987: 223; and Denis Condon, 'Touristic work and pleasure: the Kalem Company in Killarney,' *Film and Film Culture*, 2003: 7–16. **11** *Freeman's Journal*, 13 March 1917: 3. **12** 'A story of Rome', *Irish Limelight* 1: 3, March 1917: 8. **13** *Irish Times*, 13 March 1917: 3. **14** *Freeman's Journal*, 13 March 1917: 3. **15** 'Dublin Film Hire Case', *Irish Limelight* 1:7, July 1917: 20.

Ireland a Nation (1914–20)[16]	*Aimsir Padraig (1920)*
A. Framing devices	1. Prologue
(i) Players introduced	a. Opening titles
(ii) Old man begins story	b. Emblematic shot of Patrick
B. Act of Union passed	c. Angels venerate Patrick
C. Fr Murphy leads rebellion	2. Patrick's early life
1. Robert Emmet and Michael Dwyer	3. Patrick brought to Ireland as a slave
2. Daniel O'Connell's duel	4. Patrick heeds call to return to Ireland
3. Emigration	5. Patrick's first conversions
4. Newsreel	6. Patrick's struggle with Laeghaire
a. A 1914 Home Rule meeting	7. Other important elements of the legend
b. De Valera's visit to America	8. Epilogue (Actualities)
c. Unrest during hunger strikes	a. Sites associated with Patrick
d. Terence MacSwiney's funeral	b. 1919 Croagh Patrick pilgrimage
e. Ireland today	c. Armagh Cathedral and Cardinal Logue
5. Framing device	
a. The story told	

Although *Ireland a Nation* had been shot substantially in Ireland in 1914, it took more than two years to reach Irish screens.[17] As submitted to the press censor in late 1916, the film dramatized moments in the early nineteenth-century history of Ireland, ranging from the debates on the Act of Union in the Irish parliament in 1800, through the rebellion of 1803, to the actions of Daniel O'Connell. It included newsreel of political events relating to the passage of the Home Rule bill through the British parliament that were occurring as the film was being made in 1914. The longest sequence of the film concerns Robert Emmet and contains many of the features of his story as it is dramatized in Dion Boucicault's *Robert Emmet* (1884).[18] Among the common features are Emmet's relationships with Wicklow insurgent Michael Dwyer, and with Sarah Curran and Anne Devlin. The censor passed the film on condition that six cuts were made, including all of the newsreel material. While the film had been booked to play for a week at the Rotunda, which was twice the

16 The capital letters and Roman numerals indicate lost sections of *Ireland a Nation* that are here recreated from contemporary sources. 17 Before a print of the film arrived in Ireland in late 1916, two previous prints had run afoul of German submarines patrolling the Atlantic, including one that went down with the *Lusitania* in May 1915. See *Irish Limelight*, February 1917: 19. 18 A recent edition of this play appears in Andrew Parkin (ed.), *Selected plays of Dion Boucicault*, Washington, DC: The Catholic University of America Press, 1987: 331–97.

length of the normal cinema run, it had just opened on 10 January 1917, when the military authorities revoked their permission for its screening because 'the seditious and disloyal conduct [of the audience], make it clear that the further exhibition of the Film in Ireland is likely to cause disaffection to His Majesty, and to prejudice the recruiting of His Majesty's forces'.[19] The ban covered all of Ireland, and the film was not shown in the country again until the end of January 1922, under the changed political circumstances that followed the ratification of the Anglo-Irish treaty by the Dáil earlier that month. The film that was exhibited at this point included newsreel of some of the political events in Ireland at the time it had been reissued in the United States in 1920. These events include de Valera's visit to the United States in 1919–20, the hunger strikes of Michael Fitzgerald and Terence MacSwiney, and MacSwiney's funeral.

Aimsir Padraig/In the Days of St Patrick premièred in early 1920, between the two showings of *Ireland a Nation*. While this was in the midst of an increasingly bitterly fought Anglo-Irish war and Dublin was under curfew, the film experienced no official restrictions on its exhibition because it was different to *Ireland a Nation*. This cinematic hagiography was released in Dublin on 15 March to coincide with St Patrick's Day. It dramatizes events in the life of the Irish patron saint as they were represented in the popular imagination.[20] Certain scenes, however, principally the landing and selling of Patrick as a slave, owe much to the conventions of the cinematic biblical epic.[21] It closes with a sequence of actuality footage, including travelogue material of sites associated with Patrick, newsreel of the 1919 pilgrimage to Croagh Patrick, and staged shots of Cardinal Logue at Armagh Cathedral.

These brief synopses show that while cinematic history and hagiography may be quite different, they have common structural elements that make it feasible to compare them. Because they try to cover a relatively long time-span, for example, both films are more or less episodic. Parts of both films display strong causal links between scenes and sequences, but these connections weaken in the later dramatized sequences. Of more immediate interest

19 Official involvement with *Ireland a Nation* is detailed in file CSORP/1919/11025, National Archives of Ireland. For a narrative account based on these documents, see Rockett et al., *Cinema and Ireland*, 12–16. **20** The Catholic Truth Society widely disseminated a series of hagiographies in the form of penny pamphlets, including Canon Arthur Ryan's *St Patrick: Apostle of Ireland*, London: Catholic Truth Society, 1901. **21** Films of the life of Christ were popular in Ireland, and like Passion plays before them, they were generally shown at religious holidays. The iconography of the Passion play was transformed by the Kalem Company's location shooting of *From the manger to the cross* (USA, 1912), made in Palestine early in 1912 by filmmakers who produced in Ireland in the summers of 1911 and 1912. *Christus* (Italy, 1914) played opposite *Aimsir Padraig* in Dublin in March 1920. The slave market and chariot of *Aimsir Padraig* may also be influenced by the marriage market and chariots of the Babylonian story in D.W. Griffith's *Intolerance* (USA, 1916), which premièred in Ireland at the Gaiety Theatre during St Patrick's week 1918.

here, however, is the placement of the actuality material. The table above, which outlines the main sequences of the two films, makes it apparent that the actualities come at the end of each of the films. This implies that the moment depicted in the actualities, which is marked as generically and temporally immediate to its audience, is, if not the endpoint of a particular trajectory, then a crucial stage in an historical development. It also raises questions about the status of the 'reality' of the drama. If the actualities (including, notably, newsreel) represent contemporary reality, does the drama constitute a valid re-creation of a period before the existence of moving pictures, even though it clearly relies on the conventions of theatrical melodrama, in the case of *Ireland a Nation*, and biblical epic, in the case of *Aimsir Padraig*? While a relatively large body of documentation exists on the conduct of the audiences at *Ireland a Nation* in 1917 because it eventually led to the banning of the film, it is not helpful on this question. This documentation does, nevertheless, offer insights into the reception of the film in general. Official accounts of audience behaviour show that the film played to enthusiastic audiences. '[T]he Picture was received with applause throughout', reports Inspector George Love of the Dublin Metropolitan Police of the first day's exhibition, 'except some slight hissing, when Lord Castlereagh and Major Sirr were exhibited.'[22] The main daily newspapers carry brief reviews of the opening. The reviewer of the unionist *Irish Times* focused on the brief section of the film that depicts constitutional nationalist Daniel O'Connell rather than on the much longer sections concerning nationalist revolutionaries. The writer is disturbed by the audience appreciation only of the film's nationalism at the expense of its psychological subtleties:

> The film, which treated the rebel cause with sympathy, and the music, which included a number of Irish patriotic tunes, were received with loud and frequent applause by the audiences, who were not the least demonstrative when D'Esterre fell to the pistol of 'The Liberator,' and who did not seem to appreciate the mental anguish from which O'Connell was subsequently depicted as suffering.[23]

'From a historical standpoint, and indeed, from the standpoint of realism', writes the reviewer of the nationalist *Freeman's Journal*, 'the film is undoubtedly excellent, and will attract numerous visitors to the Rotunda during the week [...] Irish airs were discoursed by the orchestra while the film was being screened.'[24] Both reviewers complimented the live music as providing continuity to the screening.

22 CSORP/1919/11025. 23 *Irish Times*, 9 January 1917: 3. 24 'Irish History Films: "Ireland a Nation" at the Rotunda', *Freeman's Journal*, 9 January 1917: 3. With its motto of 'Ireland a Nation,' it is not surprising that the *Freeman's Journal* was particularly important in promoting

Although narrative cohesion is already under severe strain in the final dramatic sequences of both films, this does not make the change from drama into representations of the contemporary moment any less abrupt. The effect of this abruptness is not only to destroy any remaining narrative illusion but also to highlight the urgency of bringing the historical into contact with the contemporary. The films work through the drama towards the newsreel, showing that the historical process in some sense culminates in the present and emphasizing the relevance of the past to the current process of defining the Irish nation.

The films are constitutive of the national on different levels. *Ireland a Nation* concerns itself with the struggle for national self-determination and with the legitimacy of armed resistance in pursuit of this goal. An article in the *Freeman's Journal* begins, 'The very phrase "Ireland a Nation" is sufficient to conjure up thoughts of daring deeds and splendid memories of the cause in the days when Robert Emmet, Michael Dwyer, Father Murphy, Wolfe Tone, and their followers were making the history of their country glorious.'[25] This emphasis on the use of force is highlighted by the decision to concentrate the section dealing with the constitutional O'Connell on his duel with D'Esterre, the one event in his public life in which he could be said to have killed for his country. As the film was targeted primarily at an Irish-American audience, it takes care to account for the Irish who belonged to 'greater Ireland beyond the seas'.[26] Collapsing the differences between several strands of nationalism, its argument is that after the brave but failed attempts of Father Murphy, Emmet, Dwyer, and O'Connell to achieve independence, many Irish people had to emigrate. A new hope arrived in 1914 with the apparent success of the Home Rule party, a hope seemingly fulfilled by the visit of de Valera to the USA in 1919–20. At home, however, continuing British intransigence on independence was causing further unrest, epitomized by the death on hunger strike of Terence MacSwiney and others. Given these ongoing problems, the Irish continue to board the emigration ship to the United States. As Chris Morash puts it, the film 'creat[es] an extended narrative of Irish history in which the stage world of Whitbread's *Wolfe Tone* bleeds into the real world of the War of Independence'.[27]

Aimsir Padraig constructs Irish national identity as Catholic and Irish-speaking. As such, it is an intervention in a long-running debate on the confessional

the film. Advertisements were placed in the newspaper's 'Amusements' column from the Thursday of the week before the film opened and favourable articles on the production appeared in the Friday, Saturday, and Tuesday issues. It also published an interview with Frederick Arthur Sparling, the exhibitor of the film, after the film was banned. **25** 'The '98 Rebellion: interesting film production', *Freeman's Journal,* 5 January 1917: 2. **26** 'The U.I.L. in Dublin,' *Evening Telegraph,* 1 January 1912: 5. **27** Christopher Morash, *A history of Irish theatre, 1601–2000*, Cambridge: Cambridge University Press, 2002: 155.

status of St Patrick. From 1829, the participation of the viceroy in festivities on 17 March lent official sanction to St Patrick as the symbol of national unity for both Catholics and Protestants.[28] Despite this, sectarian struggles continued throughout the nineteenth century over which tradition could claim descent from Patrick. By beginning with an emblematic shot of Patrick and ending with a similar portrait of the Catholic primate Cardinal Logue, *Aimsir Padraig* leaves its allegiance in no doubt. The final section of the film's actualities reemphasizes the links between Patrick and the cardinal. It begins with the intertitle 'St Patrick's Cathedral Armagh, and Cardinal Logue, Head of the Catholic Church in Ireland'. It includes a full shot of a statue of Patrick on the cathedral wall that dissolves to a shot of Cardinal Logue in full clerical garb and is followed by the intertitle 'Cardinal Logue successor to St Patrick'. As the final image in the film, this shot makes clear that Patrick has been appropriated for the Catholic Church in Ireland.

Cardinal Logue is also significant in relation to the film's discourse on the Irish language. While he opposed Sinn Féin for its use of violence, the Donegal-born cardinal supported the Gaelic League.[29] Of the film's interventions in the construction of the Irish nation, the equal use of Irish and English intertitles is the first feature that confronts the spectator. This seems particularly striking for a film largely shot in 1919 and released in early 1920, in view of the fact that the increasingly politicized Gaelic League had been declared illegal in September 1919. Like its future status in the Free State, Irish in the film is privileged by being placed first in the title, credits, and intertitles.

The importance of the fact that the ends of both films include newsreel footage lies in the depiction of moments of 'real' contemporary public participation in the defining of Irish identity. It is through these participatory moments, rather than through absorptive narrative, that the films attempt to engage their audiences. These shots show how the cinema audience can enter history, following the example of Father Murphy's congregation in *Ireland a Nation* by transforming themselves into an 'insurrectionary band'.[30] In *Ireland a Nation*, such moments are numerous, particularly in the long section on the funeral of Terence MacSwiney. Many of these shots are taken from among the crowd, or 'throng' as several of the intertitles put it, giving a sense of what

28 Jacqueline R. Hill, 'National festivals, the state and "Protestant ascendancy" in Ireland, 1790–1829', *Irish Historical Studies*, 24:93, May 1984: 30–51. 29 On the Irish Roman Catholic hierarchy's ambivalence towards armed rebellion, see Patrick Murray, *Oracles of God: the Roman Catholic Church and Irish politics, 1922–37*, Dublin: University College Dublin Press, 2000: 7–10; on the involvement of clerics in the Gaelic League, see Kevin Collins, *Catholic churchmen and the Celtic Revival in Ireland, 1848–1916*, Dublin: Four Courts Press, 2002: passim. 30 The phrase comes from an article on *Ireland a Nation* in *Irish Limelight*, February 1917: 3. This indicates the film's historical inaccuracies.

a participant would have seen. In *Aimsir Padraig*, such moments are chiefly confined to the scene on the pilgrimage to Croagh Patrick.

If these newsreel images show the contemporary Irish masses playing their part in the creation of history, these shots are prepared for in the drama by depictions of the historical Irish masses playing their part. Embedded in the dramatic sequences are scenes that in different ways court the participation of the cinema audience. This occurs in the case of Father Murphy's congregation and in the emigration scenes of *Ireland a Nation*. By employing the representational conventions of stage melodrama, the film succeeded in eliciting responses from its audience that ultimately led to its prohibition. By hissing at the villain, the audience at the Rotunda was following an established practice of Dublin theatre audiences, but, in the context of the First World War and the Easter Rising, the military authorities considered the hissing of representatives of the crown to be 'seditious and disloyal'.

Two scenes in *Aimsir Padraig* are worth mentioning in this connection. The first is an approximately six-minute shot of Patrick's investiture. This single shot with a stationary camera is taken from behind a line of priests, who watch from the middle distance the deliberate movements of the more senior clerics performing the ceremony in the background. For the many Irish Catholics who saw the film, this scene must have reminded them of the rituals of the mass. The second dramatized participatory scene concerns Patrick's learning of Irish, the only positive experience that the saint-to-be undergoes during his period as a slave in Ireland. Patrick, the intertitles explain, 'working as an ordinary labourer', 'learns the Irish Language at the foot of Mount Slemish from his companions'. When Patrick attempts to pronounce the Irish words they mouth for him, they laugh uproariously. By showing that the saint also had to learn Irish, the film offered a point of identification for the many Irish people who were struggling to learn the language at the time.

The structure of these polemical screen histories has precedents elsewhere in Irish cultural production. Formal similarities exist between the films and popular Irish histories of the nineteenth century, often titled *The Story of Ireland*, that have been analyzed by Joep Leerssen and Roy Foster.[31] Foster stresses their mythological status by showing how they conform to the narrative strategies of Russian folktales examined by Vladimir Propp.[32] Unlike professional histories, Leerssen argues, the popular histories are not progressive, that is, they do not engage critically with the work of their predecessors but merely update them to the time of writing. He contends that '[p]opular, illus-

31 Joep Leerssen, *Remembrance and imagination: patterns in the historical and literary representation of Ireland in the nineteenth century*, Cork: Cork University Press, 1996; and R.F. Foster, *The Irish story: telling tales and making it up in Ireland*, London: Penguin, 2002. 32 Foster, *The Irish story*, 5–8.

trated histories of Ireland, from Milesian antiquity to the present day, are for the Irish reading public what George Eliot and Thomas Hardy are in England.'[33] These texts occupy the place in the literature of Ireland that nineteenth-century realist novels do in the literature of England and, like the novel, they are not considered to be in need of revision by the next author who comes to work on the story.

In relation to the newsreel content of the films, Foster's comment on the 'mercilessly present-minded preoccupation' of the popular histories in offering narratives that stretch from Ireland's mythological past to the moment in which the book is published is interesting.[34] For example, after outlining the events of the recent Fenian rebellion of 1867, A.M. Sullivan ends his *Story of Ireland*: 'Here abruptly pauses "the Story of Ireland"; not ended, because "Ireland is not dead yet". Like that faith to which she has clung though ages of persecution, it may be said of her that, though "oft doomed to death," she is fated "not to die"'.[35] Linking religion and politics, Sullivan draws attention to the ongoing nature of the story and the necessity of incorporating events relevant to the struggle against persecution that occurs in the contemporary moment. In these circumstances, any closure is contingent.

The films show different degrees of closure. *Aimsir Padraig* ends, as already mentioned, with a shot of Cardinal Logue that echoes the emblematic shot of Patrick with which the film begins. The effect of this is to stress the continuity of the church in Ireland, but it does this by promoting Catholicism as Patrick's true bequest, eliding sectarian differences within Christianity. There is a strong sense, however, that the story of Patrick's church is ongoing.

Ireland a Nation seeks stronger closure. Leerssen writes that 'Emmet's statement that his epitaph is not to be written, that his biography is to remain open-ended, until the day of Ireland's independence, is implicitly echoed by all these open-ended histories with their Fenian or Parnellite sympathies'.[36] *Ireland a Nation*, however, contains a scene just after Emmet's execution in which Erin leaves off playing her harp at his graveside to write his epitaph. The scene may suggest that Emmet's self-sacrifice is somehow constitutive of the independent nation, but the inclusion of a narrator in the film makes this less likely. Shots of the narrator, an elderly man telling a story to a boy and girl, frame the film. He initiates the historical drama with the intertitle 'Once upon a time Ireland had a parliament of its own'.[37] Laughing heartily, he reappears, with his charges, after the newsreel material, introduced by the intertitle 'The Story Told'. Like Erin's chiseling of Emmet's epitaph, these scenes imply that a significant period of time has passed in which the inde-

33 Leerssen, *Remembrance and imagination*, 154. 34 Foster, *The Irish story*, 5–8. 35 A.M. Sullivan, *The story of Ireland*, Dublin: M.H. Gill, 1867: 581–2. 36 Leerssen, *Remembrance and imagination*, 154. 37 'Irish Heroes the on Film [*sic*]: from Robert Emmet to Daniel O'Connell,' *Freeman's Journal*, 6 January 1917: 2.

pendent nation has been established and the painful events depicted lie sufficiently far back in the past for them to become suitable for a grandfather laughingly to tell his grandchildren. Because of the composite nature of the text, this attempt at neat closure fails, and the frame becomes just one more of the film's heterogeneous elements.

The great escape?: *The Islandman* (1938)

EMILIE PINE

In 1898 John Millington Synge went westward to the Aran Islands to, in W.B. Yeats' words, 'express a life that has never found expression'.[1] On a similar pursuit in May 1937 Patrick Keenan Heale and Donal O'Cahill went to the Blasket Islands to make a film called *The Islandman*, from an original story by O'Cahill. The 1930s was the first decade in which there was sustained indigenous film production in Ireland and *The Islandman* is a good example of the kind of film that writers and directors made, taking advantage of Ireland's beautiful scenery and rich cultural history.[2] In 1936 O'Cahill had been involved in another film-making project, *The Dawn*, directed by Tom Cooper. *The Dawn* is set in Kerry and dramatizes one year in the Irish War of Independence. The film was received very well and, in line with the political sympathies of the decade, was nationalist and pro-Fianna Fáil in tone.[3] *The Islandman*, though different in its focus, is likewise a homage to the Irish nation. The Blasket Islands represent the ideal of Catholic, Gaelic, traditional Ireland and signify 'a common bedrock of Irish culture, before the sectarian splits of more recent centuries'.[4] This is illustrated by the popularity of the literature that emerged from the islands in the 1920s and 1930s, such as Tomás O'Crohan's *The Islandman* (*An tOileánach*) (1929), Maurice O'Sullivan's *Twenty Years-a-Growing* (*Fiche Blian ag Fás*) (1933), and Peig Sayers' *Peig* (1936). The islands thus also embody a Catholic alternative to the Anglo-Irish Protestant literary tradition embodied by Yeats and Synge, which centred its nationalism on the Aran Islands.[5]

1 W.B. Yeats first told the story of his advice to Synge, to go westward, in his preface to the 1905 edition of Synge's *The Well of the Saints*, London: Maunsel, 1905. 2 For example, at the same time as *The Islandman* was on release, tourist films were also being made in Kerry. For a discussion of full-length indigenous films made during this period, see Kevin Rockett, John Hill and Luke Gibbons, *Cinema and Ireland*, London: Croom Helm, 1987. 3 For a discussion of the socio-political and cultural tone of the 1930s, see Terence Brown, *Ireland: a social and cultural history, 1922–1985*, London: Fontana, 1985; F.S.L. Lyons, *Ireland since the Famine*, London: Weidenfeld & Nicolson, 1971; J.J. Lee, *Ireland, 1912–1985: politics and society*, Cambridge: Cambridge University Press, 1998; and Joost Augusteijn (ed.), *Ireland in the 1930s: new perspectives*, Dublin: Four Courts, 1999. 4 Declan Kiberd, *Irish classics*, London: Granta, 2000: 520. 5 Though Synge also visited the Blasket Islands and travelled widely along the whole west coast of Ireland, he is primarily identified with the Aran Islands, in particular because of his play *Riders to the Sea* and the dialect of his plays which is popularly assumed to have come from Mayo and the Aran Islands. Synge's work on the islands also identifies the islanders as a deeply

The Islandman follows in the footsteps of that best known of island films, Robert Flaherty's *Man of Aran*, a British production, released in 1934. Indeed, one review went so far as to say that *The Islandman* took Flaherty's film as a model for some of its seascapes.[6] Both films lay great emphasis on the simplicity of the islanders' pre-modern, traditional way of life and both seek to place this island life at a remove from the rest of the world. Though *The Islandman* initially appears to be presenting a subtly different message to modern Ireland, ultimately it maintains an image of island life and of the islanders as a 'race apart'.

The story of the film is fairly simple. Neal O'More (Cecil F. Ford) is a young medical student from Trinity College, Dublin who, upon reading O'Crohan's *The Islandman*, decides to go to the Blasket Islands himself; Neal tells his drinking friends that he may even 'go native' and that is exactly what he does. After a long hike, Neal arrives at Dunquin, on the Kerry coast. Meeting Father O'Sullivan (Gabriel Fallon), the priest from An Blascóid Mór or, the Great Blasket, he is persuaded to cross the choppy seas in an island currach. Once on the island Neal tends to a local fisherman's injured hand and, in gratitude, the islanders hold a céilí in his honour, at which Neal meets and falls in love with Eileen Guheen (Eileen Curran). Eileen happens to be the island's best singer and, in a cruel twist of fate, is already promised in marriage to Liam (Brian O'Sullivan), the very fisherman that Neal had earlier helped. However, Eileen will not abandon Liam and, when he is called back to Trinity College, Neal leaves the island and returns to his louche lifestyle in Dublin. Several months pass and one day Neal hears, through his drunken stupor, Eileen singing on the radio. This has the power to summon him back to the island. Eileen is delighted to see Neal and, despite his protests, tells Liam of her love for Neal. Soon after, Liam is hurt in a fishing accident and though Neal manages to get him to shore, he dies almost immediately. Before he dies, however, he takes Neal and Eileen's hands and brings them together and the film ends with Neil and Eileen gazing out over the stormy seas.

URBAN-RURAL

Before going to the Blaskets, Neal is a drunken wayward student. As the narrator puts it, there 'were too many nights that were mornings, too little sleep,

spiritual yet not primarily Catholic people, embodied for example by the tradition of women keening at wakes. In contrast, the first image of the Blaskets in *The Islandman* is twinned with the first encounter with Father O'Sullivan, the island's priest. Neal is rowed to the island by the priest, implying that access to the Blaskets is available through the figure of the parish priest. The other use of the Aran Islands as a backdrop is Robert Flaherty's *Man of Aran* but this does not contain any reference to the religion of the island, and focuses almost exclusively on the age-old struggle with the sea. 6 *Evening Herald*, 1 April 1939: 9.

not enough study'. The film shows Neal walking out of Trinity College one morning with O'Crohan's book under his arm and heading for the Phoenix Park to 'get a grip on himself'. In the park Neal sits next to the monument to Arthur Wellesley, the first duke of Wellington. Wellington was of course a hugely successful Irishman in England, both militarily and politically. However, as his famous comment that 'Just because one is born in a stable does not make one a horse' implies, his Irish heritage was not one of which he was particularly proud and, indeed, one from which he distanced himself. Neal, reading *The Islandman*, is thus a striking contrast to this image of the Irish leaving or denying their roots in Ireland. Rather than choose the path that Arthur Wellesley chose and journey eastward to England, traditionally seen as the route to success and escape from a troubled Ireland, Neal walks westward, thereby becoming, as it were, more Irish than before given the west of Ireland's identification with traditional Gaelic culture.

Once on the Great Blasket, Neal realises that he has an affinity with island life, strengthened by his growing love for Eileen. Yet, early in the film Eileen tells Neal that she will only consider marrying an island man because they make life possible for the island women which, as she says, 'is no easy task'. Key to Eileen's later realization of her love for Neal and her rejection of Liam is that Neal changes to accommodate himself to island life. Upon his return to the island in the second half of the film, Neal declares to Eileen and Liam that he will not be leaving again and that he intends to become an island man. Neal enlists Liam's help and Liam teaches him to row, fish and farm like an islander. Eileen's transfer of her affections from Liam to Neal is thus in response to Neal's transformation.

By adapting to the traditional way of life Neal shows Eileen that he is capable of making life possible for her on the island yet, as he says to her, he can bring his medical knowledge to the island as well, adding his own skills to the community. It is not only Neal who is shown to be adaptable; Eileen also is capable of accommodating change. When Neal returns to the Great Blasket it is because he has heard her sing on the radio. As she tells him, after he had left the island she had gone to the mainland to record a traditional island song. Eileen is thus able to move between the island and mainland while still being rooted in the traditional island life. Eileen has not heard the record herself, however, and it is only Neal who makes this possible by bringing both the record and a gramophone to the island. Neal is once again illustrating that he will adapt to the island but bring the positive aspects of modernity with him.

Throughout the film Liam represents the traditional ways of island life, skilled in currach building, fishing and farming. When Neal first leaves the island Eileen and Liam accompany him to the mainland. Neal persuades Eileen to go to Dingle with him in a hired car, to buy presents for the islanders. However, the car breaks down and Neal and Eileen are late in returning to meet Liam at the shore. When Liam hears of the reason for their delay he laughs, saying, 'A currach never breaks down'. It seems at least at the beginning that Liam's traditional perspective has won him both the day and the girl.

Yet, from the beginning of the film Liam is in a weakened position. It is Liam whose hand is injured and Neal whose medical knowledge heals it. When Neal returns and becomes an island man himself, he demonstrates both his love for Eileen and his capacity to change and forge a new identity. Liam has no such capacity. In fact, while a currach may never break down, when Liam makes this statement the shot shows that the sea, in the background, is rough and stormy and this visually belies the safety and reliability of the currach. Liam's death in a currach accident acknowledges that the pure and uncompromisingly traditional way of life is dangerous for the islanders. In order to survive it seems that the islanders must learn to accept aspects of modern life into their traditions. Yet, the film further, and perhaps more strongly, suggests that in order for modern Ireland to survive it must reacquaint itself with its traditions. *The Islandman* thus epitomizes the anxieties of the Free State and the tension between tradition and modernity prominent in its first few decades.

CULTURE

Neal first encounters the idea of going to the Blaskets by reading some of the literature that emerged from the islands in the 1920s and 1930s. When Neal sits reading *The Islandman* the film cuts to a long shot of one of the islands. The book therefore has the power to summon up images of the island that are so powerful they cause Neal to pack up immediately and hike across the country to Kerry. The same phenomenon occurs when, back in Dublin, he hears Eileen sing on the radio. The film dissolves from a shot of Neal sprawled drunkenly in his rooms in Trinity to shots of Eileen, the Great Blasket, and sheep being carried from currachs onto the shore. Following this sequence the film cuts back to the island where Liam is telling Eileen that he hopes Neal will one day return. Overhearing him, Peg (Daisy Murphy) shakes her head and tells him that 'Neal lives in a different world'. This statement is refuted when, in the next scene, Neal arrives back on the island. In this, his second trip, there is no time lag between him leaving the city and arriving at the Blaskets and we are not shown Neal walking or indeed even leaving Trinity. This suggests the power of culture in general, and in particular, modern communications such as the radio, to perform a cohesive function. While Neal is first attracted to the idea of the Blasket Islands by literature, it is the power of the radio that drives him to overcome the obstacles between him and Eileen and return to the island. The film is thus implying that radio creates such a strong imagined community that it collapses spatial boundaries and distances. By extension, film is even more powerful as it can carry a cinema audience to the Blaskets without their ever leaving the cinema. Modern modes of culture can thus create a space within which the rural-urban divide can be overcome.

The image of unity is one that the film strives to promote and this comes across most obviously when Liam joins Neal and Eileen's hands while the community looks on. The film effectively uses island life to make this point. The islanders of An Blascóid Mór are not only a close-knit community but inhabit an undivided island, a symbol that, for Ireland in this period, must have been greatly evocative. Moreover, the powerful currents and choppy seas between the island and the mainland ensure that it is a sealed community. As Neal tells Eileen, one of the things he loves most about the island is its 'isolation from the outside world'. This comment and Neal's renunciation of mainland life imply that, though the island culture must accept new developments in order to survive, it is too important culturally to give up its separateness.

The Islandman was praised by reviewers for advocating the wholesomeness of island life, in comparison with 'the sordid half-life of the city'.[7] It came under fire, however, for its introduction of the dreaded 'red triangle' of Hollywood films to the Blaskets.[8] Yet, though Neal and Eileen's relationship does lead to a 'red triangle', Neal behaves entirely honourably, declaring that he is satisfied just being near Eileen and that he would not hurt Liam as 'an island man must not gain over another'. While introducing a love story in order to adhere to the classical Hollywood style, the film maintains its integrity and places the 'triangle' in the context of the community's customs. It thus endorses the power of the island's morality to limit the damage caused by the intrusion of modern decadence, identified with America, into their traditional way of life and to maintain the same codes of behaviour as before. This is a strong sign that the islands will not fall prey to the perceived evils of modernity, such as the promiscuity of the dance hall.

Indeed, both temperamentally and morally, the islanders appear to be a 'race apart'. Though they welcome Neal and his modern capabilities into their midst, once he becomes an island man there is no implication that he will maintain contact with his previous city life. This is the fundamental contradiction at the heart of the film. While Neal's move to the island and Liam's death both seem to imply that the island must move on from its ultra-traditional past the island remains essentially unchanged. The ultimate proof that modernity has not transformed the island is that Neal's modern medical knowledge fails to save Liam's life, as it had done previously. In becoming an island man, it seems that Neal has jettisoned his previous identity, not forged a new inclusive one. Moreover, the failure of Neal's medical knowledge is a bitter

7 Liam MacGabhann, '*The Islandman*: what worlds away', *Irish Press*, 4 April 1939: 5. 8 The *Dublin Evening Mail* also criticized the sacrifice of pure island life for the story of a 'tippling Dublin medical student', 1 April 1939: 4.

pre-echo of the fact that the last inhabitants of the Blaskets left the islands due to the lack of a doctor.

The final image of the film is of Neal and Eileen on the cliffs, facing the stormy sea. This image echoes Flaherty's earlier film, *Man of Aran*, which extolled the virtues of the island people who face the elements alone, with no help from technology. The film's visual echo of *Man of Aran* implies that it too endorses the notion of the islanders as a pre-modern race. It seems that unity can be brought about by modernity but only fully achieved by sacrificing it.

This undercurrent points to the real agenda of Heale's film. The most important transformation is not the modernizing of the islands but rather the renaissance of traditional Irish, rural culture and its potentially positive influence on modern Ireland. Neal is in his room in Trinity when he hears Eileen's 'The Spinning Song' announced by the radio presenter as a 'novelty'. Upon his return to the island Neal realises that none of the islanders have heard the song, not least Eileen herself. The audience for traditional Irish culture is thus not the rural population, but the urban. As Luke Gibbons argues, 'the idealizations of rural existence, the longing for community and primitive simplicity, are the product of an *urban* sensibility, and are cultural fictions imposed on the lives of those they purport to represent'.[9]

The film's most effective demonstration of the renaissance of traditional Irish culture is in its translation of images of colonialism into images of Catholic, Gaelic Ireland. So, Neal the Protestant, Trinity student becomes a Blaskets' island man. His early comment to fellow students that he may 'go native', a traditionally colonial remark, indicates the cultural re-appropriation going on in the film. The most striking example of this has already been alluded to. When sitting in the Phoenix Park, Neal is occupying a space conventionally associated with colonialism. Yet, since the 1932 Catholic Eucharistic Congress, held in the park, it had also become associated with Catholic nationalism, and Neal's reading of O'Crohan's book while there, further translates the park into a symbol of traditional, Gaelic Ireland. Furthermore, by exchanging the urban pastoral space of the park for the pastoral reality of the Blaskets, the film also advocates a move from the virtual quality of urban experience to the realities of rural life.

REALITY

The film thus uses modernity, paradoxically, as a medium through which to return to a less modern world. This idea is echoed only four years later in Éamon de Valera's now famous St Patrick's Day radio broadcast, in which he spoke of an idealized, pre-modern Ireland. Yet, for de Valera, as for the Blaskets, this ideal was already in the past and, when held up against the harsh

9 Luke Gibbons, *Transformations in Irish culture*, Cork: Cork University Press, 1996: 85.

economic reality of Irish rural life, the rhetoric of both film and speech comes across as empty.

While the signs of rural life – nationalism, Catholicism and community – may have been in the ascendant, the reality of rural life in Ireland, particularly in the west, was that it was declining. Between 1926 and 1936 the population of Irish towns grew by 10 per cent, while the rural population of Connaught decreased by 6.2 per cent, and both the rural *and* town population of Munster declined.[10] The social atrophy of the west was compounded by economic contraction as small farmers found it increasingly difficult to survive. Furthermore, due to these harsh economic circumstances marriage was at an all-time low with over half of women between 25 and 34 unmarried in the west and more than one quarter of all Irish women never marrying at all.[11] Indeed, based on the 1926 Census, Ireland had 'a larger proportion of unmarried persons of all ages than in any other country for which records are kept'.[12] In real life then, Eileen, if she had remained on the island and not migrated to the east as many Irish women did, far from having two eligible suitors, would more likely have had none.

In fact, rather than halting the decline of the west, Fianna Fáil's modernizing campaigns to make Ireland self-sufficient by increasing both industrial growth and farm sizes, may have hastened the decline. As Tony Varley and Chris Curtain argue, Fianna Fáil's 'rhetoric and campaign pledges were not matched by performance [... and] by the closing years of the 1930s' this 'had become the source of considerable disappointment in the West of Ireland'.[13] Though the Blaskets were not directly affected by the lack of policies favouring small farmers and controlling land redistribution they were not helped by them either and there were no policies aimed at keeping the Blasket Island population steady. As Éamon de Valera put it in Fianna Fáil's economic policy, the Irish were 'going to have to give up the luxuries of a certain kind' in order to maintain independence. He further advised that 'we should forget as far as we can what are the standards prevalent in countries outside this'.[14] Following this line of logic, living on the Blaskets was one of the luxuries that had to be sacrificed. By the 1950s the islands were completely depopulated.

NOSTALGIA

Rather than resulting in the migration of city dwellers to the margins of Ireland, books like *The Islandman* by Tomás O'Crohan were assimilated by

10 Father Felim O'Briain, 'Rural depopulation', *Rural Ireland*, 1949: 74. 11 Ibid., 76. 12 Conrad Arensburg and Solon Kimball, *Family and community in Ireland*, Boston: Clasp, 2001, 3rd edition: 99. 13 Tony Varley and Chris Curtain, 'Defending rural interests against nationalists in twentieth century Ireland: a tale of three movements', in John Davis (ed.), *Rural change in Ireland*, Belfast: Institute of Irish Studies, 1999: 59. 14 Éamon de Valera, *Fianna Fáil and its economic policy*, Dublin, 1928, quoted in Kieran Kennedy, *Population and development: Ireland since Independence*, Extract from the Annual Report of the Central Bank of Ireland, 1975: 4.

the mainland culture and read as an elegy to the island way of life. Thus, despite its upbeat tone there are many hints in the film that island life is not as buoyant as it first appears. One version of the film, entitled *Eileen Aroon*, has an extended voice-over prologue. The voice-over informs the viewer that, while the islanders 'speak of themselves as the next parish to America' they are so isolated that they represent 'the last outpost of the Celts and of their unique and ancient culture'. The elegiac tone continues when the prologue quotes O'Crohan, saying, 'Our counterparts the future cannot hold.' Indeed, some parts of the film imply that not even the current islanders are O'Crohan's counterparts. While some Gaelic is spoken in the film the dominant language is English. At his first introduction to island culture, the céilí held in his honour, Neal asks Eileen if all the islanders speak Gaelic. In reply she says, 'Oh yes, but we understand your language too'. She then goes on to sing in Irish but Peg sings in English and the song that Eileen records for the radio is 'The Spinning Song' which she sings twice during the film, both times in English. The dominance of English in the film suggests that the island culture being expounded by it is not as pure as it wants viewers to believe and that modernity has already affected island life. Indeed, Eileen is played by Eileen Curran, a well-known traditional Irish singer and actress from Cork. These elements of the film undermine the usual romanticization inherent in the journey west and imply that audiences need a more realistic vision of rural and western Ireland.

The acknowledgment of the romanticization of the islands is evident from the beginning of the film and the way Neal's story is framed. *The Islandman* opens in a cottage, as an islander is telling the story of Neal's arrival on the Great Blasket to a visitor from Dublin. As the storyteller continues, the film dissolves from the cottage scene to Neal's rooms in Trinity. By framing the narrative in this way, Neal's story becomes mythic; a story told around the fireplace by the seanchaí. The narrator, however, is absent from the end of the film. This lack of closure leaves the film's ending open, just as Neal and Eileen's future will be, and enables the audience to draw their own conclusions.

When Neal and Eileen face the stormy waves together at the end, it seems as if myth has triumphed and that Neal has totally assimilated into the island culture, thereby replacing Liam. Neal's medical knowledge fails to save Liam, indicating the fallibility of modernity and the triumph of the elements. This is underlined by the inexorable quality of the waves crashing against the rocks. Yet, in this scene Eileen is not dressed in traditional island dress and this, combined with the positive effects of modernity throughout most of the film and the dominance of English, undermines the notion of a return to a 'pure' Irishness.

The vision that Heale and O'Cahill present in *The Islandman* is thus one which sees the future of Ireland not in regressing to an era of pre-modernity, nor of uncritically accepting modernity, but of fusing the sense of community, traditional skills and values with the advantages that modernity has brought to Ireland. Neal's transformation refutes the islanders' early opinion of him as belonging to a 'different world'. As Neal and Eileen's relationship shows, bridges can be built between different worlds and a new and better one forged. The film's strategy is thus to suggest that happy endings are made from the richness of the differences between cultures and that, by recognising this, the Irish can overcome the divisions in their society, most notably the rural–urban divide. Accordingly, the emphasis of the film is on creating a balance and harmony between different ways of life, the cultural riches of the island balanced by the difficulties of island life, and the novelties of modernity such as the radio are balanced by the bittersweet nature of Liam's death.

The Islandman is thus a cultural fiction, but a knowing one, aware of the nostalgic impulse unavoidably inherent in such a project. Yet the project is still worthwhile. *The Islandman*, despite its acknowledgement that romantic Ireland is, if not dead and gone, then at least illusory, does not invalidate its underlying message. The implication is that it is better for the island to survive as a hybrid, between modernity and tradition, and to sacrifice some aspects of modernity in order to achieve this, rather than to become entirely extinct. The film thus seems to suggest that, while purity is not possible, hybridity presents an attractive alternative. Though island life and its pristine, traditional culture may never be attainable in reality, Neal's journey, the film seems to say, is still one that modern Ireland needs to undertake.

A frayed collaboration: Emmet Dalton and the Abbey Theatre adaptations at Ardmore Studios, 1957–60

BARRY MONAHAN

A few years after he retired, Emmet Dalton, the film producer who was responsible for the establishment of Ardmore Studios and its collaboration with the Abbey Theatre, was asked why the nine completed Abbey Ardmore films had not made much of an impact on the international cinema market. Explaining that the productions had not been properly distributed because of inadequately drawn contracts, Dalton described how 'the completed pictures did not get releases', and then suggested that the films 'were presold, but on the wrong basis, because initially I intended to make second features but the requirement was asked then for co-features'.[1] If he had been asked about the demise of the relationship between his production company and the National Theatre – the collaboration on which the Ardmore project was based – the answer would not have been so straightforward.

There was no reason to have expected failure when Taoiseach Seán Lemass officially opened the studio complex on 12 May 1958. The ceremony marked the culmination of two years of negotiations between Dalton and Louis Elliman, the accomplished entrepreneur who was managing director of Amalgamated Cinema (Ireland), Irish Cinemas Ltd and Odeon (Ireland). From the earliest phase of their discussions, they had hoped to involve the National Theatre in order to film some of their successful productions with the Abbey players in many of the roles, using them both for their creative influence and marketability. After some hesitation, the board of directors of the theatre consented to the cooperation and an intermediary company – Dublin Film Productions – was established. With Ernest Blythe as the theatre's representative on the board of the holding company, the Abbey directors were satisfied that they would have adequate control over the number of players that would be released at any given time on film contracts.

In the months before the official opening a series of articles appeared in the *Irish Press* optimistically announcing the significance of the project for the development of an indigenous film culture and proudly describing its tech-

1 Emmet Dalton interview with Cathal O'Shannon, *Emmet Dalton remembers,* Documentary, Radio Telefís Éireann (Niall McCarthy, 1977).

nological capabilities and superb settings.[2] Earlier that year, a well-received pilot production, *Professor Tim* (Henry Cass, 1957), had been released, and *Boyd's Shop* – an adaptation of the St John Ervine play by the same director – was already in post-production. In fact, Dalton and Elliman were so assured of the success of the collaborative venture that they informed Blythe that there had been nine bookings before the studios had been opened and that it was likely that a further two sound stages would have to be added to the three already built to cater for the demand.[3] There seemed, from the outset, no reason to question that the partnership marked a potentially valuable contribution to film production in Ireland, even if the emphasis was less on film culture and more on the Irish word-based dramatic tradition. In spite of this, however, within three years of opening it was evident that the studio was failing to serve as anything other than an overseas facility for British and American producers, and that it had made little effort to foster indigenous filmmaking, or the training of Irish film technicians, directors or producers.

Across the many factors that contributed to the collapse of the association on which the Ardmore venture was based, one common theme emerges. In this paper I want to suggest that the project faltered and ultimately failed because it was built on an insecure foundation that was destabilized by latent ideological conflicts among policy makers and cultural activists in Ireland at the time. I will consider the Ardmore scheme within a context of the ideological uncertainty that was central to how government officials had regarded the evolution of film in Ireland since the Censorship of Films Act, 1923. I will place the development against a political background that was weakened by a conflict between a liberal cultural outlook and an innately essentialist nationalism; an ambiguity which was at the heart of the transition from the de Valera to the Lemass administration. I will deal with the three influential factors in chronological order: starting with the area of policy creation, moving to deal with the ideological aspects of Ireland's phase of development at the time the collaboration began, and finishing with a consideration of the internal conflicts between the collaborators.

When he described Eamon de Valera as an 'adroit tactician, a master of international and interpersonal relations',[4] J.J. Lee was making reference to the leader's characteristic political flexibility, and chameleon-like ability to bring diverse groups together under his unifying influence. For many, even the beginning of his career was marked by a desire to show himself as the individual representative of opposing ideological forces in the country. If this

2 Julia Monks, 'Ireland's first big film studios opened', *Irish Press*, 13 May 1958. Other articles appeared in the paper on 29 January, and on 13 March 1958. 3 Ernest Blythe, National Theatre board of directors minutes, 11 December 1957. File P24 Document 756, Archives Department, University College Dublin. 4 J.J. Lee, *Ireland, 1912–1985: politics and society*, Cambridge: Cambridge University Press, 1989: 333.

trait was evident in his dealings with the Gárda Síochána, the Irish Free State Army, the IRA, and the Catholic Church, it was no less apparent in his ability to conceal his contradictory attitude towards the development of an indigenous film industry. While, on the one hand, strict censorship was persistently posited as an appropriate cultural and moral protectionist measure against the corrupting influences of British and American films, paradoxically, nothing was done to counteract the allegedly negative consequences through the establishment a native film industry. Having referred to the 1923 Censorship of Films Act as a 'sin filter', the conservative film censor James Montgomery wrote in 1942 of an earlier paper he had delivered: 'At that time I read a paper ... pointing out that Anglicization was not the greater evil, but that Hollywood from its film factories in Los Angeles was waging a fight with national cultures everywhere'.[5]

Suspicion of the foreign product and producer was echoed in political circles every time a film company approached the Abbey Theatre directorate with a view to artistic collaboration. When the board of the Abbey was approached in 1937 by Milton Shubert, a director of Warner Bros., and partner in the Shubert Theatrical Group, at the time responsible for backing the latest Abbey Theatre tour of America, it was proposed that an association would be made forming an equal-rights partnership with the intention of establishing a film studio in Dublin. However, because the contract stipulated that each party had to provide £20,000 to inaugurate the deal, and this was far more than the resources of the theatre could provide, the board asked the Minister for Finance, Seán MacEntee, for assistance. The minister refused to support the venture, and de Valera noted, as the proposed project evaporated, that

> it will be necessary to keep carefully in mind in reaching a decision [...] the type of film which will be produced. We must guard against the danger of the enterprise being used for the production of plays which would be regarded as hurtful from the national point of view.[6]

Although there was much enthusiasm surrounding the first official screening of Tom Cooper's 1936 feature film *The Dawn*, with political acclaim accorded to the enterprise, little was done by policy makers to encourage or foster a native film industry in the years after its release. Kevin Rockett has summarized the enthusiasm of many at the time by citing Maud Gonne MacBride's review of the film in *An Phoblacht*: *The Dawn*, she said, 'establishes not the possibility but the certainty that Ireland will be able to compete in film production with Hollywood'.[7]

5 James Montgomery, 'The menace of Hollywood', *Studies*, 31, December, 1942: 420. 6 Memo. from Taoiseach, 25 November 1937, Department of Taoiseach File S14342A, National Archives, Dublin. 7 Kevin Rockett, 'From radicalism to conservatism: contradictions within the Fianna

The widespread belief that the establishment of a strong, competitive film industry in Ireland was not only possible but also imminent following the reception of Cooper's film proved to be premature. In spite of the praise and encouragement, there was no sustained consideration of policies that might assist the development of an indigenous film industry or support individuals seeking assistance with production. As with Robert Flaherty's *Man of Aran* (1934), it soon became apparent that it was the ideological resonances in the representations of the films – and not the fact of their production – that had resonated most strongly in political circles. It may not be wholly inaccurate to assume that in many traditionalist circles the cinematic medium was distrusted as embodying – even at the level of apparatus – some corrupting influence of modern international capitalism. It was convenient for those in government that film producers approached the board of the National Theatre directly about collaborative projects because it suited a general attitude of 'arms length' and policy avoidance when it came to discussions about the establishment of an indigenous industry. The central contradiction here was between those who favoured a modest indigenous film industry, many of whom were associated with the Irish Film Society (founded in 1936), and state policy as articulated by the Minister for Industry and Commerce Sean Lemass, who favoured the establishment of a 'film factory' for the use of foreign film producers, not indigenous filmmakers. The establishment of Ardmore Studous was the culmination of Lemass's policy. By the time he succeeded de Valera as Taoiseach in 1959, Ardmore had received financial support from his department.

As Minister for Industry and Commerce Seán Lemass may have been both a proponent and executor of many of Eamon de Valera's earlier measures of economic protectionism,[8] but as Taoiseach he was keen to distance himself from the industrial, if not always the ideological, standpoint that was characteristic of de Valera's period in office. The former regime had been marked by a tendency to mobilize images of tradition and the past. As J.J. Lee has stated: 'Fianna Fáil extended its emotional sway over past as well as present, establishing a virtual monopoly on the historical mythological market.'[9] By the time the Abbey/Ardmore collaboration was established, Ireland's international outlook was more open-minded and less isolationist then at any time since independence.

The recently opened studio facility at Ardmore was perfectly positioned at the dawn of Lemass' administration for his strategic employment of the project as a symbol of industrial progress, and in his introductory speech he was quick to foreground the economic and industrial aspects of the scheme over its cultural and social value.[10] However, as Luke Gibbons has noted, Ireland's

Fáil film policies in the 1930s', *Irish Studies Review*, 9: 2, 2000: 155. 8 Lee, *Ireland, 1912–1985*, 190. 9 Ibid., 183. 10 Kevin Rockett, 'An Irish film studio', in Kevin Rockett, Luke Gibbons, John Hill, *Cinema and Ireland*, London: Routledge, 1988: 99.

modernization in the 1960s was not as definitive and homogenous as it might first appear, nor was the projection of certain images of Irishness without ambiguity. Gibbons draws attention to the inherent contradictions of the time when he is critical of subsequent accounts of the period because they

> convey the impression that the pull of the past is due solely to the traditional sector, as if the metropolitan centre, by contrast, could only impel a society towards the future. What is not acknowledged is the possibility that it is the modernization process itself [...] which is the source of the social and cultural 'backlash' of the 1980s.[11]

The implication in this comment is that certain aspects of Irish history, identity narratives and national artefacts were preserved and mobilized in the 1960s in the newly-emerging project of industrializing Ireland, as ideologically useful remnants of an ostensibly homogeneous past. For many Irish critics, the association between the traditional dramatic medium and its modern cinematic counterpart in the Ardmore association, was highly problematic, and further underscored the precarious ideological contradictions of the time. Liam O'Laoghaire (later O'Leary), who, both as a filmmaker and as an Abbey Theatre director in the 1940s, had been consistently critical since the 1930s of an alliance between theatre and the cinema, and objected to the use of stage plays and theatre actors in film production. He frequently claimed, as he put it in 1936, that several of those 'recruited to the talkies ... never considered the differences between stage and film'.[12] Moreover, the National Theatre was perceived by many commentators as being too rooted in a tradition of narrow-minded cultural nationalism, and as having become so detached from any meaningful artistic project,[13] that it could never have been considered seriously as an acceptable creative associate in the construction of a healthy film industry in the new 'modern' Ireland. In comparison with the independent experimental and progressive Pike Theatre managed by Alan Simpson – who had been arrested in 1957 for his production of Tennessee Williams' *The Rose Tattoo* – members of the board of the National Theatre were perceived to be aligned ideologically with the more conservative elements in society. While activities surrounding the controversial staging at the Pike Theatre provoked strong political as well as police reaction, and Dublin's archbishop, John Charles McQuaid, personally intervened in the affair, there had never been any reason to arbitrate on the suitability of productions by the artistically and politically anodyne national theatre company.

11 Luke Gibbons, 'Coming out of Hibernation? The myth of modernization in Irish culture', in Luke Gibbons, *Transformations in Irish culture*, Cork: Cork University Press, 1996: 88–9. 12 Liam O'Laoghaire, 'Cinema as cinema', *Ireland To-day*, I–III, June 1936–March 1938, 'Films', 67. 13 For two examples of this criticism, one contemporary and another more recent, see: Ulick O'Connor, 'Dubliner's dilemma' *Theatre Arts XL*, July 1956: 65, and Robert Welch, *The Abbey Theatre, 1899–1999*, Oxford: Oxford University Press, 1999: 157.

There may have been some reason for optimism when the Irish Film Society announced its general aims in 1936, and Liam O'Laoghaire promised screenings of 'the best contemporary films from all countries not otherwise available to foreign filmgoers'.[14] However, his desire to screen films 'which we were not allowed to see',[15] stood in marked contrast to the aims of the National Film Institute of Ireland, under the patronage Archbishop McQuaid, outlined almost a decade later, which sought 'to acquire, encourage, promote, produce, and distribute films of educational, cultural, and recreational value, with particular reference to the principles laid down in the encyclical, *Vigilanti Cura*'.[16] As Kevin Rockett has noted, although the latter organization fought persistently for more severe film censorship, it ultimately had no lasting influence on state policy, film production or film culture in Ireland,[17] at least until its secularization in the 1980s as the Irish Film Institute. In 1958 as Ardmore Studios was opened, Archbishop McQuaid led a successful campaign against an attempt by government officials to liberalize the Censorship of Publications Board, and although the argument was centred on productions in the Dublin Theatre Festival,[18] the repercussions would not have been lost on the more conservative members of the National Theatre board as they embarked upon a long-term partnership with Emmet Dalton's production company.

Writing on Irish literary criticism in the early stages of the de Valera government, John Zneimer noted an obsessive and narrow-minded inclination to search for any possible means by which a sense of 'Irishness' could be defined through the literary text.[19] In later critical pieces, another manifestation of this method was the *a priori* assumption of the existence of some essentially Irish characteristic that, if ultimately discovered and properly harnessed, could stimulate any number of creative and cultural projects in the country. The elusive national characteristic was evoked in even the most sophisticated commentaries by writers campaigning for a film industry in Ireland. Rex MacGall's essentialist-based conviction was justification enough of the viability of an indigenous cinema when he told readers of *The Bell* in 1946 that 'the Irish film should be a distinct and individual medium of expression, having its own characteristics, expressing the spirit, faith, character and mind of the Irish people'.[20]

Seven years later in the same publication, Hilton Edwards questioned the possibility for a small country of ever having the financial support for the development of its own cinema. Having recently produced two films with Mícheál MacLiammóir – *Return to Glennascaul* in 1951 and *From Time to Time*,

14 Liam O'Laoghaire, 'Aims of the 1936 Film Society movement', *The Bell*, 15: 3 December 1947. **15** Ibid. **16** 'Aims of the National Film Institute', *Scannán*, 1: 1 December 1945: 4. **17** Rockett, 'From radicalism to conservatism', 164. **18** Lionel Pilkington, *Theatre and the state in twentieth-century Ireland: cultivating the people*, New York: Routledge, 2001: 157–8. **19** John Zneimer, *The literary vision of Liam O'Flaherty*, Syracuse, New York: Syracuse University Press, 1970: 16. **20** Rex MacGall, 'Towards an Irish film industry', *The Bell*, 12: 3 June 1946: 241.

the following year – he suggested the strength inherent in national identity, in essentialist terms:

> If it be asked how can a country like Ireland compete with the vast machinery of Hollywood or the English studios, I would answer that I am gambling upon the existence in Ireland of some quality particularly and authentically national that could give to Irish pictures an individuality; a uniqueness which other countries could not supply.[21]

Paradoxically, even as Ardmore was announced as 'Ireland's first big film studios'[22] and nationalized as the 'All Irish Studio',[23] three of the most popular plays adopted from the Abbey repertoire, would consciously question the essentialisms on which national identities, myths and historical narratives were founded.

The most successful Abbey plays adapted by Dalton were *This Other Eden*, based on the play by Louis D'Alton, *The Big Birthday* from the play by Hugh Leonard, and *Home Is the Hero* by Walter Macken. Each one establishes in its plot an 'outsider' character through whose point of view images of national identity and historical narratives are seen. The formal structure of the 'outsider narrative' works in the Dalton films to facilitate examination of the concept of 'Irishness' on thematic levels, and highlight the elasticity of concepts such as identity, nationality, and history in light of the problematic and flexible notion of perspective. In the three films, the introduction of the foreigner into the community provides the interface of novelty and history, fact and fiction, and self and other in the establishment of a protreptic discourse, which, as defined by Eugene O'Brien,

> can be seen to produce a critique of the essentialist and mythopoeic aspects of Irish identity, a critique which will see a position of heterogeneity and alterity as achievable if only as a negative, regulative notion from which an ethnicity of Irish identity can be fashioned and debated in a dynamic manner.[24]

In *This Other Eden* the outsider is the Englishman Crispin Brown, and a series of questions relating the national to ideas of personal history and identity are reassessed through his point of view – an ironically idealistic reading of Ireland – for the spectator. In *The Big Birthday*, another Englishman, this time a television producer, Tony Randall, becomes involved in the quest to produce a documentary based on the life and times of Ireland's oldest patriarch. As he arranges

21 Hilton Edwards, 'An Irish film industry?', *The Bell*, 18: 8 January 1953: 461. **22** Monks, 'Ireland's first big film studios opened'. **23** 'All Irish film studio by May', *Irish Press*, 15 January 1957. **24** Eugene O'Brien, *The question of Irish identity in the writings of William Butler Yeats and James Joyce*, Lewiston, Queenston, Lampeter: The Edwin Mellen Press, 1998: 11.

the nature of Irish representation, the truth about the age claim of the 110-year-old comes under question and, with it, the consequence of the means by which Randall is 'framing' the nation and national identity. Once again, history, nation and identity are displayed as performances, and the production of realism and narrative discourses based on verisimilitude are exposed as constructs. In the third of the films the position of the 'outsider' is altered. In *Home Is the Hero* the patriarch is 'othered' in the process of the narrative through his rejection by his family and community following the involuntary manslaughter of a neighbour. He renegotiates his standing in the community and relationship with his family after his release from prison and, in doing so, challenges the myths that have been developed around his heroism. The questions raised on the level of national history and identity by virtue of the foreign 'outsider' in *This Other Eden* and *The Big Birthday* are reduced to the more local levels of community and family in *Home Is the Hero*. Nevertheless, myth and identity, the authenticity of authority and paternity, still operate as central facets of the film.

The plays for adaptation were chosen because of their popularity at the Abbey. This fact displays a certain sophistication among spectators, who were clearly sensitive to the parodic undermining of national essentialisms and the satirical way in which the plays criticise the hypocrisy of many of the characters. It is ironic, therefore, that Ernest Blythe, who represented the Abbey board of directors in the Ardmore partnership, would, when writing six years after the demise of the relationship, continue to echo his 1920s' Gaelic League ideals in reference to the role of the National Theatre in Ireland:

> The continued existence of the Irish nation, as a community with coherence and a character of its own, can be ensured only by saving the ancestral language and by thus giving the country the possibility of retaining a vigorous and distinctive living culture.[25]

The collaboration between Dalton and the Abbey ended when *This Other Eden* director Muriel Box refused to cast as many of the theatre players as had been called upon for the earlier films. One month before filming began, Blythe had confidently told board members that

> Except for the part of the girl Maire McRoarty which will be played by Audrey Dalton, Emmet's daughter and the part of Captain Crispin which will be played by a British star the majority of the parts will [...] be filled by members of the Abbey Company.[26]

This was not to be the case, however, and only Harry Brogan and Geoffrey Golden were cast in substantial roles. Having bemoaned throughout the 1940s

25 Ernest Blythe, *The Abbey Theatre*, Dublin: The National Theatre Society, 1966: 28. 26 Board of directors minutes, 7 January 1959, file P24 Document 758, Archives Department,

and 1950s the hazard to the theatre caused by players' absences on film contracts, Blythe was now expressing disapproval of the fact that more of the Abbey talent on offer had not been used in the film, though some of the Abbey performers had also complained about the casting when the film's producer Alec Snowden had met the actors. He explained that although Dalton was anxious to use as many of the Abbey players as possible, frequently the artistic decision on casting was made by the director of the project and that certain choices could not be overruled. Blythe felt that the decision to cast Hilton Edwards as Canon Moyles would weaken the character by making him 'more earthly',[27] and argued on the phone with Muriel Box as he tried to get her to consider casting either Tom McKenna or Vincent Dowling in the role of Conor Heaphy. Despite the fact that the affair provoked tension between the parties, there was almost unanimous agreement among the performers *not* to dismantle the collaborative arrangement between Emmet Dalton Productions and the Abbey Company. Blythe informed the board of the general sentiment among the company, noting that apart from a minority, 'the rest of the players are anxious that no drastic decision such as withdrawing the Abbey participation should be taken',[28] no doubt reflecting the generous remuneration and wider exposure they received from films. Of course, Blythe's motivation was also driven by the hope of getting money for the Abbey from film production companies.

When *This Other Eden* had its première at the 1959 Cork Film Festival, in an unexpected move Emmet Dalton announced that he had plans 'for a non-Irish story', with locations in London and Cornwall, which he hoped to start shooting at Ardmore in January 1960.[29] Dalton never again employed players from the theatre – apart from a small number of individual performers – and the collaboration between the Abbey and Emmet Dalton Productions was ended. The fact that Dalton placed the interrogation of national mythology at the centre of his desire to produce a 'non-Irish' film is perhaps indicative of the difference in approach to Irish and international culture that had led to the uneasy alliance between the pair, with Blythe more concerned to promote a distinctive, if traditional, Irish-language and conservative theatrical culture at a time when Ireland was leaving behind such social, economic and cultural protectionism.

Ardmore was primarily embraced as another one of many symbols that were mobilized and projected to demonstrate the modernization of Ireland in the 1960s. Whatever the immediate outcome of many of the developments of Lemass' outward-looking political, social and industrial strategies, the latent ideological contradictions among certain cultural and governing groups in the country at the turn of the decade created an insecurity that ultimately challenged the stability of the alliance on which the project was based.

University College Dublin. **27** Board of directors minutes, 21 January 1959, file P24 Document 758, Archives Department, University College Dublin. **28** Ibid. **29** 'More plans for Ardmore Studios', *Kinematograph Weekly*, 15 October 1959: 9.

From no wave to national cinema: the cultural landscape of Vivienne Dick's early films (1978–1985)[1]

MAEVE CONNOLLY

> MAC DONALD: How about the title *Visibility: Moderate.* Does it refer to the view from the [World] Trade Center?
> DICK: No, just to the weather reports you hear all the time on the radio: 'visibility moderate to fair'. It's like a little comment of my own on the film, which I felt was really a surface thing; it was the best I could do under the circumstances, moneywise and with the pressures on me. While I was doing it, and as I was finishing it, I met all these other people; it could have been quite different. I was just getting into living in Ireland again. I want to make more films there, better films.
>
> Vivienne Dick interviewed by Scott MacDonald[2]

At the beginning of the 1980s the Irish filmmaker Vivienne Dick was perhaps the most celebrated figure in New York's 'No Wave' or Punk cinema. She had produced a series of Super-8 film narratives, which were 'hailed as contemporary underground classics'[3] and her work featured prominently in a special 1982 issue of the journal *October*, focusing on contemporary developments in avant-garde film. It included an interview, by Scott MacDonald, and an article by *Village Voice* critic J. Hoberman, dealing with the development of No Wave cinema since its emergence in 1978.[4] Yet, as the above quote sug-

1 This paper forms part of a larger study of Irish film in the 1970s and 1980s. My research is funded by a Government of Ireland Scholarship, awarded by the Irish Research Council for the Humanities and Social Sciences. I would also like to gratefully acknowledge the assistance provided by the Irish Film Archive, by Vivienne Dick and by Luke Gibbons and Stephanie McBride, who provided comments on an earlier version of this paper. The extended earlier version is included in a forthcoming special issue of *Boundary 2*, edited by Seamus Deane, under the title '*Visibility Moderate*? Sighting an Irish avant-garde in the intersection of local and international film cultures'. 2 Scott MacDonald, 'Interview with Vivienne Dick', *October*, 20, Spring 1982: 98. A revised version of this interview is also reprinted in Scott MacDonald, *A critical cinema: interviews with independent filmmakers*, Berkeley: University of California Press, 1988: 191–200. 3 Eric Knorr, 'Vivienne Dick', *Moving Image*, September/October 1981: 13. 4 J. Hoberman, 'A context for Vivienne Dick', *October* 20, Spring 1982: 102–6. Earlier articles by Hoberman include 'No wavelength: the para-punk underground', *Village Voice*, 21 May 1979: 42–3 and 'Notes on three films by Vivienne Dick', *Millennium Film Journal* 6, Spring 1980:

gests, the focus of Vivienne Dick's work was already shifting towards Ireland and in the same year she left New York for Dublin.

Another journey is also signalled by this special issue of *October*; the migration of No Wave cinema from its birthplace in the bars and rock clubs of the East Village, towards the established institutions of avant-garde film. No Wave cinema did not retain its position at the critical edge of avant-garde practice for very long. By 1984, the movement (if it ever had any such coherency) had dissipated and its history was being re-written by formerly supportive critics such as Hoberman. In an overview of developments in American filmmaking, entitled 'After Avant-garde Film', Hoberman dismissed No Wave cinema as a 'postmodernist repetition' of an earlier cultural moment, associated with pop art and underground film and compared this repetition to the nostalgic 'genre pastiches', such as *American Graffiti*, *Star Wars* and *Body Heat*, produced by Hollywood during the same period.[5]

The No Wave movement retains a place within American film history, however, and in recent years a number of major retrospective exhibitions have been staged. Vivienne Dick's work has featured in two: *No Wave Cinema, 1978–87* at the Whitney Museum (1996) and *Big as Life: An American History of 8mm films* (1999), at the Museum of Modern Art. Even though she has not lived in the US since 1982, these events have confirmed her status as an important 'American' filmmaker. But Dick's prominence within the No Wave has also worked to limit analysis of her work in the US and in Ireland. For the most part, American curators and critics have paid little attention to her later films, made in Ireland and in London.[6]

No Wave cinema has always been theorized in terms of a definitively *American* tradition, not least because of the fact that Vivienne Dick and her contemporaries Beth and Scott B, James Nares and Eric Mitchell were all based in New York during the late 1970s and early 1980s. J. Hoberman was also instrumental in shaping the processes of reception and historicization, through his articles in the *Village Voice* and an influential programme of screenings at Anthology Archives in 1981.[7] He consistently situated the movement in relation to a specifically American tradition of narrow-gauge filmmaking, an approach that did not allow for an extended analysis of either Dick's feminism or issues of cultural specificity.

It was only when Vivienne Dick began to focus on overtly 'Irish' themes, in *Visibility: Moderate – A Tourist Film* (1981), that critics such as Hoberman

90–4. 5 J. Hoberman 'After avant-garde film', in Brian Wallis (ed.), *Art after modernism: rethinking representation*, New York: New Museum of Contemporary Art, 1984: 68–9. Hoberman seeks to define the No Wave movement through reference to a definitively *American* avant-garde, which in his account seems to have developed largely in isolation from European practices. 6 With the notable exception of a 1988 screening at San Francisco's Pacific Cinemathèque. 7 Hoberman curated *Home movies: towards a natural history of narrow gauge: avant-garde filmmaking in America*, Anthology Film Archives, 1 May–30 June, 1981.

began to emphasize the fact that she was Irish.[8] Her association with No Wave cinema has also presented problems of categorization for Irish curators and critics, particularly in relation to the dominant practices in Irish cinema or visual art.[9] Until relatively recently, her work was outside the canon in its most literal sense: the national film archive.[10] This is despite the fact that she has made a large number of films in Ireland since the early 1980s and has represented Ireland in a small number of international exhibitions and festivals.[11]

A critical analysis of Vivienne Dick's work, from the late 1970s to the present, is clearly long overdue. But my own research centres on avant-garde currents in Irish filmmaking during the 1970s and 1980s and, as such, this paper deals only with a small selection of Dick's films. My aim is to highlight thematic parallels between her work and that of contemporary Irish filmmakers and I focus on the representation of the family and on the relationship between public and private space. In the process, I identify continuities between Dick's 'American' and 'Irish' films, centring on the notion of a cultural landscape that is mediated by Hollywood and by the experience of migration. *Visibility: Moderate – A Tourist Film* provides a focal point for my analysis because it is explicitly concerned with Dick's own position as a migrant filmmaker, positioned between Ireland and the US.

My analysis of Vivienne Dick's work, and Irish filmmaking in the late 1970s and early 1980s, is informed by reference to contemporary theories of the avant-garde. In particular, it relies heavily upon Paul Willemen's 'An Avant Garde for the Eighties' and Claire Johnston's analysis of Pat Murphy's film *Maeve*.[12] Although Willemen does not reference No Wave cinema directly, he traces a turn towards narrative across a range of feminist and anti-colonial practices. He theorizes an avant-garde that is structured by a critical engage-

8 J. Hoberman, 'Partly cloudy', *Village Voice*, 4 March 1981: 44. Dick's nationality was noted, however, in earlier interviews. See, Amy Taubin, 'The other cinema', *Soho Weekly News*, 12 July 1979: 44, and Stephen Barth, 'Not your ordinary dick', *East Village Eye*, 18 March 1980: 10. 9 Vivienne Dick is not mentioned in either Martin McLoone's *Irish film: the emergence of a contemporary cinema*, London: BFI, 2000 or Lance Pettitt's *Screening Ireland: film and television representation*, Manchester: Manchester University Press, 2000. To be fair, neither publication claims to address avant-garde practice and Dick's work is also absent from surveys of Irish media art such as Shirley McWilliams's, 'Screen and screen again', *Circa, 100*, Summer 2002: 42–8. 10 It was only in the late 1990s, following the retrospectives at MoMA and the Whitney, that a number of Vivienne Dick's films were acquired by the Irish Film Archive, in the form of preservation prints. 11 *Images/Ireland* (1988) was included in *Selected Images*, an exhibition of Irish film (curated by Declan McGonagle and James Coleman) at Riverside Studios in London, as part of the 1988 *Sense of Ireland* cultural festival. This event explored the intersection between visual practice as narrative and situated Dick's work in relation to the work of Irish poets and writers as well as artists. More recently, *She Had Her Gun All Ready*, *Rothach* and *London Suite* were included in a season of Irish films (curated by Sheila Pratschke) included in the Island-Arts from Ireland festival at John F. Kennedy Center for the Performing Arts in 2000. 12 See Paul Willemen, 'An avant garde for the eighties', *Framework* 24, 1984: 53–73.

ment with specificities of cultural production *and* reception and he focuses, in particular, on the representation of landscape. Noting a shift away from modernist aesthetics and towards a critical engagement with the conventions of realism, he emphasizes that the new avant-garde may mobilize landscape 'as a layered set of discourses, as a text in its own right'.[13] This contrasts with conventional representations of landscape:

> In conventional narrative [...] a tourist's point of view is adopted as opposed to the point of view of those whose history is traced in [the landscape], or for whom the land is a crucial element in the relations of production that govern their lives. The tourist sees in the landscape only mirrors or projections of his/her own phantasms.[14]

Many of the filmmakers foregrounded by Willemen (Chantal Akerman, Cinema Action, Pat Murphy, Thaddeus O'Sullivan) are positioned *between*, rather than firmly within, national formations. Vivienne Dick's work, which transects a number of quite distinct contexts for avant-garde practice, also seems to have been formed by this productive position of 'outside-otherness'.

FROM THE MARGINS TO THE METROPOLIS

Before turning to the analysis of specific films, it may be useful to provide a brief biography of Vivienne Dick, tracing her various journeys between Ireland and the US. Born in Donegal in 1950, Vivienne Dick studied arts (Archaeology and French) at University College Dublin and then toured Europe, India and Mexico before finally moving to New York in 1975. There, she joined the Millennium Film Co-op and began exploring Super-8 film. It was not until she became involved with the Colab film collective, which included Beth B, Scott B, James Nares and Eric Mitchell, that she began to make and exhibit her own work. At this time she was also heavily involved in the Punk music scene and she collaborated with performers such as Lydia Lunch and Pat Place on film, performance and music projects.[15]

In the late 1970s New York was at the centre of the American avant-garde. It was home to a number of established institutions, from the Filmmakers' Co-op and Anthology Archives (associated with New American Cinema and the 'structuralism' of Michael Snow and Hollis Frampton) to the Whitney Museum (associated with the feminist and conceptual film of Yvonne Rainer and Vito Acconci, among others). The Lower East Side also hosted an increasing number of artists' studios, galleries and performance spaces. The No Wave

13 Ibid., 53. 14 Ibid., 69. 15 Details on Dick's musical career can be found in Alan Licht, 'The Primer', *The Wire: adventures in modern music* 225, November 2002: 34–41.

filmmakers, however, rejected both the established and 'alternative' art spaces, in favour of bars such as Max's Kansas City, temporary storefront cinemas, such as the New Cinema on St Mark's Place, as well as newer film clubs such as the Collective for Living Cinema and the Millennium. Instead of Anthology's reverence towards the medium of film and the Whitney's critical rigour, No Wave filmmakers sought to recapture something of the populist appeal of 1960s underground cinema by screening their films in rock clubs between the bands.

Super-8 appealed to the No Wave filmmakers because of its accessibility and its long association with home movies. In the mid-1970s it also became possible to record sync sound and the 'anti-aesthetic' of Super-8 became associated with Punk. The No Wave featured a number of prominent women performers and this was highlighted in Vivienne Dick's first completed film, *Guérillière Talks* (1978), which consists of a series of 'interviews', each running for the length of a three minute reel. Despite this 'structuralist' approach, however, *Guérillière Talks* is clearly less concerned with the specificity of film than with issues of gender.[16] Her subsequent films, *Staten Island* (1978), *She Had Her Gun All Ready* (1978), *Beauty Becomes the Beast* (1979) and *Liberty's Booty* (1980) retain something of this quasi-documentary quality. Yet, with the exception of *Liberty's Booty*, they are also notable for the way in which they cast No Wave 'stars', such as Lydia Lunch and Pat Place, as characters in trash melodrama.

Although all of these works were produced on a very low budget, funded entirely by Vivienne Dick's earnings, their circulation was supported by an established network of clubs and societies and by the early 1980s, Dick was touring with her work to film clubs and colleges throughout the US.[17] Her films were shown on Manhattan Cable, a public access television station, at international festivals such as Berlin, Genoa and Edinburgh [18] and, in 1981, a programme of her films was screened at San Francisco's Pacific Cinemathèque. Finally, in 1983, *Visibility: Moderate* (1981) was included in the film programme of the Whitney Biennial, a prestigious survey of contemporary art.[19] But by this time, however, Vivienne Dick had relocated to Ireland.

16 Dick's work during this period was specifically informed by Monique Wittig's critique of gender. 17 These include the Walker Arts Center and Cal Arts. Dick discusses the distribution of her work in the US and in Ireland when interviewed by Scott MacDonald. See Scott MacDonald, 'Interview with Vivienne Dick', 98–9. 18 Karen Kay, 'New York Super-8: Edinburgh Event, 1980', *Idiolects*, Winter 1980: 7–9. 19 Commenting on his own experience of seeing the film in New York in the early 1980s, Tom Gunning has pointed out that *Visibility: Moderate* was not shown in Punk venues. I am indebted to Gunning for pointing this out because my subsequent research suggests that a shift in exhibition (and possibly in Dick's approach to practice) *did* take place around this time. But it may have happened even before 1981 since only *Guérillière Talks* and *She Had Her Gun All Ready* were actually first shown in rock clubs. Each of the subsequent films, including *Visibility: Moderate,* was shown first in dedicated film clubs (either in the Millennium or in the Collective for Living Cinema).

Her decision to return to Ireland was prompted, in part, by positive encounters with Irish filmmakers in New York and in Ireland. She met Bob Quinn and later Thaddeus O'Sullivan and Pat Murphy in New York, while attending screenings of Irish film, including O'Sullivan's *A Pint of Plain* (1975) and Murphy's *Rituals of Memory* (1977).[20] On a brief visit to Dublin, in 1979, she followed Quinn's recommendation to contact Project Arts Centre and arranged screenings of her own work for filmmakers such as Cathal Black. At this time, Project was at the centre of a vibrant indigenous film culture, which was supported by new initiatives in arts policy.[21] When Dick returned in 1982, however, Project Cinema Club was less active and, although the Irish Film Board had been established, the facilities for low budget avant-garde production were underdeveloped at best. Dick continued to exhibit her work at film clubs such as the Ha'penny, at festivals outside Dublin and in colleges. She also became involved in running one of Ireland's first film production courses, at the College of Commerce, Rathmines (now part of DIT).

While in Ireland, Vivienne Dick completed a number of short Super-8 films, including *Trailer* (1983) and *Like Dawn to Dust* (1983). The latter film, set within the Irish rural landscape, features a performance by Lydia Lunch and was subsequently broadcast by Channel Four. But in the absence of recognition from funding agencies for her previous Super-8 work, she found it difficult to continue her film practice.[22] In 1984 she left Dublin for London, where she became a member (and later a director) of the London Film-makers' Co-op. Almost immediately after arriving in London, she received funding from the British Arts Council to complete *Rothach* (1985), a 16mm film photographed in Donegal. She subsequently secured a number of commissions and awards from both Irish and British agencies and continued to explore Irish subjects in films such as *Images/Ireland* (1988) *Pobal-Portrait of an Artist* (1988) and *A Skinny Little Man Attacked Daddy* (1994).[23]

BETWEEN THE PUBLIC AND PRIVATE: VIVIENNE DICK'S NEW YORK

As I have already noted, New York occupied a key place within the American avant-gardes of the late 1970s. It boasted both the established cultural insti-

20 Vivienne Dick, interviewed by the author, 23 June 2001. **21** See Kevin Rockett, 'Constructing a film culture: Ireland', *Screen Education*, 1978: 23–33. **22** Vivienne Dick, interviewed by the author, 23 June 2001. **23** The *Pobal* series was produced by Bob Quinn for RTE. *London Suite* (1989) was funded by an 'Experimenta' award and was shown on Channel Four and RTE. *New York Conversations* (1991) was funded by the Arts Council of Great Britain. Vivienne Dick has since returned to live in Ireland and is currently based in Galway. Her most recent work, *Excluded by the Nature of Things*, made in 2002, is a multi-screen video installation funded by the Irish Film Board.

tutions, such as MoMA and the Whitney, and the alternative spaces of the Lower East Side, some of which had witnessed the emergence of underground cinema. But the city also served as the privileged symbol, if not the actual centre, of globalized capitalism and it remained a focal point for migrants from all parts of the world. New York's doubled identity, as both 'subcultural' haven and global trade centre was, of course, most evident in the Lower East Side, located in close proximity to the twin towers. Towards the end of the 1970s these contradictory aspects of New York city life became particularly pronounced when rents in the Lower East Side began to rise, driven by a process of gentrification to which artists had perhaps (unwittingly) contributed.[24]

Vivienne Dick's early Super-8 narratives figure New York as a site of conspicuous consumption and waste. One of her first films, *Staten Island* (1978), is actually set in what appears to be a dump. In this short work, an androgynous female figure (the No Wave musician and performer Pat Place) investigates various abandoned objects, adopting the manner and wearing the costume of a visitor from outer space. The distinctive No Wave or Punk 'anti-aesthetic' becomes more pronounced in later films, through the accumulation of mass-produced goods and the referencing of retro fashion and pop music (as well as Punk). This aesthetic seems to suggest a convergence of formerly distinct eras, a form of time-space compression that David Harvey has identified as characteristic of postmodernity.[25]

Pat Place also features in *She Had Her Gun All Ready* (1978) which remains one of Vivienne Dick's most acclaimed films. This is a narrative of obsessive desire focusing on the relationship between Place and the 'femme fatale' Lydia Lunch. It is set within iconic New York settings such as East Village diners and Coney Island and it explores the dark side of American culture, with fleeting references to serial killers and stalkers. Dick's next film, *Beauty Becomes the Beast* (1979), also explores the flip side of the American dream and it shares some of the same themes as *Taxi Driver*. The central character in this mock-documentary (played by Lydia Lunch) is a teenage runaway, turned prostitute. Much of the action takes place in the contemporary Lower East Side, complete with vacant industrial lots, but this 'realism' is disrupted by the casting of Lunch, and by the use of melodramatic flashbacks which hint at a history of abuse.

Liberty's Booty (1980), Vivienne Dick's subsequent film, also explores the theme of sexual exploitation, focusing on a group of prostitutes working in a New York brothel. This film developed out of a series of interviews and many

24 Many New York-based artists were politicised by the rent crisis and they participated in benefit gigs, exhibitions and rent strikes. For an analysis of the gentrification process, see Craig Owens, 'The Problem with Puerilism', *Art in America*, 6, 1984: 162–3 and Rosalyn Deutsche and Cara Gendel Ryan, 'The fine art of gentrification', *October*, 31, 1984: 91–111. 25 David Harvey, *The condition of postmodernity*, Oxford: Blackwell, 1990: 201–326.

of the participants are not actors. But, like much of Dick's work, it resists easy categorization as the 'documentary' sections are framed by a short animation and interspersed with some obviously staged elements. Despite the apparent sensationalism of its subject matter, the narrative is resolutely focused on the everyday, calling attention to the domestic details of these women's lives. The women are, in fact, represented primarily as exploited *workers* and in the latter part of the film the critique of gender relations is displaced by a broader interrogation of US capitalism, when Dick suggests an analogy between the brothel and employment practices of McDonald's restaurants.[26]

Despite an evident fascination with American culture, Vivienne Dick's early films offer a number of thematic and formal parallels with the work of Irish contemporaries. For example, *Beauty Becomes the Beast* and *Liberty's Booty* both explore memories of abuse, exploitation and violence, as do Cathal Black's *Our Boys* (1981) and Joe Comerford's *Traveller* (1981). Yet, while the films of Black and Comerford have been theorized as explorations of national identity and national history[27] Dick's work seems to lack any overt reference to foundational narratives or myths of the Irish nation. But in *Liberty's Booty*, the exploration of gender stereotypes is informed by a critique of the mythic tropes through which the American nation has been imagined. The figure of 'Liberty'[28] becomes a symbol of exploitation as well as freedom and is aligned with another signifier of globalized capitalism, the golden arches of MacDonald's.

The representation of public and private space in Dick's New York films might also be read in terms of an exploration of Irish identity. *She Had Her Gun All Ready*, *Beauty Becomes the Beast* and *Liberty's Booty* are initially set within domestic environments. Yet, despite the deeply personal character of the themes explored in the two earlier films, the central characters end up playing out their fears and fantasies on the street. *Liberty's Booty* also disrupts fixed concepts of personal space because it is set within an apartment that doubles as a brothel. In *Transformations in Irish Culture*, Luke Gibbons highlights a 'blurring of boundaries between the personal and the political', associated with the experience of colonization.[29] He notes both that the colonized nation may be conceptualized as a literal 'body politic' and that an 'alternative "feminised" public sphere (imagined as the nation)' can serve to turn the colonial stereotype against itself, providing a critique of the official patriarchal order of the state. The confusion of public and private in Dick's work could

26 A fascination with the sex industry, in terms of its relationship to other forms of commerce is also evident in the films of Beth and Scott B, such as *G-Man* and *Black Box*, which reveal sado-masochistic desires at the heart of corporate and security agencies. 27 See Kevin Rockett, Luke Gibbons and John Hill, *Cinema and Ireland*, London: Routledge, 1988: 127–44 and McLoone, *Irish Film*, 131–50. 28 Marjorie Keller (a filmmaker loosely associated with the No Wave project) employs a home movie format to critique this symbol from a feminist perspective in *Daughters of Chaos* (1980). 29 Luke Gibbons, *Transformations in Irish culture*, Cork: Cork University Press, 1996: 21.

be read in these terms, as an attempt to negotiate the relationship between the nation, the state and the female body. Arguably, however, this project is also informed by the No Wave's particular investment in New York as both a site of cultural opposition and a global symbol.

LOOKING TOWARDS IRELAND: MYTH AND MEMORY

> Tourist Land is always make-believe land in a certain way. You work most of the year and in America you get two weeks off, only two weeks. [...] You escape into this fantasy land, where everything has to be beautiful and fabulous. If it's Ireland you see lush green countryside and horses and carts and the Blarney Stone. [...] It's totally unreal; it's all memory and myth.[30]

The final section of *Liberty's Booty* features a number of references to Ireland, and specifically to a strike by Irish McDonald's workers, which was apparently broken by 'heavies from America'. Ireland is represented initially by images of rolling fields viewed from above, and by a tourist postcard of Irish dancing. In the closing shots, however, news coverage of Pope John Paul II, identified by the newscaster as 'the superstar Pope', seem to suggest a convergence between Irish and American popular culture, mediated by communication technology. Vivienne Dick's next film, *Visibility: Moderate,* examines this mediated relationship between Ireland and the US in further detail, focusing on advertising and tourism. But it also considers the way in which the lived experience of place is structured by traditions of representation associated with the colonial state and with projects of resistance.

Visibility: Moderate is perhaps Vivienne Dick's most self-reflexive work. Although the title is taken from a weather report overheard at one point in the narrative, it could also be said to describe the prospects for avant-garde filmmaking in Ireland and the economic interdependencies between Ireland and the US. The first part of the film follows an American woman, dressed in fashionably retro clothes, on a tour of Irish landmarks and seems to take the form of a home movie. This 'tourist' poses in the ruins of Irish monasteries, visits the Puck Fair, kisses the Blarney stone and travels on a horse drawn cart, recalling images from iconic John Hinde postcards and, most obviously, the romantic landscape of John Ford's *The Quiet Man* (1952). The 'tour' is, however, punctuated by a montage of TV ads (ranging from the amateurish animation of '*Jack Ryan* truck rental' to the slick suburban fantasy offered by *Blueband* margarine) and by several comic interludes in which the tourist imagines herself as a 'Celt' running through a mystical rural landscape.[31]

30 MacDonald, 'Interview with Vivienne Dick', 97. 31 The soundtrack also provides a coun-

As the tour progresses it becomes apparent that the visitor is in fact Irish-American, and her fantasies acquire an even greater resonance. But *Visibility: Moderate* is not exclusively concerned with cultural tourism, or even ethnicity, and the journey to Ireland is book-ended by images of the twin towers of the World Trade Center. The pre-credit sequence introduces the connection between power and vision; the camera pans from the spectacular view over New York city back to the central character, who is slicing a pineapple, a graphic symbol of global trade. This alignment between spectacle and power becomes overt in the second part of the film, which deals primarily with surveillance. The tourist embarks on an alternative sightseeing journey through the urban spaces of Dublin and Belfast. She encounters a series of unlikely characters, from kitsch religious singers to labour activists and Hare Krishnas. These sequences, and specifically the street protests against the H Block prisons, are reminiscent of certain sections in Thaddeus O'Sullivan's *A Pint of Plain* (1975), just as the earlier images of the Puck Fair echo scenes from O'Sullivan's *On a Paving Stone Mounted* (1978).[32]

The tour ends with an interview with the former political prisoner Maureen Gibson. It is filmed straight to camera, in the manner of a press conference. But the inclusion of a visible microphone is also reminiscent of Dick's earlier 'interview' film *Guérillière Talks*. As Gibson describes the ritual humiliations[33] enacted by prison authorities, the discourse of the interview is disrupted, by the motion of the camera (slowly zooming in and out) and by the insertion of computerized titles, detailing Gibson's history. So, despite an initial focus on tourism and performative ethnicity, *Visibility: Moderate* is ultimately concerned with the politics of representations, both in relation to the 'troubles' and the experience of women.

Like Dawn to Dust, made two years later, takes up the exploration of the rural landscape initiated in *Visibility: Moderate* but it is characterized by a very different mode of address. Instead of appropriating from radio, television or film, Dick develops a more overtly 'poetic' aesthetic, through performance, cinematography and sound. The opening shots of a decaying 'Big House', bearing the scorch marks of a fire, are accompanied by an off-key piano, recalling stage melodrama or early cinema. The house, most likely a remnant of Anglo-Irish society, is abandoned but for the figure of Lydia Lunch, wearing her signature New York 'Goth' make-up and clothes. Lunch delivers a poetic monologue, both on screen and in voice-over, over a traditional soundtrack

terpoint to the imagery, including a segment from RTÉ's *Glenabbey Show*, with the character of Festy (played by Frank Kelly) engaging in the kind of double-meaning commentary that has traditionally divided the tourist from the local. 32 For a discussion of the theme of the 'visual' in O'Sullivan's film, see Cheryl Herr, 'Addressing the eye in Ireland: Thaddeus O'Sullivan's *On a Paving Stone Mounted* (1978)', *Historical Journal of Film, Radio and Television*, 20: 3, 2000: 367–74. 33 No Wave filmmakers Beth and Scott B also explore media constructions of political violence, but, in contrast with *Visibility: Moderate*, their work tends to mythologize (and sexualize) terrorism.

and her final words emphasize the circularity of Irish narratives: 'the past never dies, it just continually repeats itself'.

Rothach (1985), Vivienne Dick's next film, extends this exploration of narrative and the poetic. It was filmed on 16mm in the Donegal countryside and is composed of a rhythmic series of pans across a barren rural landscape that recalls the setting for Michael Snow's monumental work *La Region Centrale.* Unlike Snow's rocky landscape, however, *Rothach* is filled with evidence of activity. Scenes of a child playing the fiddle are interspersed with shots of farm machinery and turf-cutting on the bog. Many of these images are strikingly picturesque and reminiscent of iconic Irish colour postcards. But the serenity of the location is gradually undercut, both by the soundtrack, which changes from a melody into a series of shifting electronic pulses, and by the uncanny presence of the same child in different locations. It soon becomes apparent that this landscape is highly constructed.

The word 'Rothach' can be translated from Irish to mean cycle or wheel and the film closes with a recitation of Seán Ó Riordáin's Irish-language poem 'An Roithleán', which evokes a moment between sleep and wakefulness. Despite the relatively conventional nature of the images, this use of oral narration (particularly in the Irish language) seems to work against a 'tourist' perspective. In the process, the film seems to mobilize the landscape as a text to be read. So while *Visibility Moderate* foregrounds the difficulty of finding a vocabulary adequate to the representation of the landscape, *Rothach* seems to privilege an historical relationship between image, language and landscape.

CONCLUSION: FROM NO WAVE TO NATIONAL CINEMA

There are pronounced differences, in setting, format and mode of address, between Vivienne Dick's 'American' and 'Irish' films. But her practice, through the late 1970s and early 1980s, remains structured by the need to develop a filmic vocabulary adequate to the articulation of Irish experience. Of necessity this vocabulary encompasses, but is not limited to, the genres and conventions of narrative cinema. As I have already noted, J. Hoberman categorizes the No Wave aesthetic as a 'postmodern' return to Warhol and underground cinema. I would argue, however, that Vivienne Dick's work calls for a more complex interrogation of cultural exchange, with respect to avant-garde practice and popular culture.

Hoberman's account explicitly aims to counter Peter Wollen's influential genealogy of 'the two avant-gardes', which theorizes distinct aesthetic and political currents in American and European practice. But this attention to the history of avant-garde practice was itself informed by what Andreas Huyssen has identified as the postmodern 'search for tradition'.[34] Huyssen calls attention

34 Andreas Huyssen, 'The search for tradition: avant-garde and postmodernism in the 1970s', *New German Critique,* Winter 1998: 23–40.

to the cultural and historical factors structuring the emergence of pop and underground film in the 1960s and he notes that what might have seemed new, or even revolutionary, to a US audience could also signify mere repetition to Europeans. His analysis highlights the fact that the avant-garde's alignment with the popular (and the oppositional) can take the form of a rejection *or* an endorsement of modernist aesthetics.

The parallels between Vivienne Dick's work, and that of her Irish contemporaries, must be situated in relation to a reconsideration of narrative form in avant-garde practice in the late 1970s and early 1980s. Since No Wave cinema emerged as a rejection of institutional formations particular to the American context, its re-appropriation of Hollywood genres formed part of a populist mode of address. In the Irish context, however, the 'popular' was located in a revival of Brecht and in a recuperation of narrative forms associated with the anti-colonial project. But the work of filmmakers such as Bob Quinn, Pat Murphy, Joe Comerford and Thaddeus O'Sullivan *also* responded to a tradition of representation associated with Hollywood cinema. As such, No Wave and the emergent Irish national cinema share a certain investment in generic form and in the recuperation of earlier modes of oppositional practice.

While critical analysis of the intersections between the neo-avant-gardes and the emergent national cinemas of the 1970s and 1980s remains limited, Miriam Hansen has provided a useful account of the relationship between Hollywood and the historical avant-gardes of the 1920s and 1930s.[35] She theorizes classical cinema as a form of 'vernacular modernism': an aesthetic idiom encompassing elements of the American everyday or quotidian which mediated competing cultural discourses on modernity and modernization.[36] As she points out, Hollywood film appealed to avant-garde artists and intellectuals in both the USA and 'the modernizing capitals of the world' and she goes on to trace this vernacular through the work of Eisenstein, among others.

The 'Americanism' of classical cinema may have intensified its appeal for European avant-gardes but, by this time, many Irish audiences were already familiar with aspects of the American everyday. Before the advent of cinema, mass emigration to America had contributed to the 'disintegration and fragmentation' of Irish society and, as Luke Gibbons notes, it had accentuated the premature 'shock of modernity' on Irish culture, even in its most remote rural outposts.[37] Hollywood's subsequent incorporation, and mediation, of images

35 Miriam Hansen, 'The mass production of the senses' in Christine Gledhill and Linda Williams (eds), *Re-inventing film studies*, London and New York: Arnold and Oxford University Press, 2000: 332–50. 36 Hansen, 'The mass production of the senses', 333–4. 37 Gibbons, *Transformations in Irish culture*, 6. While literature and music articulated the trauma of exile, the letters, remittances and commodities sent home by Irish emigrants structured Irish perceptions of America. See Kerby A. Miller, *Emigrants and exiles: Ireland and the Irish exodus to North America*, Oxford and New York: Oxford University Press, 1985: 357–61. 38 Hansen, 'The mass production of the senses', 332.

of Ireland and Irishness only added a new dimension, then, to an already complex relationship between Irish and American modernity.

As theorists of recent Irish cinema such as McLoone have noted, America continues to retain a hold over the Irish imagination. It is this cultural landscape, emerging at the intersection of rural and metropolitan spaces through a process of exchange, that Vivienne Dick's films seem to chart. Miriam Hansen notes that the 'postmodernist challenge' has opened up a space for the understanding of 'alternative forms of modernism [...] that vary according to their social and geopolitical locations, often configured along the axis of post/coloniality and according to the specific subcultural and indigenous traditions to which they responded'.[38] Vivienne Dick's work, existing on the margins of avant-garde practice and national cinema, seems to constitute an important contribution to this critical project.

Part 2: Film Form, Representation and Culture

'Pigs!':[1] polluting bodies and knowledge in Neil Jordan's *The Butcher Boy*[2]

ELLEN E. SWEENEY

Recent writing[3] on Neil Jordan's 1997 film, *The Butcher Boy*, has suggested that the film is a visualization of the confrontation between tradition and modernity in Ireland in the 1960s that gave birth to the globalized Ireland of the Celtic Tiger of the 1990s. Although it depicts rural Irish society at a particular historical period – the height of the Cuban Missile Crisis – it is not a heritage film, but an exploration of the way in which the recent past is 'remembered and interpreted' in contemporary Ireland.[4] Martin McLoone characterizes the Ireland depicted in the film as one in which empty nationalist rhetoric masks a society 'riven by poverty, complacency, hypocrisy and neglect',[5] and that is haunted by traumatic histories of colonial oppression, famine and emigration and oversaturated by American popular culture. In their study of the film, Emer and Kevin Rockett argue that the particular issues with which the film deals – the sexual abuse of children by clergy, the crisis of cultural identity, modernization, 'aspiration and representation', globalization, and Ireland's ambivalent relationship to Britain[6] – are more relevant to today's Ireland than the Ireland of the 1960s. The film can thus be read as a kind of 'state of the nation' piece in which the affluent nation of the 1990s looks back at the period when the process of Ireland's modernization began.[7] Reading the film's protagonist, Francie Brady, the abused child[8], as an allegory for Irish history, Martin McLoone argues that the boy's 'increasingly unhinged and psychotic behavior' is in 'direct proportion' to the psychosis of the world around him.[9]

1 I would like to thank Cheryl Herr at the University of Iowa and Tom Gunning at the University of Chicago for their suggestions regarding the development of this paper. I am grateful to Jessica Scarlata at New York University and Henry Sussman at the State University of New York at Buffalo for sharing with me their unpublished essays on the film. Most particularly, I thank John Hill at the University of Ulster at Coleraine and Kevin Rockett at Trinity College Dublin for inviting me to present at the seminar in 2003 and for their incisive comments regarding an earlier draft of this paper. 2 A version of this essay, 'Mrs Nugent's little piggy went to town: abjected identities and the traumatic return in Neil Jordan's *The Butcher Boy*', has been published in *Cultural dynamics* 15: 3. 3 Martin McLoone, *Irish film: the emergence of a contemporary cinema*, London: British Film Institute, 2000: 213–23; Emer Rockett and Kevin Rockett, *Neil Jordan: exploring boundaries*, Dublin: The Liffey Press, 2003: 179–203. 4 McLoone, *Irish film*, 217. 5 Ibid., 221. 6 Rockett and Rockett, *Neil Jordan*, 181. 7 McLoone, *Irish film*, 217. 8 Ibid., 220. 9 Ibid.

The film's utilization of the structure of return, associated with the traumatic event of Francie's interpellation as a pig, emphasizes a non-linear conception of history in which a colonial past continues to influence the experience and perceptions of the postcolonial present. In its reference to a long-repressed historical event that came to light decades afterward – the sexual abuse of industrial schools children by clergy in postcolonial Ireland – Jordan's film, like the pig into which Francie is interpellated, troubles the boundaries separating 'fact' from 'fiction'. As a fictional narrative that testifies to a repressed history, *The Butcher Boy*'s contaminated text allows us, the viewers, to gain an understanding of the punishment that the most vulnerable in society had to bear in the clash between old and new Ireland.

Briefly, Neil Jordan's *The Butcher Boy* is a film adaptation of Patrick McCabe's 1992 novel of the same title. The film and novel concern twelve-year-old Francie Brady's exploits in and eventual exclusion from society in 1960s small-town Ireland. The film's paradisiacal beginning in a luscious rural Ireland abruptly ends with Francie and his mother being castigated as 'pigs' by the middle-class Mrs Nugent, the mother of Francie's prissy classmate from whom he stole comic books. This epithet, which evokes a history of English anti-Irish caricatures, will haunt Francie throughout the film. Life in the Brady home is characterized by abuse and neglect, as Francie is the son of an alcoholic, unemployed trumpet player and a psychologically unstable mother. Fleeing an abusive home environment to find freedom in Dublin, Francie returns after a short period to discover his mother has committed suicide. Following his mother's suicide, Francie focuses his anger on the Nugents, and breaks into the Nugent home and defaces it. Francie is sent to an industrial school to be reformed, but finds himself subject there to molestation by a priest and visions of the Virgin Mary. After attacking the priest who had been molesting him, Francie is sent home and takes a job as a 'butcher boy', working in the slaughterhouse and living on the margins of society as an alcoholic and violent troublemaker. After Francie's father dies and the police discover that Francie has not reported the death, but has left the body in the home, Francie is sent to a psychiatric institution (where he is given electric shock treatments) and from which he eventually escapes. Hearing that his best friend Joe is going to boarding school near where his parents had honeymooned, Francie goes off to visit the only place his parents said they were ever happy and to renew his friendship with Joe. In the course of his journey, Francie discovers that his parents' stories were lies and Joe rejects Francie's friendship. The end of his friendship with Joe causes Francie to return home to kill Mrs Nugent whom he blames for all his troubles. At the height of the Cuban Missile Crisis, the time when the town is awaiting an apparition of the Virgin Mary to deliver them from the impending nuclear holocaust, Francie Brady provides the town with an alternate vision: Mrs Nugent's dismembered corpse found in the bottom of the brock heap – the feeding place for pigs – and the name 'Pigs,' written in Mrs Nugent's blood, covering the walls of the Nugent home. The film ends with the middle-aged Francie's release from the mental institution in which he had been incarcerated following his murder of Mrs Nugent.

The Butcher Boy, both as a literary and film text, belong to a subgenre of Irish writing, and documentary and fiction films, that emerged in the 1980s and 1990s that dealt with the legacy of the industrial school system, which was in operation from the late Victorian era until the 1970s, when it was phased out following the publication of the Kennedy Report, which condemned its treatment of children.[10] Run by religious orders but funded by the state, the industrial school system was the most financially expedient model for the care of poor children.[11] In his study of writings on the industrial school system, Michael Molino argues that a system conceived to offer a solution to the Victorian workhouse evolved into one in which the poor were criminalized and exploited for commercial gain.[12] Ultimately, the schools operated as a kind of plantation system, with the children working as ill-fed, uneducated, and physically and sexually-abused indentured servants. Memoirs such as Paddy Doyle's *The God Squad* (1988), Patrick Touher's *Fear of the Collar* (1991), novels such as Mannix Flynn's *Nothing to Say* (1983) and Patrick McCabe's *The Butcher Boy* (1992) (shortlisted for the Booker Prize), and television documentaries such as *Dear Daughter* (1996) and *States of Fear* (1999)[13] worked to create a consciousness of abuse within Irish culture which had been 'ignored or disbelieved' while the schools were still in operation.[14] In particular, the public outcry caused by RTÉ's (Radio Telefis Éireann, the state-run television station) airing of *States of Fear* impelled the taoiseach to issue a formal apology to the victims of abuse in the schools and to set up the Commission to Inquire into Childhood Abuse in 1999.[15] The airing of this documentary is proof of a change within Irish culture; for ten years, RTÉ had refused to air a drama-documentary which it had funded, Cathal Black's *Our Boys* (1981), for fear that the film's representation of the Christian Brothers' system of education as '(physically) abusive and controlling' would 'offend the still dominant Church".[16] Like Peter Mullan's *The Magdalene Sisters* (2002), *The Butcher Boy* is a cinematic intervention that allows for repressed images and voices finally to be seen and heard in Irish society.

Francie's interpellation as a pig is a metaphor for the way in which Ireland's colonial past as an abjected people continues to influence the way in which

10 Michael R. Molino, 'The "House of a Hundred Windows": industrial schools in Irish writing', *New Hibernia Review*, 5: 1, URL (consulted March 2002) http://muse.jhu.edu/journals/nhr/. 11 Mary Raftery and Eoin O'Sullivan, *Suffer the little children: the inside story of Ireland's industrial schools*, New York: Continuum, 1999: 38. 12 Molino, 'The "House of a Hundred Windows", 41. 13 Ibid., 33–52. 14 Ibid., 34. 15 Ibid. 16 Rockett and Rockett, *Neil Jordan*, 187.

Irish society conceives of itself. According to literary critic Anne McClintock, the process of abjection was a 'formative aspect of modern industrial imperialism' in the nineteenth century, in which 'certain groups [were] expelled and obliged to inhabit the impossible edges of modernity', such as the slum, and are those 'industrial imperialism cannot do without'.[17] In her thesis, she draws on Kristeva's theory of abjection, which suggested that subjects were fundamentally constituted through the abjection or expulsion of 'impure' matter.[18] Objects that are considered filthy are those that have been expelled from a boundary to a (bodily) margin,[19] such as 'spittle, blood, milk, urine or tears'.[20] It is abjected matter's 'composite' or ambiguous identity, which troubles the boundary between inside and outside that 'disturbs identity, system, order,'[21] and thus renders it threatening. For Kristeva, abjection is the fear that this 'border matter' constantly threatens the subject with annihilation. She writes that when 'weary of fruitless attempts to identify with something on the outside, [the subject] finds the impossible within; when it finds that the impossible constitutes its very being, that is nothing other than abject'.[22] In this reading of society, the socially marginal becomes symbolically central.[23]

In British colonial discourses from the sixteenth to seventeenth centuries onward, the Irish had been associated with the boundary-troubling pig, which was considered almost human because of its physical resemblance to a Caucasian baby, similar dietary habits, and living in the household with the family.[24] For the British, the Irish were abject because of their own racial ambiguity; they were a 'white' colonized race.[25] In nineteenth-century England, the Irish were blamed for the filth of the slums because of their habit of having pigs live in their homes, despite this also being a common English practice at the time.[26] The commonplace association of the Irish with the pig found its way into representations in nineteenth- and early twentieth-century British and American popular cultures. In response to the rise of militant Fenianism and emigration to Great Britain in the nineteenth century, the Irish were stereotyped as pigs or monkeys in the pages of *Punch*.[27] In early American cinema, a main character in a Thomas Edison serial was a stereotypically 'impetuous, stupid and drunk' Irishman.[28] In one instalment of the serial, *Casey's Twins* (1903), a pig (dressed in clothes) and a human infant share the same crib and fight over a bottle.[29] In later American cinema, a young Irish girl is shown playing with pigs in *Smiling Irish Eyes* (1929).[30] Despite the pig's

17 Ann McClintock, *Imperial leather: race, gender and sexuality in the colonial conquest*, New York: Routledge, 1995: 72. **18** Ibid., 71. **19** Mary Douglas, *Purity and danger: an analysis of concepts of pollution and taboo*, New York: Frederick A. Praeger, 1966: 121. **20** Julia Kristeva, *Powers of horror: an essay on abjection*, trans. Leon S. Roudiez, New York: Columbia University Press, 1982: 69. **21** Ibid., 4. **22** Ibid., 5. **23** Peter Stallybrass and Allan White, *The politics and poetics of transgression*, London: Methuen, 1986: 5. **24** Ibid., 132, 47. **25** McClintock, *Imperial leather*, 59–60. **26** Ibid., 132. **27** Rockett and Rockett, *Neil Jordan*, 195. **28** Ibid. **29** Ibid. **30** Kevin Rockett, Luke Gibbons and John Hill, *Cinema and Ireland*, London: Croom

negative significations, Emer and Kevin Rockett suggest that there is a positive ambiguity to the Irish association with the pig; the Irish habit of keeping pigs in the home was a sign of their economic independence as the pig enabled the Irish a level of 'independence and self-sufficiency', serving 'the family rather than the Empire'.[31] The Rocketts read Francie's interpellation as a pig not simply as being 'uncouth', but as being 'too Irish and too rooted in the past', and therefore the opposite of Mrs Nugent, who with her 'sophistication' acquired from living in England, is representative of the 'new social and economic smugness of the Lemassite era'.[32] In terms of the film's narrative, Francie's first reaction to Mrs Nugent's interpellation and his eventual marginalization can be read as a shift from an anarchic celebration of the pig's more empowering significations – the Pig-Toll tax sequence turns the affectations of the Nugents' against them – to the most negative as Francie becomes society's pariah as the butcher boy (of both pigs and Mrs Nugent).

The Butcher Boy is in many ways a creation story that depicts how one emotionally and economically impoverished child became Irish society's nightmare figure. The film begins with a montage sequence of various comic-book characters and ends with a mummy in a hospital bed. The image dissolves onto the cinematic image of Francie Brady – the mummy – lying in the hospital bed, being asked by his former employer, the pig butcher, why he did what he did. The image then cuts to what is a cinematic quotation from Genesis, the theft of the forbidden fruit, which is followed up by one from the Odyssey, with Mrs Nugent as Circe[33] turning the Bradys into pigs. Although the film begins in a euphoric spirit, Francie's interpellation into a pig becomes the point of origin of his journey into darkness as Francie's proliferating identities – drawn from American and British popular culture – lose their power to sustain Francie and he becomes confined to a single, essentializing identity: the boy-pig. In an action that is a metaphor for the treatment that Francie and his family will receive from Irish society throughout the film, the middle-class Mrs Nugent's epithet draws a *cordon sanitaire* around the Bradys in order to protect herself and her family from the Bradys' contaminating influence, which she sees as poverty, alcoholism, and shiftlessness. Mrs Nugent's conflict with the Bradys is a confrontation between the post-Independence nationalist ideal, epitomized by the Catholic middle class, with the reality of Ireland's underclass whose existence challenges the essentialism of that conception of the Irish nation. In order for this ideal to remain 'pure', Mrs Nugent must exclude the Bradys from the body politic by categorizing them as subhuman. In being interpellated as a pig, Francie is pulled out of one existence – a carefree boyhood – and categorized into another that denies him his very humanity.

Helm, 1987: 54. 31 Rockett and Rockett, *Neil Jordan*, 196. 32 Ibid. 33 Henry Sussman, 'On the butcher block: a panorama of social marking,' unpublished essay, 2001: 8.

Francie's interpellation as a pig is an extreme example of the violence inherent in being named, which is one of the fundamental ways in which a subject is constructed in language because a subject's existence depends on the 'address of the Other'.[34] In being named, the subject both acquires and becomes responsible for the history inherent in the name. Judith Butler underscores that we are all ultimately powerless in determining the names by which we are hailed.[35] Writing about interpellation[36] as hate speech, Butler suggests that, 'Injurious names have a history … [in the way] such histories are installed and arrested in and by the name',[37] the name's historicity is the 'sedimentation of its usages' that 'gives the name its force'.[38]

In her speech act, Mrs Nugent calls on a history of domination and invalidation of the underclass that is incorporated in the name 'pig', which had once been used by the English colonizers to legitimate their subjugation of the native Irish, but is now appropriated by the post-Independence native middle class to support its own social agenda and to distance themselves from Ireland's seedy underside. This historicity not only empowers Mrs Nugent's diatribe against the Bradys, but also transforms the speaker into an instrument of oppression as Mrs Nugent herself becomes incorporated into the historicity of the name. As a proper middle-class Catholic woman whose experiences of living in England have given her an elevated social standing in the community, Mrs Nugent's hybrid identity suggests that the ongoing influence of the Irish colonial past is further magnified by its reinterpretation into the post-Independence present. Mrs Nugent also appears to need to distance herself from her 'roots' – her bogmen brothers – and so Francie and his family are the victims of a kind of displaced abjection,[39] in which Mrs Nugent displaces her sense of inferiority onto her socio-economic inferiors, the Bradys. In being named a 'pig' by Mrs Nugent, Francie finds himself inscribed into a certain social position, with a history from which he cannot free himself, and a predetermined destiny from which he cannot escape.

Francie's interpellation becomes the structuring topos of his narrative; after his naming, Francie reads the time before and after the 'naming ceremony' in terms of events that relate to his family's and his own porcine nature. It is important to note that the word 'pig' does not have the same historicity for Mrs Brady as it will have for her son. Operating as a sign, the word as interpellation has countless significations, any one of which can be read and assigned as the truth of the name. In short, Mrs Brady reads one interpretation into the interpellation while Francie will read another. Most importantly, while

34 Judith Butler, *Excitable speech: a politics of the performative*, New York: Routledge, 1997: 5. 35 Ibid. 36 In this work on hate speech as interpellation, Judith Butler draws upon Louis Althusser's theory of interpellation as explored in his work 'Ideology and ideological state apparatuses'. 37 Butler, *Excitable speech*, 36. 38 Ibid., 3. 39 Stallybrass and White, *The politics and poetics of transgression*, 53.

Mrs Brady reads the truth of the interpellation in terms of her present, Francie will read the future events that befall him, which render him a pig in the eyes of the town and of himself, in terms of a curse being fulfilled.

The force of Francie's interpellation underscores the temporal and spatial dimensions of the national story that 'resists the transparent linear equivalence of event and idea that historicism proposes …'[40] Rather, the historicity of the name is worked upon, revisited, through the re-experiencing of the traumas that Francie associates with Mrs Nugent's speech act. Judith Butler argues that interpellation's traumatizing power comes from its working through 'an encoded memory or trauma, one that lives in language and is carried in language'.[41] The interpellation operates as a social trauma, which 'takes the form, not of a structure that repeats mechanically, but rather of an ongoing subjugation, the restaging of injury through signs that both occlude and re-enact the scene'.[42]

Francie Brady's interpellation as a 'pig' is the originary trauma of *The Butcher Boy*; it is the one from which all other traumas emanate. Following Mrs Nugent's interpellation of the Bradys, Francie's narrative undergoes a metamorphosis from being the story about a young boy's 'adventures' with his best friend in a bucolic Ireland to a terrifying vision of the ordeals to which the marginalized were subjected in 1960s Ireland. The force of the interpellation increases in Francie's imagination during the course of the boy's journeys to different places of incarceration in Irish society that follow upon the death or loss of a loved one in Francie's life, beginning with his mother's suicide. In his work on the chronotope (meaning literally 'time space'), Mikhail Bakhtin writes about the interconnection of time and space in the novel: 'Time, as it were, thickens, takes on flesh, becomes artistically visible; likewise, space becomes charged and responsive to the movements of time, plot and history'.[43] Homi Bhabha takes up this thread in his own work, writing that 'the origin of a nation's visual presence is the effect of a narrative struggle … National time becomes concrete and visible in the chronotope of the local, particular, graphic, from beginning to end'.[44] *The Butcher Boy*'s locales – the idyllic rural home, the psychiatric ward, the police jail, the city of Dublin, the movie house – are a mix of 'respectable' (middle class) spaces with liminal ones,[45] and produce a counter-narrative to the Irish middle-class nationalist 'imagined community'.[46] The crisis of *The Butcher Boy* is the emergence of

40 Homi K. Bhabha, 'DissemiNation: time, narrative, and the margins of the modern nation', in Homi K. Bhabha (ed.), *Nation and narration*, New York: Routledge, 1990: 292. 41 Butler, *Excitable speech*, 36. 42 Ibid., 36–7. 43 M.M. Bakhtin, 'Forms of time and chronotope in the novel', trans. Caryl Emerson and Michael Holmquist, *The dialogic imagination*, Austin: University of Texas Press, 1981: 84. 44 Bhabha, *Nation and narration*, 295; Jessica Scarlata, 'Carnivals and goldfish the end: history and crisis in *The Butcher Boy*,' unpublished essay, 2001:1–25. 45 Scarlata's reading of Francie's categorization as transgressing the borders between human and animal and his relationship to Ireland's sanitized and liminal spaces, temporality and history influenced my own thinking on the topic. 46 Bhabha *Nation and narration*, 300.

these liminal spaces into view and the troubling of the boundaries that separate them from the 'pure' spaces of middle-class Ireland. Francie becomes the link between the picture-postcard Ireland promoted by Irish nationalism and the liminal spaces rarely witnessed in popular representations or historical documents. It is Francie's movement through 'the wastes of time and space' that connects them to each other, dissolving the boundaries between them.

The Butcher Boy is 'structured around crises in the linear aspect of time'[47] with the repetition cycle of the death or loss of a loved one, transgression, incarceration and return, subverting the film's narrative progress. Into each chronotope he enters, Francie carries with him the past history that is further acted upon by the new chronotope. In *The Butcher Boy*, time is fractured and 'deprived of unity and wholeness'[48] because the spaces into which Francie is incarcerated are outside of the parameters of national space and time. These liminal spaces are disconnected from the world outside their doors, operating according to their own spatio-temporal laws. Francie has belonged, at some point, to all of them – from the film's opening sequence of a rural paradise to the end of the film with his release from the psychiatric hospital. The problem is that once Francie returns from these liminal spaces he can no longer 'belong' to the idyll or to the town as he once had because his experiences have marked him as belonging to outside of the nation as one of its pariahs, and the traumatic knowledge that he carries with him (of sexual abuse by a priest) prevents him from reentering the halcyon world to which he so desperately wishes to return.

In *The Butcher Boy* film text, an aspect of the traumatic is the infusion of more than one 'scene' of localized history in one place and time. The juxtaposition of chronotopes in *The Butcher Boy* represents both Francie's increasingly traumatized mental landscape as well as the dissolving of the boundaries of class, history (the sanitized and the repressed), and national borders. During the 'pig school' sequence in which Francie the Pig invades the Nugent's perfect home, Francie imagines he is teaching the Nugents how to be pigs. In the background, the Nugents' television plays images of atomic bomb detonations in the American west, of American children hiding under desks, and of squealing pigs running free from their pens. Writing on the mirrors and on the television set, 'PIGS,' Francie both leaves his mark on the Nugents' pristine house – a place devoid of all signs of a contaminating world – and inscribes the Nugents' curse back onto them. This scene is built on the topos of return, with Francie the Pig marking the Nugents' immaculate home with the truth that lurks behind the pristine façade. At a national level, Irish society's relegation of Francie to the margins of society refers to Ireland's own peripheral position during the Cuban Missile Crisis.

The film's overdetermined spaces and the narrative's topos of return symbolize the 'peculiar temporal structure of the historical experience' associated

47 Scarlata, 'Carnivals and goldfish', 11. 48 Bakhtin *The dialogic imagination*, 128.

with trauma in which the traumatic event is experienced 'in connection with another place and in another time'.[49] Cathy Caruth argues that traumatic flashbacks tell a 'history that literally *has no place*, neither in the past, in which it was not fully experienced, nor in the present, in which precise images and enactments are not understood'.[50] In the sequence where Francie is sedated by a doctor's needle, the boy experiences a hybrid hallucination of the various chronotopic topoi in the text: the explosion of an atom bomb cloud over the lake and pastoral idyll; the destruction of his hometown and the transformation of the town's inhabitants and his antagonists into cooked pigs; and the appearance of the invader – an alien with a giant green insect head dressed in a priest's cassock who comes riding into town on a horse. The dreamer drowns in the images of the multiple imperialisms of his world, both past and present: American, English, and Catholic. Francie's nightmare vision underscores his powerlessness, while rendering those in power as inhuman forces, either as 'pigs' or as terrifying half-human/half-insect monsters. In the sequence's conflation of temporalities and connotations, the oppositions between past and present, alien and human, centre and periphery, disappear because Francie's traumatic vision reveals that these signifiers all refer to the same truth: history does not progress, but unceasingly repeats itself, with new countries taking the place of empires and a native class stepping into the role of the oppressor, all the while the effects of the past continue to determine the present and future.

The film's sole 'saving' vision is a contaminated version of the kitschy, middle-class images of the Virgin Mary found in many Irish Catholic homes. A far cry from the 'saintly silent' apparition at Knock, Francie the Pig's "Missus" (as he calls her) uses profanity, speaks in a working-class Dublin accent, and appears in 'dirty, liminal spaces'[51] (one of which happens to be the screen of a broken television set in a junk heap) 'to a dangerous and wounded child'.[52] Played by pop singer Sinéad O'Connor, an outspoken critic of church and state in Ireland in regard to issues of reproductive rights for women and child abuse,[53] Francie's 'Missus' can be read as a testimony to the hypocrisy of the Church in Ireland that exploits the powerless. Yet, because of her 'polluted' nature and his own highly suspect mental state, Francie's 'Missus' provides the boy with yet another 'vision' that cannot be incorporated into the national narrative, and so further relegates Francie's knowledge beyond society's borders. Francie's traumatic visions raise the question whether all testimonial knowledge is 'dirty' – polluting, contaminating – causing those who bear such knowledge to be cast out of society. It is significant that Francie's attempt to tell Joe about his abuse in the industrial school is met by

49 Cathy Caruth, 'Introduction: Trauma and experience', in Cathy Caruth (ed.), *Trauma: explorations in memory*, Baltimore: Johns Hopkins University Press, 1995: 5. 50 Cathy Caruth, 'Introduction: Recapturing the past,' in Cathy Caruth (ed.), *Trauma: Explorations in memory*, 153. 51 Scarlata, 'Carnivals and goldfish', 25. 52 Ibid. 53 Ibid.

Joe's running away and leaving Francie in the country, at the margins of the town and the societal mores that it represents.

The collision between Ireland's pure spaces and contaminated ones is most visceral in Francie's fraught attempts to negotiate between the identities read onto him by the various communities that have marked him. For Father Sully, the priest who sexually abuses him, he is both the Virgin Mary's interlocutor and his 'wife'; for his hometown, Francie is the boy pig; for the mental hospital, he is an insane child; for the police he is a delinquent, for Francie himself he was a good son and Joe's best friend. Francie's loss of the more positive identities, accompanied by the magnification of the negative ones, lead him to believe that he has become the composite metamorphosis of all epithets by which he has been hailed: pig, sinner, monster, bad son. Like the experience of the traumatic event that is beyond the borders of memory and knowledge, Francie occupies a space beyond any socially sanctioned identity. The film's climax of Francie's brutal murder and dismemberment of Mrs Nugent parallels Francie's own psychic dismemberment by the various communities, which have contributed to his ostracism.

The topos of traumatic return can be seen in the film's organizing structure: the voice-over narration by the adult Francie Brady. By having the actor Stephen Rea play both the adult Francie and Benny Brady, Francie's father, Neil Jordan suggests that the lives of the father and son mirror each other in significant ways. Both suffer from abuse inflicted on them during their incarceration in religious-run homes for boys, although Benny's experience occurred in Belfast, while Francie's took place in the Republic. Father and son's similar experiences suggest that the lines dividing separate national spaces and different chronological periods are an illusion, as both Benny and Francie both follow the same path of abused becoming abuser as seen in Benny's physical violence towards his wife and son, and Francie's towards Philip and Mrs Nugent. Although Benny's violence is limited towards his family, Francie focused on Mrs Nugent as a metonym for the body of Irish society that has violated and excluded him. It is Francie's discovery that his father had 'behaved like a pig' on his honeymoon which brings about the film's climax. The curse inflicted by Mrs Nugent 'turns out to be an action that has been happening all along, such that the forward movement of time is precisely what is inverted by the temporality of the curse'.[54] Mrs Nugent's curse, in a sense, brings 'into the future what has always already been happening'.[55] It is this ambiguity between past and present that influences the temporal confusion in Francie's narrative and underscores its placelessness within Irish society.

In the opening sequences of the film, Rea's voice-over indicates Francie's temporal confusion: 'When I was a young lad twenty or thirty or forty years ago I lived in a small town where they were all after me on account of what I

54 Judith Butler, *Antigone's claim*, New York: Columbia University Press, 2000: 61. 55 Ibid.

done on Mrs Nugent'. Francie's uncertainty as to the date of the events narrated as opposed to the 'now' of the narration alerts us to the fact that the most significant aspect of his narrative will be that the past is essentially not over for him. In fact, the voice-over narration in no way indicates an adult's distance from his younger self. Rather, it appears that Francie never grew up, but remains trapped in the reliving of his childhood traumas, with the past remaining ever before him, while the actual 'present' time is simply *not present to him in any significant way*. The absent division between past and present is most clearly visualized in the 'Pig School' sequence in the Nugent home when the adult Francie's voice actually enters into the diegetic world to teach the young Francie how to act like a pig. In the elder Francie's entrance into his 'past' history, the film foregrounds the arbitrary division between past and present that characterizes Francie's narrative.

Situated on the boundary between historical fact and fiction, *The Butcher Boy* is a border text whose own ambiguous identity testifies to what Shoshana Felman calls the 'radical impossibility of testimony', which 'confronts us with the question in what ways, by what creative means (and at what price), would it become possible for us to witness the-event-without-a-witness'.[56] In making the central character a middle-aged man institutionalized half his life in a psychiatric hospital, Jordan possibly suggests that a testimony from 'within the event' is one that would inevitably be touched by madness. Francie's 'madness' further underscores the placelessness of his testimony, for madness has been associated with 'non-being'.[57] How can a person who does not exist testify to his non-existence? How can there be a testimony to a 'loss of mind' by one who is already mad? In another work, Felman writes that madness has come to occupy a 'common discursive place' in contemporary society because it points to the 'radical' ambiguity of the border between the inside and outside of culture.[58] She writes, 'madness usually occupies a position of *exclusion*; it is *outside* of a culture. But madness that is a *common place* occupies a position of *inclusion* and becomes the *inside* of a culture.'[59] In my view, Francie the Pig's madness foregrounds that of the world around him, as seen in the anti-communist hysteria of the 1960s and the omnipresent fear of nuclear annihilation, as well as exploitative religious orders' and prejudiced townspeople's concern with appearances of the Virgin Mary, but not with the welfare of poor children. In his film, Jordan integrates the outside of the national text of Irish society – the poor, women, and children – into the inside by depicting at what cost this marginalization occurred and its influence on Irish history and contemporary Irish society.

56 Shoshana Felman, 'The return of the voice: Claude Lanzmann's *Shoah*,' in Shoshana Felman and Dori Laub (eds), *Testimony: crises of witnessing in literature, psychoanalysis, and history*, New York: Routledge, 1992: 227. 57 Shoshana Felman, *Writing and madness (literature/philosophy/psychoanalysis)*, Ithaca: Cornell University Press, 1985: 39. 58 Ibid., 13. 59 Ibid.

Finally, the ambiguity of the film's border identity ultimately lies in both its identity as a fictional work that testifies to a historical event and, until recently, Irish society's repression of the knowledge of its occurrence. In witnessing a fictional testimony based on an historical event, I would inquire if fictional works such as *The Butcher Boy* created a space – a place of recognition – in Irish culture for the real histories of the survivors of abuse in the industrial school system to be seen and heard during the 1999 airing of the documentary *States of Fear*. In my view, the power of *The Butcher Boy* lies in its own placelessness as a border text that operates on the border of the inside (the historical event) and the outside (the fictions that bear witness to that history). In taking responsibility to bear witness to a repressed history, such a text challenges the validity of the clear-cut inside/outside dichotomy.

Fighting within the rules: masculinity in the films of Jim Sheridan

JOSEPH MOSER

Referring to Irish literature and film, the film director Jim Sheridan has observed a significant absence: 'In *My Left Foot* I was always thinking of the oedipal bit and in *In the Name of the Father* I was thinking of the Good Father ... I had to think when was the oedipal story ever told, when was the Good Father [story] ever told in Ireland?'[1] Sheridan also suggests that his last 'troubles' film, *The Boxer*, fills a crucial void as an 'Irish love story': 'There's no love stories in Irish literature ... In repressed ... broken cultures love stories have not much prominence ... It's very difficult to do'.[2] In response to these absences, it can be argued that Sheridan's films attempt to reconstitute affirmative figures of masculinity in a post-colonial culture. In his three 1990s films – *The Field* (1990), *In the Name of the Father* (1993) and *The Boxer* (1997) – Sheridan seeks to reclaim Irish masculinity from a heritage of patriarchal violence, and through his use of widely appealing story structures such as the coming-of-age tale, the prodigal son, and the star-crossed lovers, he endeavours to trace a path away from the endemically violent masculinity that has stereotypically defined Irish identity.

THE FIELD

In *The Field*, for example, the identity of a young rural Irishman hangs in the balance, as Tadgh (Sean Bean) seeks an alternative to his father Bull McCabe's (Richard Harris) tyrannical, primordial attachment to land and honour. According to Declan Kiberd:

> the evidence of Irish texts and case-histories would confirm the suspicion that the autocratic father is often the weakest male of all, concealing that weakness under the protective coverage of the prevailing system ... Patriarchal values exist in societies where men, lacking true authority, settle for mere power.[3]

1 Sheridan quoted in Ruth Barton, *Jim Sheridan: framing the nation*, Dublin: Liffey Press, 2002: 144. 2 Sheridan, Director's commentary, *The Boxer*, Collector's Edition DVD, Universal, 1997. 3 Declan Kiberd, *Inventing Ireland*, Cambridge, Mass.: Harvard University Press, 1995: 390–1. Kiberd is also quoted in Barton, *Jim Sheridan*, 55–6.

In this regard, *The Field* may be seen to offer a bleak critique of the fundamental 'weakness' underlying the exercise of patriarchal power. Tadgh seems destined to live under the oppressive aegis of his father and the code passed down from Bull's 'father's father's father's father'. Though the film is set in the 1930s, Bull's repeated polemics about the potato famine and the British 'echo a narrow, nationalist interpretation of history'[4] which suggests the hardline Republicanism characteristic of the IRA.[5] As Ruth Barton observes, 'the film sees history not as linear, but as circular and repetitive … both older and younger generations are trapped in time and in a cycle of violence'.[6]

However, if we focus on Tadgh, as opposed to the more obviously central figure of Bull, we can also identify *The Field* as a tragically stunted *Bildungsroman*. During the film Tadgh gradually forges the will to resist Bull, and towards the end he nearly cuts his ties with his father and the land. His growth as a man, however, is limited by the lack of a positive model of masculinity within his family and community more generally. Thus, even as he throws off the yoke of his father, he appropriates Bull's violence against the Yank (Tom Berenger) to aid his wooing of Katie (Jenny Conroy), the tinker's daughter. Apart from Bull, the only other prominent male figures in the film are the bumbling and cowardly 'Bird' (John Hurt), the dim-witted Yank, and a priest fool enough to attach himself to an exploitative outsider. Ultimately, Tadgh fails to escape his father, as his final attempt to reach the increasingly volatile Bull precipitates his own demise. Tadgh's death serves as the final indictment of a community devoid of affirmative models of masculinity. Indeed, 'manhood' here is identified with futility and impotence, as we last see Bull furiously striving to beat back the encroaching tide. Here Bull plays out the tragedy of the Cuchulain myth,[7] as the patriarch unwittingly destroys the last of his line. In the world of *The Field*, the past consumes the future, the sins of the father are visited on the son and successive generations *ad infinitum*.

IN THE NAME OF THE FATHER

Sheridan's subsequent films, *In the Name of the Father* and *The Boxer*; pursue a similar theme but in each case the *Bildungsroman* element is fully realized and a positive male figure plays an essential role in establishing the character of the protagonist. *In the Name of the Father* pits the deadly slick provo Joe McAndrew (Don Baker) against gentle consumptive Guiseppe Conlon (Peter Postlethwaite) who vie for control over Guiseppe's son, Gerry (Daniel Day-Lewis), the quintessential angry young misfit. Because Gerry in his youth has

4 Barton, *Jim Sheridan*, 48. 5 Sheridan notes this connection in Barton, *Jim Sheridan*, 153. 6 Barton, *Jim Sheridan*, 47. 7 For a fuller discussion of this point, see Elizabeth Butler Cullingford, *Ireland's others: gender and ethnicity in Irish popular culture*, Cork: Cork University Press, 2001: 181–2, 231.

felt intense shame over his father's physical decrepitude – 'Why'd you have to be sick all your life?'– he also assumes his father to be weak and irresolute in spirit. Thus, when father and son are confined to the same prison cell, they revert to their previous relationship on the outside. Gerry defies his father's advice to maintain dignity in the face of adversity and becomes attracted to the charms of militant ideology.

However, midway through the film, Gerry cuts his ties with McAndrew and Guiseppe clearly emerges as the 'Good Father'. Gerry's change of allegiance may be linked to Kiberd's remarks on the position of the father under colonialism who relies on patriarchal modes to emphasize his potency. Gerry's fundamental error is to mistake Guiseppe for a 'weak father', when in fact he is neither weak (in spirit) nor patriarchal (he is a loving husband and gentle father). Gerry initially lacks concern for his family and community: in the film's opening Belfast sequence he threatens the security of his family by incurring the wrath of the local IRA, and he endangers the lives of all those in the community by helping incite a riot to evade capture by British paratroopers. Forced into shared confinement with his father, Gerry observes the respect that Guiseppe commands among prison officials and inmates alike as well as the effectiveness of his pacifist resistance in the form of his letter-writing campaign for their release. Gerry ultimately rejects McAndrew in the wake of his horrendous maiming of a prison warden. His deeply ironic statement, 'You've done a good day's work, McAndrew', disavows the type of ineffectual, self-perpetuating violence that the action represents. Though Guiseppe's passive resistance to their imprisonment takes years to bear fruit, and he himself never lives to attain freedom, Gerry ultimately recognizes his father's strength. As Kiberd argues, the recognition of an assertive (but non-patriarchal) father can steer the child away from rebellion towards 'the task of achieving a vision of society as a whole and the even more exhilarating challenge of framing an alternative'.[8] Gerry chooses to follow Guiseppe's model as it becomes increasingly apparent that it is only in his father's form of action, as opposed to violent resistance, that the potential to accomplish 'a good day's work' and enact a change in their situation becomes possible.

Although Martin McLoone argues that *In the Name of the Father*'s 'engagement with dominant narrative forms is a problem in terms of making a film about politics',[9] the film may also be seen to use the genre conventions of the coming-of-age film, the prison film, and courtroom drama to make a statement about the process of self-discovery that leads a young, oppressed man

8 Kiberd, *Inventing Ireland*, 391. Sheridan himself makes a similar point when he argues that most of his films are 'about the son not being able to look up to the father and the father not being an authority figure'. See Gary Crowdus and O'Mara Leary, 'Getting past the violence: an interview with Jim Sheridan', *Cineaste*, 23: 3, Summer 1998: 13. 9 Martin McLoone, *Irish film: the emergence of a contemporary cinema*, London: British Film Institute, 2000: 73.

to reject extremism in favour of a mode of masculinity that values community over militancy. Indeed, for Margot Gayle Backus, 'the film's father/son dynamics shed considerable light on the very real problem of postcolonial masculine identity and self-representation, and could even be seen as offering insight into the emergence of a new political praxis'.[10] One might argue, then, that it is, in fact, the film's very engagement with 'dominant narrative forms' that expresses, rather than obscures, the film's political perspective.

THE BOXER

As Sheridan points out, *The Boxer* begins where his previous film ends.[11] Danny Flynn (played, as was Gerry Conlon, by Daniel Day-Lewis) emerges from prison in the opening title sequence. If *In the Name of the Father* plays out the successful mediation of male aggression within prison walls, *The Boxer* concerns itself with addressing violence on the outside. According to Sheridan, 'the film came to me after the IRA let off the bomb in Canary Wharf after the ceasefire, and I thought, "the hell with this … (I'll) make a film about … violence and what I think about it"'.

As in *In the Name of the Father*, Sheridan addresses masculinity in *The Boxer* through the use of a triangular pattern. Danny Flynn embraces his boyhood trainer Ike (Ken Stott), while he rejects his old IRA comrade, Harry (Gerard McSorley). However, the later film does not so much dramatize the process of self-discovery that leads away from violent patriarchy, as the struggle to live within a community in which violence still prevails. As *The Boxer* begins, Danny Flynn has already tried the way of the gun, seen it fail, and done time for his past association with the IRA. Danny has become alienated from his natural family during his fourteen-year imprisonment (none of his blood relatives play a part in the film), and the story ultimately propels him towards the formation of a new family based on tolerance and reconciliation. As Sheridan points out, 'the film … crosses from the politics into the personal and becomes […] a family story, which is what the Greeks understood […] that you could basically reduce everything down to the family and […] see what was wrong with society'. In this regard, *The Boxer*'s dramatization of the family is itself intended as a commentary on the broader dynamics of society.

Like Tadgh in *The Field*, Danny is initially all but silent; but as his identity solidifies so his voice emerges. His reunion with Ike Weir, his childhood

10 Margot Gayle Backus, 'Revising Resistance: *In the Name of the Father* as postcolonial paternal melodrama' in James MacKillop (ed.), *Contemporary Irish Cinema: from The Quiet Man to Dancing at Lughnasa*, Syracuse, NY: Syracuse University Press, 1999: 58. 11 Sheridan, Director's commentary, *The Boxer* DVD. Unless otherwise noted, all subsequent Sheridan quotes come from the same source.

trainer, acts as the catalyst that leads Danny towards the use of boxing as a unifying emblem, offering the possibility for mediating sectarian tensions. The destructive force of violence maintains its power in the community in the person of Harry, the hard-line provo. He maintains his militant stance despite the onset of a ceasefire and continues to influence the younger generations of Belfast, including Maggie's son, Liam (Ciarán Fitzgerald). Harry's weapons are guns and rhetoric, while Ike's only weapons are his hands and 'a bit of truth', as Danny puts it.

Ike functions not only as a paternal figure, but as a dramatic soothsayer. His two drunken outbursts of cathartic truth-telling frame the film. In the first, he lectures Danny, 'You tell them, Ike Weir doesn't need a gun to fight. [...] Put your gun down, Danny Flynn, fight me like a man'. Here Ike sets up the ethical framework that Danny employs throughout the film: he fights within the rules of the ring, and, in his final bout against a Nigerian opponent, refuses to extend the contest to the point of brutality. In Ike's last speech, he confronts Harry, Danny's one-time friend turned nemesis: 'I know you, Harry. You're only interested in hurtin' people. [...] You killed this district, Harry. You killed the one thing you loved. Your own son. You filled his head full of shit, and you sent him out to die.' Harry responds by killing Ike. However, this murder is the action of a weak man, an exercise of 'mere power' in the face of actual male authority. Although, as an alcoholic, Ike conforms to a negative characteristic shared by both the 'stage Irishman' and Kiberd's weak, colonized father, he nevertheless functions as an agent of change among men like Harry, who are insulated from their own self-deceptions by violent, patriarchal rhetoric; the same sort of rhetoric that his enemies, the British, use to justify their continued presence in the North. Thus, Sheridan uses Ike's bouts of drunkenness as an outlet for this good father to reveal the suppressed truth that Danny and Harry, as well as their community at large, will not articulate.

Ike's identification as spiritual 'Good Father' becomes clear in Sheridan's long, soaring helicopter shot of Liam cradling the trainer's body. Like Tadgh in *The Field*, Liam is a character whose masculine identity hangs in the balance throughout the film. In this scene, he clearly chooses his ideological alignment and subsequently accepts Danny, Ike's disciple, as a father figure. Here Sheridan reclaims and reconstructs masculinity by uniting three generations of Irish manhood in a spirit of familial peace and reconciliation in the face of patriarchal violence.

Sheridan's programme of reconstructing affirmative masculine figures in a post-colonial setting is illuminated by the film's relationship to the conventions of the boxing film. Although *The Boxer* has been described as an 'overtly generic work',[12] it resists narrow categorization and its deviations from other boxing films are significant. For Ike, Danny and Liam, boxing acts as a means

12 Barton, *Jim Sheridan*, 99.

to personal and community empowerment. In other boxing films, however, the sport promotes vices like boozing, drug use, philandering, and gambling (as in *The Champ* and *Body and Soul*) or encourages ethical decline. Thus, boxers often develop a taste for violence (as in *Champion* and *Raging Bull*) or 'forget their roots' and alienate family and friends (as in *Raging Bull*, *Body and Soul* and *The Great White Hope*). Physical decay also often overtakes boxing-film heroes, as they commonly fight past their prime and, in some cases, die in the ring. In conventional boxing films, the one thing that the sport does generate is money, though money itself almost invariably leads to the corruption and downfall of the boxer.

In Sheridan's film, Danny never covets the money and fame that appeal to professional athletes in film and in reality. He is past his prime and only wants to get a few fights and 'set the record straight'. Even though it is a common trope of boxing films that once-great fighters make a comeback, Danny never speaks of pursuing a title or public acclaim. Rather he seeks personal redemption through a sport that also has the potential to transcend religious and ideological differences in his community.

Unlike the conventional boxing-film hero (or, as is often the case, antihero), Danny doesn't win many fights. He loses his first fight, wins his second, and is disqualified from his third, and presumably last, fight. As one might expect, most boxing films focus on men who win most of their fights, more often than not champions. However, Sheridan's film promotes ethical over material success, as in the England episode when Danny leaves the ring rather than continue a bout that he believes he has already won. When the officials fail to uphold the rules, he enforces them himself, asserting that 'the fight's over'. He refuses to allow his sport, potentially full of generative power, to become a spectacle of brutality. In this way, Danny also avoids the material exploitation dramatized in many boxing films (such as *Body and Soul*).

Along with ethical and material corruption, Danny also resists political exploitation. Early on, he warns Ike not to accept donations of equipment from 'cops' – the predominantly Protestant Royal Ulster Constabulary (RUC) – and later, when a sneaky cameraman snaps a publicity photo of the boxer and a police captain shaking hands, Danny complains, 'I don't like being used'. Accepting the police sponsorship ultimately costs Ike and Danny dearly, as it gives Harry a pretext for blowing up the police captain (as he leaves Danny's second fight) and setting off a riot that renews sectarian tensions, momentarily nullifying all the positive communal effects of the Holy Family gym. In a community where one wrong move can ignite a blaze of hatred, Danny learns to be absolutely uncompromising in his vision and representation of peace, as he finally determines to rebuild the gym. Daniel Day-Lewis says of the film's message: 'There's always the possibility that you can regain your life; no matter to what extent it's been ruined through your own actions or the actions of others, you can have it back.'[13] Indeed, *The Boxer* is deeply concerned with psychic, as well as physical, resilience in the face of devastation and bitterness.

An essential intertext for *The Boxer* is Elia Kazan's *On the Waterfront* (1954). Both films centre on a boxer past his prime (Danny Flynn is thirty-two, Terry Malloy is 'pushing thirty') whose career has been compromised by his personal affiliation with a violent organization (Danny with the IRA, Terry with mobsters). Kazan's film, like *The Boxer*, sets up a triangular construction of masculinity, with Father Barry representing male moral authority and Johnny Friendly embodying the powerful masculine figure of violence. Both men find redemption in loving a woman (in both cases, a Catholic woman) and in enduring a particularly traumatic process of disavowing violence, as Danny loses his friend/mentor and Terry loses his brother. Each of these characters ends up physically battered – Danny by Harry, Terry by Johnny Friendly – but with his integrity intact. Finally, both films dramatize and vivify the maxim, spoken by Father Barry at the end of *On the Waterfront*, 'You lost the battle, but you have a chance to win the war'. In each case, we are left with a hero staggering into the distance, defeated physically yet spiritually intact, embodying a peaceful figure of masculinity in a community beset by violence.

Undoubtedly, the unabashed idealism clearly reflected in Sheridan's work leaves the politics of his films vulnerable to criticism by those seeking a more realistic or sympathetic portrait of Irish Republicanism. However, rather than discount the filmmaker's work as politically inadequate, I would argue that Sheridan's films should be read as cogent responses to the ideologies of extremism and patriarchy. As he says of *The Boxer*, 'I wanted to endorse the people who were giving up violence [in Northern Ireland]. That's what it is about. It's a propaganda film made with Hollywood money and, OK, it lost money but it did some social good, I think, I hope.'[14] One might argue therefore that, as imaginative works, Sheridan's films not only reflect the world, but also seek to play a productive role in shaping it.

Invariably, Sheridan manages to portray violence as an intensely personal experience. He often places his characters in positions of isolation: Tadgh as an only child in a practically silent household, Gerry in prison, Danny in prison and often silent and alone outside of it. In these films, only individual responses to violence pass muster. Conversely, the rhetorics of extremism and empire both employ language that fails to do justice to individual loss or suffering and incorporates it into an inadequate narrative history. In *The Field*, Bull rants about the Great Famine and the evil Brits; in *In the Name of the Father* Inspector Dixon ignores the evidence of the Guildford Four's innocence; and

13 'Fighting for peace: inside *The Boxer*', feature on *The Boxer* Collector's Edition DVD, Universal, 1997. 14 Sheridan interviewed in Barton, *Jim Sheridan*, 147.

in *The Boxer* Harry invokes the Long Kesh hunger strikers to stigmatize the peace negotiations as a betrayal. Sheridan encourages us to mistrust such perspectives, which trivialize individual experience in the interests of ideology. Indeed, the only language that he seems to value comes from individuals speaking, not as part of a group, but for themselves (consider, for example, Gerry's speech in the final scene of *In the Name of the Father* and Danny's speech to Joe Hamill near the end of *The Boxer*). The director's progressive portrayal of maleness reaches its apex in *The Boxer*, as only in the last film does a man ultimately move out of isolation and begin to live as part of a community.

Sheridan portrays the tragedy of destructive masculinity in *The Field*. As the sins of his father finally condemn Tadgh, he cannot free himself from patriarchy: 'the tyranny wrought by weak men'.[15] However, in *In the Name of the Father* and *The Boxer*, Sheridan constructs a viable alternative mode of masculinity in which individual experience and conscience contribute to a vision of the future rather than a perpetuation of the destruction of the past. His work exposes the weakness of violent men and the strength of the peaceful.

15 Kiberd, *Inventing Ireland*, 391.

Memory and mapping in *Bloody Sunday*

MARGARET O'NEILL

When Paul Greengrass presented *Bloody Sunday* at the Chicago International Film Festival in 2002, he defended his aesthetic strategy with recourse to a reference to memory. When asked about his use of fades-to-black within scenes and as transitions, his response was that 'memory is a series of shards of different lengths … a collage and not a smooth continuity'.[1] Whilst I do not want to over-emphasize a correlation between Greengrass' authorial intentions and the actual meanings in the film, I am taking this rhetorical claim as the starting point for an analysis of the relationship between the structure of knowing and telling in the film and the use of maps within the narrative.

Bloody Sunday was one of two films made for the thirtieth anniversary of the murder of fourteen civilians on a Civil Rights march in Derry, 1972. The memorializing impulse informs both films, and the ideas I'm discussing in this paper are intimately related to the issues of mourning and healing that are integral to their production. This issue of memory is an important aspect of both films for the anniversary, and some of my remarks will also apply to aspects of *Sunday* (Charles McDougall, 2002). My research is concerned with how memory of this traumatic wound becomes expressed as discourse, and my broader study of the representations of Bloody Sunday will engage with trauma and popular memory in the production of both the films. For this paper, however, I will concentrate on the Greengrass film.

In assessing why this event is associated with memory, rather than history, I am drawn to Susannah Radstone's assessment of a contemporary reaction against history in academic subjects such as Cultural Studies where 'memory is construed in opposition to history … [and] history becomes negatively associated with the authority of master narratives, with the "public" and with "objectivity", [whilst] memory has become positively associated with the embedded, the local, the personal and the subjective'. Bloody Sunday is not history in the sense of something that is over, but rather memory of an unhealed wound. And embedded in the trauma of that wound is the further injury inflicted by Lord Widgery's official version of events. Memory and history provide a politically useful opposition rather than one that can be sustained against too searching an analysis although, as Radstone continues,

1 I am quoting from the director's comments during the discussion that followed the screening of *Bloody Sunday* at the Music Box Theatre, Chicago, on 6 October 2002.

'Memory becomes a rich source … for those seeking alternatives to dominant versions of the past.'[2]

However, as the title of my paper implies, this suggestive contrast between memory and history is not the main topic of my discussion. My central interpretive focus is the relationship between mapping and memory. In my discussion of *Bloody Sunday* I explore the use of real maps and the map as metaphor and allegory in order to delineate the relationship between memory and maps as two topographies of knowledge.

The map and memory as ways of knowing and ways of telling imply polarized epistemologies. The map as grid, framework, and disciplined organizing structure is delimited in its conception and execution, and reasoned in form. It is a deliberate or conscious construction. By contrast, memory seems to arise as a reflex or reaction, rather than as something consciously predetermined. It is protean and labile and, although cognitive science would try to chart the location of memory in some rational way, it does not seem to be contained in an unchanging, immutable form, nor easily to be marshalled into a fixed structure. Perhaps, as Greengrass says, it is made up of 'shards of different lengths'. Certainly a common perception of memory is that it is characterised by crisis.[3] Sporadic and discontinuous, it has seismic faults where things drop out. Technologies of memory, such as systems of mnemonics which have been in use since the Greeks, testify to this instability and to our perception of memory as fragile, weak and, above all, uneven.[4] The fades-to-black in *Bloody Sunday* are an attempt to replicate this uneven operation in the aesthetics of the film, depicting omissions of knowledge and the intermittent functioning of recall. If memory is a way of knowing, then it is knowledge that is subject to slippage and to the crisis of forgetting. It is also a way of knowing that is organized by narrative, through processes of telling and re-telling. Thus, for Marita Sturken, 'memory is a narrative rather than a replica of an experience that can be retrieved and relived' and she posits re-narrativization as its defining quality.[5]

The central defining aspect of the memories of Bloody Sunday is that they are memories of trauma. Cathy Caruth has written extensively on trauma and narrative, arguing that trauma is 'much more than a pathology, the simple illness of a wounded psyche: it is always the story of a wound that cries out, that addresses us in the attempt to tell us of a reality or truth that is not otherwise available'. In describing how trauma recurs, she argues that 'what returns to haunt the victim…is not only the reality of the violent event but also the reality of the way that its violence has not yet been fully known'.[6]

2 Susannah Radstone (ed.), *Memory and methodology*, Oxford: Berg, 2000: 84. 3 Marita Sturken, *Tangled memories: the Vietnam War, the AIDS epidemic, and the politics of remembering*, Berkeley: University of California Press, 1997: 17. 4 Rusiko Bourtchouladze, *Memories are made of this*, New York: Columbia University Press, 2002: 2. 5 Sturken, *Tangled memories*, 15. 6 Cathy Caruth, *Unclaimed experience: trauma, narrative, and history*, Baltimore: John Hopkins University

And for the psychiatrists Kolk and Hart, 'traumatic memories are the unassimilated scraps of overwhelming experience which need to be integrated with existing mental schemes, and be transformed into narrative language'.[7]

In summer 2001, *Screen* opened a debate on what they termed 'trauma cinema' and I think this discussion is also of relevance to this film.[8] For me a significant aspect is how the film expresses Caruth's traumatic 'crying out' of the event, a crying out that has seen the appearance of many discursive references and expressions of Bloody Sunday over the past three decades. What I find particularly compelling in the theories of trauma is their reference to narration: how the wounding repeats, and finds expression as discourse. And in the film, *Bloody Sunday*, the crying out of the wound is a repetition of the trauma in a particular cultural form. The traumatic event recurs because it cannot heal; it is neither wholly narrated nor fully understood. How appropriate, therefore, that Caruth's proposal for the mastery of trauma through narration should be the primary operation of memory itself. Greengrass's film is not only part of this narrativization of people's memory; it is also an example of the repetitions of trauma.

The various cultural narrations of the event have been both repetitive and re-scriptive. The early narratives of Bloody Sunday are different in tone and purpose to the film. An early work such as Thomas Kinsella's poem *Butcher's Dozen* is more reactive and angry, the poetic purpose of which is to marshal vernacular anger into an explosive condensation of accusation and lament. A year after the event Brian Friel's play, *Freedom of the City*, was produced. Its subject is the killing of three Civil Rights marchers: but it is not about *this* particular march, nor *these* particular victims, and not *this* specific chain of events. It *is* Bloody Sunday, but expressed as analogy. The play feeds on the anger of injustice piled on injury in its study of a group of unarmed victims, and many elements of its narrative speak to the events of 30 January 1972, so it is a *transparent* analogy. Its dramatic inclusion of a mendacious inquiry provides an ironic channel for the anger and frustration towards that injustice.

In Greengrass's commentary we can see how the 'meaning' of Bloody Sunday, as re-scripted in this particular anniversary story, is quite specific. It is something of a commonplace that any look to the past is an attempt to recoup it for the present, and underlying this narrative of the past is a therapeutic issue. With its emphasis on memory, Greengrass's film is about remembering the past in order to facilitate healing, which in effect is to remember in order to forget. In not just giving one person's point of view, or one side's version of events, it is about an attempt to remember fully, in a 'collage' of

Press, 1996: 4–6. 7 Bessel A. van der Kolk, and Onno van der Hart, 'The intrusive past: the flexibility of memory and the engraving of trauma', in Cathy Caruth (ed.), *Trauma: explorations in memory*, John Hopkins University Press: Baltimore, 1995: 176. 8 Susannah Radstone et al., 'Reports and debates', *Screen*, 42:2. Summer 2001: 188–216.

stories. It is in validation of the local and the subjective that Greengrass's film is inspired by witness statements, and that a concatenation of individual descriptions of particular moments informs the narrative, rather than some 'master' viewpoint. A salient feature of much of the commentary about the film has been this very issue of healing; indeed, as Martin McLoone has mentioned, the very fact that *two* films have been made has helped in this way.[9] Perhaps what is significant then in this film, and in McDougall's film, is how their stories depart from the early discourses which did not actually attempt to narrate the event. Greengrass's film features performances by non-actors including ex-soldiers and members of the Derry community. For example, Simon Mann, who plays the role of Colonel Wilford, formerly served in Northern Ireland as a member of the British Army. A particularly striking aspect of the film is the casting of Declan Duddy, the nephew of Jackie Duddy, one of the victims, in another of the central roles. His sympathetic performance as Gerard Donaghy lends a poignant complexity to the re-enactment. The decision to cast the film in this way suggests a very particular attempt at a full expression of the event.[10] These elements lend strength to the thesis of the recurrence of trauma: in effect, the film is not only telling the story but, through its performances and re-enactment of the past, it involves narration as mimetic repetition.

Within this narrative of traumatic memory, the map is a significant trope. In contrast to the intermittent workings of memory, the map purports to cover the whole territory and, in so far as it does so, it is about knowledge and power. The map is a structured, rational device the purpose of which is to indicate the territory as clearly as possible. The mapping *impulse* entails a quest for knowledge and, in the nineteenth-century mapping of Ireland by the British Ordnance Survey, the colonial and capitalist impulse for acquisition and possession. That maps serve political interests is hardly a controversial suggestion: there is a heady power in what is included, in what is named and in what is omitted. The boundaries of the map's power are formed by what is given emphasis, or subtlety undermined in the scale, or blatantly excluded by the mapmaker, who is inscribing a self-portrait in the process. Denis Wood reminds us that 'all maps, inevitably, unavoidably, necessarily embody their author's prejudices, biases, and partialities'.[11] However, the aspect of the map that interests me here is its structure: the rational form it takes, and its adherence to codes, rules, and a methodology of reason and logic.

Turning to how actual maps are deployed in the film, we can see that from the outset it is the army who are associated with this form of knowledge. The

9 Martin McLoone, 'Bloody Sunday' (review), *Cineaste*, Fall, 2002: 42–3. 10 The involvement of the local community, in both the production of the script, and in performances, is a feature of each of the two films and is a central area of my larger research. 11 Denis Wood, *The power of maps*, New York: Guilford Press, 1992: 24.

film opens with the army press conference at which General Ford and Brigadier MacLellan are assembled in front of a large-scale map of the Six Counties (of Northern Ireland). In their statement about the illegal status of the proposed civil rights' march, that 'the law's the law and must be respected', they are associated by analogy with the rigid structure of the system in place. In the Brigade room they chart the route of the march, their own positions and the perceived IRA positions, and their own plan of action, with reference to another large-scale Ordnance Survey map, this time of the Bogside, which is pinned on the wall. This raises the issue of ownership of the map, and of the territory. Historically we can say that the army 'own' the Ordnance Survey maps: originally they made them.[12] Later, in a revealing turn of phrase, Colonel Wilford says of the post-shooting territory, 'I owned the Bogside in military terms: I occupied it.'[13]

During this planning stage of the military operation, the map is inscribed with the potential of the march before it begins by anticipating the route with arrows. Later in the film, once the march has begun, the map is again marked to show the progress of the marchers. This is also the army staking a claim of ownership, or control, of the march through the very process of mapping its route. The film cuts between the map and the march itself, so that the march animates the points on the map. This effect is underscored at various moments, when the film depicts events at specific places that were previously indicated on the Brigade planning map. For example, the army barriers that have been described in the Brigade room are made concrete by the action in the film, as when Cooper calls for calm and trouble then breaks out at the actual barrier. Similar to the cuts between the map and the actual spaces depicted on the map are the cuts between orders given in the Brigade room and the effect of those orders on the ground. For example, when we are shown Brigadier MacLellan giving the order to 'Send in Neptune', as the rioting at barrier fourteen becomes more heated, this is followed by shots of the water cannon being used. Likewise, his order, 'Rubber bullets at discretion', is followed by footage of the bullets being fired.

In the field, the army are also associated with maps. The Parachute Regiment, in position in the churchyard, discuss the proposed route of the march and their plan of action by referring to a small map. We see them invest the map with a verbal description of the geography, describing, for example,

12 The complete mapping of Ireland was executed by the British Ordnance Survey on a six-inch scale in a project begun in 1824. A detailed account of this project is given in J.H. Andrews, *A paper landscape: the ordnance survey in nineteenth century Ireland*, London: Oxford University Press, 1975. 13 My emphasis. The quotation is from Colonel Wilford's cross-examination by the Saville Inquiry: http://www.bloody-sunday-inquiry.org.uk/transcripts/Archive/TS314.htm: 6. This remark is taken from an interview with Colonel Wilford by the journalist Peter Taylor in the documentary 'Remember Bloody Sunday – An Insider Special' transmitted on BBC1, 28 January 1992.

the waste ground beyond the churchyard wall. The map also becomes the starting-point for their operations, when we see them embark upon their plan of action on the basis of the geography described there, the plan being to pick up 'the Derry young hooligans'.

Delving deeper, and in relation to the use of maps in the film, I will turn now to how the real space is depicted, and the differences between the army and the local people's relationship to the territory itself. We can start to uncover these differences in the significant contrast of planning styles between them, a contrast that is evocatively symbolized by the army's attachment to the map and to fixed places, such as the Churchyard and their Brigade room, and Ivan Cooper's mobility through the actual spaces depicted on the map.

The contrast is underscored effectively in the 'Normandy Landing' scene. At this stage in the film, Cooper has already been shown walking in the streets, familiar to the people he meets, and negotiating the space as he rallies support for the march. The scene has two aspects to it: firstly his meeting with Kevin McCorry in Glenfada Park, and secondly his negotiations with the army. Cooper and McCorry's relationship to the space is one of familiarity and local knowledge. Kevin interprets the space without the aid of a map: indicating the space around him with his hands, whilst verbally explaining what they see. He points out the army positions, indicating the force of their numbers in his choice of words: 'We've got the Normandy Landings down there' and 'That's going to be the flash-point'. The scene continues with Cooper addressing a local woman as she passes by. His local knowledge and acquaintance with the people in the area have been established since the opening of the film, and this is a trope throughout; indeed the reviewer for *Sight and Sound* observes how 'Cooper roves the Bogside, glad-handing and trouble-shooting, joking with old ladies who invite him to Mass, spreading the gospel of peaceful protest.'[14] In effect, Cooper personifies the contrast between the security forces and the locals, a contrast to be found metaphorically in the symbolism of the maps and memory as opposing forms of knowledge.

The meeting with the army in the second part of the scene is particularly suggestive because the response of the army sums up their ideological opposition to Cooper. When he tries to negotiate with them, he finds himself addressing a soldier who won't shift, or even listen, but just keeps saying, 'Step away from the barrier'. This rigidity and inflexibility is in sharp contrast to the civil rights' organisation's decision to re-route the march to try and avoid trouble. This opposition between them involves the playing out of the contrast between the flexible, protean operation of memory, and the brittle ossification of a particular historical paradigm. Ultimately, the film depicts the army's plans for their operation as subject to failings in the map (the three-foot drop beyond the churchyard wall is not on the map, forcing them to

14 Richard Kelly, 'Bloody Sunday' (review), *Sight and Sound*, 12:3, March 2002: 39.

change their plan to break it down) and in the power/command structure that the map symbolizes (with Brigadier MacLellan in the Brigade room losing control of proceedings, despite all the careful planning). The failure of the map is a failure of a particular epistemology, and mapping as a discursive practise is undermined in the narrative depiction of this failure. The project of the film seeks to reinstate discourse as a healing power by depicting events through collective memorial, remembrance, and performance.

The telling of the people's story as a narrative practice, like de Certeau's 'walking in the city', is a resistance to the set routes of the map.[15] It is a repetition of the trauma but also a way of making a resistant narrative cut across the official map of the event (that map being Widgery's report, and the twenty-five-year refusal to change the story, being an endless re-inscription of his version of events). All the 'local' versions of the story, such as Don Mullen's book of witness statements, repeat marches for the anniversary each year, and the re-enactment in the film by relatives, are about refusing the 'official' version, whilst insisting on the telling of their 'own' story, and the validation of their own memory. Indeed, the Department of the Taoiseach's report to the British government in June 1997 emphasizes the scepticism with which the Widgery version is perceived: 'The very disregard with which the Widgery report was viewed by nationalists, particularly those in Derry, has meant that they largely ignored it, so far removed was its version of events from the reality of what they believed happened in Derry on 30 January 1972'.[16]

For Otto Rank and Freud, the 'double' is an insurance against the destruction of the ego, 'an energetic denial of the power of death'.[17] And re-enactment, read as a mimetic doubling, can be seen by analogy as the playing out of that denial – in fact a refusal to die a second time through the insistent reminder of their continued existence in people's memories and stories of the event.

The tensions between the two topographies of the map and memory play out in the aesthetics of the film. The film is structured according to conventional forms of realist narrative. Although bracketed with the press conferences which cut into the opening and closing credits, the film proper is set within the temporal structure of one day. It begins and ends on the clock striking midnight, its form adhering to the classical unity of time, place, and action of Aristotelian tragedy, the implication being that this twenty-four-hour time period changed everything for Northern Irish history. It is a rationally framed, highly ordered dramatic form, which is lucid, balanced, and symmetrical in its formal elements and has a clear narrative trajectory. Elements within the temporal framework underscore the overall unity. There are the stories of two parallel

15 Michel De Certeau, *The practice of everyday life*, Berkeley: University of California Press, 1984. 16 Available at: http://www.taoiseach.gov.ie/upload/publications/186.doc. 17 Sigmund Freud, 'The uncanny', in *The standard edition of the complete psychological works of Sigmund Freud*, vol. 17, London: Hogarth Press, 1966: 235.

sets of inter-denominational couples with Cooper and his Catholic girlfriend, Frances, and Gerard Donaghy and his Protestant girlfriend. And the opposition between the army and the civil rights group is revealed by the film intercutting between them, as each group prepares for the march. These aspects lend a great deal of symmetry and arrangement, allowing the contrasts to be revealed.

Moreover, the film's aesthetics, in addition to its hand-held visceral and energetic mobile style, are governed by artful arrangement: from carefully framed, structured, and balanced shots, to swooping pans which manage to frame the action perfectly. For example, the opening sequence, with Gerard and his girlfriend kissing on the sofa while baby-sitting, is composed like a Vermeer domestic interior, albeit done in the Northern Irish vernacular. The shot is carefully framed through a doorway, with illumination from the left, and the voyeuristic sense of interrupting the private domestic moment is echoed in the action of the scene where the couple are being interrupted by the baby crying. And when the disturbance of this story world is wracked by the shooting, the camera is able to give fluid access to the intense scenes of violence and its aftermath.

The formal elements, then, are mobilized to make the film at once both chaotic-seeming, and so visceral that we feel we are in the action, and yet clear enough that we can apprehend that action. Given that the depiction of memory is a guiding principle behind some of the formal and aesthetic choices, and although memory is apparently a fragile thing, the film does narrate the story in a highly ordered way. The *surface* of the film depicts memory problematizing knowing through the black spaces. However, giving memory this rational, ordered form to describe the day means that the *matter* of the film, and its overall structure, builds a coherent story out of memory.

Greengrass' 'collage of shards' then is in fact more powerful than we would give memory credit for, as illustrated in the concluding scene involving Cooper's direct address to the British government. His speech is informed by hindsight, and that hindsight view embodies the power of memory in its discourse. Bernadette Devlin is given the final words in the film, 'We will not rest until justice is done'. Here memory as a way of knowing does not falter on a 'crisis' of forgetting, but is fluent and purposeful: both emotionally expressive and politically eloquent.

Imagining the future: post-Troubles comic fiction

DERVILA LAYDEN

The field of trauma studies has produced interesting insights into the function of literature[1] in expressing trauma. The focus tends to be on the unrepresentable nature of trauma itself and two inter-related loci of trauma studies are memory and the trace of the traumatic event in literature. I want to look at a way in which literature might be used, not only to investigate and analyse trauma, but to move beyond it. I'm not suggesting that trauma can be ignored – in fact, it returns insistently – but that it may be possible for a particular type of literature to have an important function in the rehabilitation process.

The type of literature to which I refer is comic fiction. I'm examining the idea that such fiction creates a space in which we can move forward, beyond trauma, to consider what life might be like in the future – a future that accepts the past but isn't controlled by it. Northern Ireland's past has been traumatic – and signing the 1998 Belfast Agreement doesn't necessarily mean that such trauma is easily forgotten. In this paper, I look at some post-agreement (optimistically termed post-troubles) fiction to evaluate how it negotiates the past and looks to the future. Two key screen texts are *Eureka Street* (Adrian Shergold, 1999) and *Wild about Harry* (Declan Lowney, 2000). *Eureka Street,* a blackly comic 1996 novel, precedes the Belfast Agreement but engages with a post-troubles society. It is set around the period of the ceasefire that began in August 1994 and charts the changes in the characters' lives and environments as peace is brokered and begins to take hold. The story concludes before the Canary Wharf shattering of that ceasefire and so seems directly linked to a post-agreement optimism – a linking confirmed by the production of a 1999 screen version (a BBC NI/RTE mini-series)[2]. *Wild about Harry* is also optimistic. Although it uses a formulaic plot of accident-induced amnesia, the Northern Ireland setting allows us to read this as creating a space between the present and a traumatic past – with the possibility of a future not overshadowed by that past. Harry is a heavy-drinking, field-playing TV chef who is beaten up one night and behaves increasingly strangely the next day, finally

1 The term 'literature' as used in this paper refers to cultural production generally and includes written, filmed and televised works. 2 For the sake of convenience, *Eureka Street* will be referred to as a film (although it is a four-part mini-series and was never publicly screened as one complete showing) for the remainder of this paper.

collapsing. When he comes around, he can't remember the last twenty-five years and thinks he is eighteen again – creating major difficulties for his exasperated wife, Ruth, who was about to divorce him.

But before proceeding further, I want to outline what I mean by comic fiction and explain its relationship to society. By comic fiction, I refer to fiction which is light in tone (unless of course it is black comedy, which uses humour but is often concerned with very shocking subjects), is humorous or satirical, which frequently operates by creating an element of distance between us and the comic characters, and generally ends happily for the main characters.[3] While many of the principles of screen comic fiction are drawn from literature, particularly drama, the cinematic form – especially early and silent cinema – lent itself to a very visual interpretation of this dynamic and one which used 'bodies as physical instruments, showing the mechanical and comic in human action and behaviour, but also interjecting both a befuddled and triumphant human soul'.[4]

How is this comic action related to our society? According to Freud, the repressed comes to the surface in dreams, verbal slips and jokes because our controlling selves won't allow it to surface in any other way. This works on a societal as well as a personal level and jokes or comedy in the public arena can be a way of protesting against constraints imposed by society. Comic film, in creating a distance between the audience and the comic characters, provides a particular type of space where we can imagine a very different world. This world is not subject to the usual rules and the comic movement 'eludes scruple just as it eludes physical obstacles; the comic decision has much in common with the comic chase in films; there is the same miraculous evasion of every blocking force, whether the stricture of reason or the traffic ahead'.[5] This suspension of rules operates like Bakhtin's concept of literary carnival, where normal ideology is suspended and authority can be mocked, satirized and subverted. And carnival, with its emphasis on satire, physical bodies and costumes, along with suspension of time is invoked by both of these comic films.

Eureka Street uses a recurring visual motif – the daubing of the meaningless letters OTG all over Belfast – to satirise the usual oppositional ideology. This gathers force throughout the film. Initially we merely notice it recurring on walls or roadways, then background news clips speculate about it, characters start to comment on it (what does it stand for? is it a slogan or an organisation? what side are they on?), one copycat character starts painting it every-

3 This definition has been drawn from an amalgam of sources: Austin M. Wright, *The formal principle in the novel*, Ithaca, New York: Cornell University Press, 1982: 149–52; Wayne C. Booth, *The rhetoric of fiction*, Chicago: University of Chicago Press, 1961: 331; and Chris Baldick, *The Concise Oxford dictionary of literary terms*, Oxford: Oxford University Press, 1991: 40. 4 Ira Konigsberg, *The complete film dictionary*, London: Bloomsbury, 1987: 59. 5 Martin Price, *Forms of life: character and moral imagination in the novel*, New Haven: Yale University Press, 1983: 72.

where, and finally it is adopted as the name of a new political party. No-one knows who started the OTG graffiti and no-one ever figures out what it stands for – which is exactly why it will become a new force in politics, 'a force for the great and lazy majority [who] will never be arsed writing anything anywhere … OTG was written for them. It could mean anything they wanted.'

Some real people are mocked through their presentation as ineffectual characters in very transparent veils – Jimmy Eve as the Just Us party spokesperson; Shague Ghinthoss as the nationalist poet writing about hedges and spades. Other characters are caricatures, such as Aoirghe – a pale, slightly undernourished and massively over-earnest supporter of the republican cause. The main narrative voice is Jake, who derides the history and ideology of all sides: 'There were three basic versions of Irish history: the Republican, the Loyalist, the British. They were all murky and all overplayed the role of Oliver Cromwell'. Jake's own, simple version is as follows: 'Eight hundred years, four hundred years, whatever way you wanted it, it's all Irish killing lots of other Irish.' He subverts ideology by submitting its language to a humanitarian and literal interpretation. When the bomb blast happens at the mid-point in the film, the shock of the bomb is portrayed through the sudden complete silence (so rare in a film soundtrack)[6] representing the temporary deafness caused to those near the blast, and the colour becomes almost monochromatic while the camera pans over the sprawled and lifeless bodies mimicking the sudden intimate invasion of photojournalism. When the dust settles and the injured gradually start to stir, Jake's voice-over denies any type of reasoning behind this atrocity, reminding us that the so-called 'historical imperative' makes no sense to the dead, wounded, traumatized and bereaved. His experience of life (and this type of death) in Northern Ireland leads him to define politics as an 'antibiotic i.e. an agent capable of killing or injuring'. This literal approach strips away ideology, exposing the hypocrisy of so-called terrorist 'mandates' for action.

Satire in *Wild about Harry* is less direct; rather than confronting political ideology, it avoids it. The purpose of film, it seems to suggest, is to tell stories and entertain, so why should films about the North have to engage with politics and religion? *Wild about Harry* contains no religious references and no political parties. Although one of the characters is a prominent politician, the party he represents is never mentioned. A flashback does show the young Harry in his job interview talking grandly about the potential of television to make a difference in a divided society, but this is one of the film's two brief references to the troubles and this youthful idealism is quickly lost in his cheesy TV chef role. As the show's producer points out, people 'like to switch on and know that their Harry will be smiling out at them'. His audience relies on television

6 We hear the blast from the perspective of a nearby office and the ensuing complete silence lasts for over a minute before Jake's voice-over begins. The background sounds of the city do not return until after the voice-over.

for company and entertainment, not politics. As the show's host, Harry entertained, flirted, filled his television patter with sexual innuendo and (as his daughter later reminds him) 'screwed everything that moved'. When he loses his memory, conveniently forgetting the last twenty-five years, we can't help feeling that this is satirizing those who define Northern Ireland in terms of its politics and its past. The tension of the domestic arena is substituted directly for the political – the film has a ceasefire (Harry's amnesia forces Ruth to interrupt divorce proceedings) followed by a period of negotiation, eleventh-hour agreement (when he convinces Ruth that he has changed), a breakdown of that agreement and finally a new legal arrangement (a divorce, but one which we sense gives both parties their own space to negotiate an eventual future together).

But carnival is not just about satire; pleasure – particularly physical pleasure – plays an important part. According to Bakhtin, 'the individual body ceases to a certain extent to be itself; it is possible [...] to exchange bodies, to be renewed (through changing costume and mask). [...] the people become aware of their sensual, material, bodily unity and community'.[7] In *Eureka Street* this is first manifested in the unlikely coupling of Chuckie and Max – Chuckie a sexually inexperienced 'fat git' (the BBC's own description), Max a svelte and cosmopolitan American woman. Their meeting only occurs after Chuckie has transformed himself during an extended sequence in front of the bathroom mirror where the camera acts as the mirror and Chuckie performs directly for us. During this sequence, Chuckie turns himself from an unkempt man with thick, unattractive glasses into a besuited businessman with contact lenses, all the time accompanied by carnival-like music with an increasingly insistent beat. As Chuckie starts to be satisfied with his appearance, he becomes visibly more confident, almost ringmasterish and swaggering. The scene closes when he sweeps out the front door, past Peggy, his astonished mother, and her friend. Peggy's amazement is such that she clings to a lamp-post for support.

Eureka Street goes on to present a late-flowering lesbian relationship between Peggy and her best friend, Caroline. Peggy has been in bed with severe shock after witnessing a bomb blast and, in the pivotal scene, we see Caroline ascending the stairs to Peggy's bedroom with a tray for the patient. The world inside the bedroom has, however, been transformed and Peggy is standing in front of the mirror dressed in assorted lingerie and feather boas. Caroline drops the tray in shock and they embrace and dance around the room. There is almost no dialogue, merely exclamations and laughter, as the camera follows their impromptu and dizzying dance accompanied by music that carries us along with them.

In both cases, a carnival-like transformation is effected which suspends normal identity and provides the impetus for the sexual union. Although car-

7 Mikhail Bakhtin, *Rabelais and his world*, trans. Helene Iswolsky, Bloomington: Indiana University Press, 1984: 255.

nival is used here within the genre of comedy, this film moves beyond the possibilities of carnival. Carnival is a temporary release following which the natural order is restored, and hence has an innate conservatism within it – a sort of safety-valve for releasing anti-establishment tension. In this film, the principles of carnival are used to destabilize the usual ideology, but the two relationships that are established become part of a new order.

In *Wild about Harry* there is lots of sex in Harry's life before his memory loss – but it is an empty habit, almost part of his job. His memory loss allows him to rediscover sexual pleasure – this time with his wife (he credits it as 'beginner's luck'!). His blank memory also erases fear, giving a sense of freedom which his son exploits by bringing him swimming (unfortunately, Harry doesn't remember that he can't swim!). In relation to costume and masks, the film neatly reverses the usual carnival tropes. The everyday appearance is sometimes the real mask. One example of this is the politician, Walter Adair, whose apparently conventional, faithful marriage covers a vigorous bisexuality. His unmasking by Harry drives him to adopt another mask, this time a carnival one – dressing as a woman to obtain entry to the TV studio and wreak revenge. For Harry, the costume and carnival of TV is the everyday routine, with the film's mission being to discover the 'old' Harry in place of the carnival clown who has become a parody of himself. The film juggles Harry's public and personal selves, with the invasion of the real and the personal at the end of the film finally catching the public imagination and achieving worldwide TV coverage. His personal life is in many ways a performance lived out in public, both for the old Harry whose sex life constantly made tabloid headlines and for the new Harry, who was divorced in court and whose wife declares her love for him on worldwide television. And while the public performance is carnivalesque, what is underneath Harry's TV mask has now changed – no longer is there merely sex and physicality, but love, something on which a future can be built.

The suspension of ideology in carnival is also linked to a suspension of time. According to Clark and Holmquist, '[t]he kind of time peculiar to carnival is the release from time, a respite from the relatively closed and rigid historical patterns that dominant ideologies impose on time's flux'.[8] This characteristic of carnival time is echoed in both films. In one Harry cannot remember the last twenty-five years; the other is set during a temporary ceasefire – a time of which Jake says 'I don't know what got into Chuckie that year, or into any of us [...] but anything seemed possible.' The comic structure sometimes allows us to see both kinds of time simultaneously (as it does in *Wild about Harry*) and suspend our disbelief for long enough to imagine a future where we may have forgotten the past. In the space created by this suspen-

8 Katerina Clark and Michael Holmquist, *Mikhail Bakhtin*, Cambridge, Mass.: Harvard University Press, 1984: 302.

sion of normal time, the usual ideologies no longer prevail and a society based on different ideologies may be imagined.

Forgetting the past is easy for Harry, but not for those around him who see the Harry they know and hate despite his change in behaviour. Part of the recovery process seems to be having a memory before the trauma. Ruth is initially hostile but soon realises that the new, nice Harry (like the one she fell in love with years before) seems to be for real. Billy (his son) finds it hardest to accept the new Harry as his memories are all bad ones. In a pivotal scene, when Billy has been reminding Harry of just how awful it was for Billy to be his son, Harry asks him what he would do in his situation and Billy aggressively retorts that he would 'stop being a self-pitying bastard'. Harry then turns the remark around, suggesting that Billy should also do the same thing. One may have bad memories but the other has none at all and yet they both have to move forward. This particular scene emphasizes the difficulties involved for all participants in building any new future.

Because he can't remember the past, Harry has to be confronted directly with its consequences – the arrival of a letter about his divorce. He can't believe that he acted as he did and sets out to win Ruth back. A sustained campaign of romance and re-invention follows, played out against a visual backdrop of the new Belfast[9] and a reinvigorated personal living space.[10] This appears to be successful, but – just as they seem to be preparing for a new future together – the past intrudes (Harry's old habits of a breakfast fry and a cigarette together with a misconstrued phone conversation convince Ruth that it is all an act). This is eventually smoothed out, and it is clear that they will have a future together – but it is equally clear that the resolution will take time and that the past must be carefully negotiated.

In *Eureka Street*, Aoirghe hangs on to the past – both the historical political dimension and the personal one (her father is wheelchair-bound after an unprovoked RUC attack). She can't forget the past and Harry can't remember his. Yet, like Harry, it is only when confronted with the human dimension of the consequences of her behaviour (in her case the punishment beating by republicans of Roche, a twelve-year-old boy) that she can regret it. To move forward to the future, they must all 'forgive' (which is the one-word letter from his ex-girlfriend that Jake opens near the film's end), not just others but also themselves.

These three aspects of carnival (satire, sexual release, suspension of time) together confront entrenched political ideology and the past. Embedding these

9 Martin McLoone points out the use of a gleaming Belfast City Hall in the background as Harry pleads with Ruth to give him another chance. The building acts as a symbol of the political and commercial renewal of Belfast that took place in the wake of the agreement and its use as a backdrop clearly links Ruth and Harry's relationship to the ongoing political process. See Martin McLoone, 'Challenging colonial traditions: British cinema in the Celtic fringe', *Cineaste*, 26: 4, Fall 2001: 51–4. **10** Harry paints a rainbow on their house and digs a huge heart shape in the field behind it. These are both representative of hopes and dreams.

within a comic structure forces us to laugh at this exposed ideology even as we see it more clearly and simultaneously distance ourselves from it. Distance is also important within the structure of comedy, particularly the perceived distance between the audience and the comic characters. In these films, the main comic characters are Harry and Chuckie. Harry differs from us, not just in his lack of memory, but also in his celebrity status while Chuckie's comic nature stems both from his appearance and his habit of talking himself into projects that he has no idea how to complete. Comic distance is typically founded on the superiority of the audience to the comic characters and we do indeed feel superior to the amnesiac Harry and the bumbling Chuckie. Yet despite our superiority, we must admit that they inhabit a recognizable Northern Ireland. However, they don't accept its rules as readily as we do and they manage to re-invent their lives and act as the catalyst for those around them to re-invent theirs. The re-invention that takes place requires dialogue with others and a building of trust – and in the final resolution, the characters are all moving from the position of comic inferiority into a new space, a space where we can respect them.

Eureka Street opens with Jake, bitter about the failure of his last relationship, who describes himself as a 'repo thug who lies to the waitresses he takes home'. During the film he re-invents himself, learning how to relate to people and his decision to leave the repo job (a job that operates on the threat of violence) is an indicator of his progress. By the final scene – showing his nocturnal contemplation of Belfast city and Aoirghe (with whom he has fallen in love) – he is a man who is honest and at ease with himself and with others. His best friend, Chuckie, starts off as a never-employed just-turned thirty-year old who has never been in love. He refuses to accept the social status thrust upon him by family and location and ends as a successful, media-savvy businessman with a beautiful girlfriend and a child on the way. Although he achieves fame and success, he realizes that this is not everything and he too learns to relate to people. One Catholic, one Protestant, neither man has much time for the distinctions of religion or for the violence and hypocrisy that those distinctions have engendered. They are more interested in a normal life – with friends, jobs and girlfriends – than agonizing over history. The film leaves us in no doubt that their reinvention is related to the wider political process. The ceasefire is announced the day that Jake gives up the repo job, which is also just after Peggy and Caroline have got together and Chuckie has found Max[11] and asked her to marry him.

Initially Harry is not re-inventing but finding himself (including playing Deep Purple and discovering the wonders of microwaves and remote controls).

11 Max had run away, sure that her own past was coming back to haunt her. Chuckie goes after her and convinces her that he loves her – regardless of her past – and that they can have a future together.

Ruth tries to reform him, telling him that he doesn't drink or smoke and that he jogs regularly and eats healthily. But these are relatively surface issues and when he discovers 'the full horror' of his TV show and that his behaviour eventually drove Ruth to seek divorce, he sets about trying to change. He also learns how to relate to people – but this is made easier for him because the intervening twenty-five years have been erased. He can continue on logically from the life he remembers (where Ruth was his girlfriend and not his wife), not so much re-inventing himself as trying to circumvent what he is told he had become.

These re-inventions all involve dealing with trauma of some sort. This may be past trauma (Jake's break-up with Sarah, Ruth's memories of Harry's philandering past) or present trauma (Harry's shock at his memory loss). The re-inventions may even cause trauma for others e.g. Chuckie's horror at his mother's lesbianism. But what is common to all is that this re-invention requires letting go of the past.

I've noted that the main characters all find new ways of relating to people. In Northern Ireland – a society that ideally no longer defines itself by the older religious/cultural groupings – these new ways of relating place greater importance on the individual and the family. Individual characters acquire freedom as they re-invent their lives. Family structures are given particular attention as new modes of being and new structures emerge. Although it appears that a conventional relationship is likely to re-establish itself in *Wild about Harry*, this is only after traditional child-parent roles have been reversed (the scene mentioned earlier where Harry asks Billy's advice; also the prompting Harry gets from his daughter Claire) and a divorce has occurred. Adults are not necessarily any surer of what to do than are their children. Family in *Eureka Street* cannot always be relied on: Jake was taken into foster care at fifteen after a tough childhood; Roche sleeps rough to get away from his abusive father and Max's mother doesn't seem to care about her. But rather than giving a negative view of family, this film offers alternatives (friends, foster-families); everyone belongs somewhere, if not within their own family within some alternative family or community.

In *Eureka Street*, a greater tolerance of sexual difference emerges. This is most notable in Chuckie's acceptance of his mother's relationship with Caroline. His initial reaction is horror; he cannot even verbalize it to Max. Luckily she knows – as all the locals are talking about practically nothing else. The two women refuse to hide their relationship, aware that they are causing scandal but determined that this nine-day wonder to the neighbours will become part of everyday life. And Chuckie gradually comes to accept that it is part of normal life.

Personal re-invention also overcomes class distinctions – particularly in *Eureka Street*. The catalyst for Chuckie's 'I Have a Dream' TV performance is the remark he overhears writing him off as 'some fat git from Eureka Street'.

His evangelical speech outlines a vision of a state where people will be judged by their character and not by their religion or class and concludes with Chuckie answering (in response to the television interviewer's question) that he will set up a political party to achieve this vision. The films provide a utopian comic space, where everyone regardless of age, religion, sexuality or class can find community and true love, make money and be happy. By comparison the comic space is used very differently in films produced during the troubles (which tend to be darker and more pessimistic) or contemporary films produced in the South (which have a less traumatic relationship with the past, sometimes parodying the relationship between past and trauma).

Comedy is useful in providing a space where we can question received ideology and re-invent ourselves, but we need to ask whether the comic mode stretches belief so far as overcome its own usefulness. In these two films the experiences of both Chuckie and Harry stretch the audience's credulity to its limits. Chuckie, despite a complete lack of resources, sets up a business empire that makes money no matter what he does. Harry loses twenty-five years of his life to find himself with the mind of a young man but a middle-aged body – an almost golden opportunity to return to his youth. They are classic comic characters, evading normal rules. With such far-fetched scenarios, can comedy really provide the necessary foil to protect society from memories of the past while simultaneously imagining a new future? Both of these films seem to think so and they work by linking each fantastic, hyperbolic character with a more realistic one. Chuckie's friend, Jake, is accorded significantly more reflection and character development. Harry's wife, Ruth, knows the sordid happenings of Harry's missing years but may be persuaded to move forward into the future with him. The optimism of the two fantastic characters and our identification with the two realistic characters drag both plot and audience towards the future.

But these new emerging identities and structures cannot exist in a time vacuum and the intrusion of the past is a notable feature of these films. At the end of *Wild about Harry*, Harry's memories of the past are starting to return. And the final scene with Walter (which triggers Ruth's declaration of love) is determined by Harry's past action – an action he doesn't remember. Although the end of *Eureka Street* skips forward to the signing of the agreement, we know that the past returned (with that first ceasefire ending). This insistent return of the past brings us back to trauma studies, reminding us that this past is traumatic, characterised by 'the literal return of the event against the will'.[12]

These comic films have created a temporary space, a space providing sufficient distance to ease the pain of the past and an open area in which to ques-

12 Cathy Caruth (ed.), *Trauma: explorations in memory*, Baltimore: Johns Hopkins University Press, 1995: 5.

tion received ideology. But like the essential parts of the Northern Ireland peace process, there is limited time available before the past intrudes on this new space. Northern Irish fiction seems to be particularly aware of the danger of this intrusion and mindful of the need to seize the opportunity to move forward. Although the past does finally intrude on the present, both films seem optimistic about the future. This temporary space now allows the past to be acknowledged and brought into the open – a place where the future is already taking shape.

The future envisaged by both films is gained through personal struggle – Chuckie's search for Max, Harry's battle against time for his wife, Jake's letting go of Sarah's memory and reconciliation with Aoirghe. It is not mere coincidence these are ultimately love stories – love is the most basic human desire. These films are not united by some idealistic desire for peace; they are united by their imagination of a future where people can live normal lives in Northern Ireland.

The musicality of film rhythm

DANIJELA KULEZIC-WILSON

The ubiquitous nature of rhythm has prompted some scholars to say that it represents the 'manifestation of the reign of law throughout the Universe'.[1] Biological rhythms govern all the processes in our body, from the continuous pulse of the beating heart and the rhythm of breathing to the body's responses to external cyclical rhythms of nature manifested in the succession of day and night, lunar influences, the change of seasons and so on. Rhythm is connected with movement and as such has been inherent to practically all man's activities, from sexual relations to social exchanges. Rhythm has also been a crucial part in either winding up or releasing and expressing all sorts of personal or collective suppressed emotions and anxieties, be they ritual dances in primitive societies, ballroom waltzes, rapping battles or techno raves.

MUSIC RHYTHM AND ITS REFLECTION IN THE ASPECTS OF FILM RHYTHM

Walther Dürr's claim that the whole world that surrounds us reveals itself in rhythmic forms has particular weight when it comes to the arts. Rhythm is an essential part in structuring any art form and, as the most reliable parameter for measuring space and time, rhythm can also act as the common denominator for all arts.

In any attempt to define film rhythm, music imposes itself as a natural reference point. Forms of both arts unfold in time, relying on rhythm as their structural 'scaffold'. On the other hand, music rhythm has been studied and analysed in depth for centuries while film theory has dealt with rhythm only sporadically.[2]

Choosing music as a reference point and role model for film was also considered to be an obvious approach by the French school of so-called 'impressionists' in the first decades of the last century. Unlike the Soviet school that concentrated on montage as the main tool in developing film language and

1 Victor Zuckerkandl, *Sound and symbol*, Princeton: Princeton University Press, 1973: 158. 2 A bibliography covering all writings about rhythm in music collected by Jonathan D. Kramer and published in 1985, has around 850 items. See Jonathan D. Kramer, 'Studies of time and music: a bibliography', *Music Theory Spectrum*, 7, 1985: 72–106.

articulating ideas through images, the 'impressionists' were more interested in the notion of 'pure cinema', which insisted on denouncing film's dependence on any other arts but music in its attempt to be formally and aesthetically self-sufficient. Music was seen as crucially important in terms of autonomy of form and immediacy of emotional impact, but most of all as the source and model for visual rhythm.

However logical the comparison between music and film rhythm seemed to the French impressionists, their approach was justifiably criticized by Jean Mitry,[3] who pointed to the main differences between the two, particularly the fact that film time is not based on periodicity which is responsible for our comprehension of rhythm in music. He also emphasized that, unlike music, film rhythm does not only involve the temporal relationships of its constituent elements but also the spatial. Although perfectly plausible, Mitry's arguments do not mean that knowledge about music rhythm cannot be applied to film in order to try and reveal relevant aspects of film rhythm itself.

On the simplest level, rhythm can be defined as the relationship between durations and accents. The first element of this relationship is a temporal category; if the same definition of rhythm is applied to arts with more prominent spatial dimensions, the aspect of *duration* could be interchanged with measures of length, distance, volume and so on. In film its description will certainly include both temporal and spatial aspects as, curiously, the perception of the temporal aspect is highly dependent on the spatial/visual aspects of the shot. Two shots of the same length may be perceived as different in duration depending on the dynamics of their content and their aesthetic characteristics, which is yet more evidence that the rhythm of editing cannot be based on the absolute durations of the shots.[4] Beside the fact that visual perception is less sensitive to temporal than to spatial stimuli, our perception of duration can change depending on the content, composition, framing and mobile framing (camera movement) of the shot, as well as on its 'density'.[5]

Things are even more complicated when it comes to the second element of the definition of rhythm, *the accent*. In music literature, accent is defined as a 'stimulus which is *marked for consciousness* in some way'. It means that

3 Jean Mitry, *Esthetique et psychologie du cinema*, Paris: Editions universitaires, 1965; *Semiotics and the analysis of film*, London: Athlone Press, 2000. 4 It is revealing that the term 'rhythmic editing' still has the same meaning in contemporary textbooks about film as in the era of the Soviet montage school: it considers the length of the shots in relation to each other implying that the actual durations of the take are the most important factors in establishing rhythmic relations between them. See David Bordwell and Kristin Thompson, *Film art: an introduction*, New York: McGraw-Hill, 1993: 256–66; 277–9. 5 A long shot full of action will appear shorter than a static close-up of the same duration. However, a dynamic close-up will be perceived as shorter than a static long shot. As Mitry concludes, 'the more dynamic the content and the wider the framing, the shorter the shot appears; the more static the content and narrower the framing, the longer the shot appears' (*Semiotics*, 2000: 223). For the relationship between mobile framing and our sense of duration in film, also see Bordwell and Thompson, *Film art*, 226–7.

accent in music can be distinguished from other stimuli because of differences in duration, intensity, pitch, timbre, and so on. The question is, though, how do we define accent in film, or more precisely, how do we decide which accents are relevant to film's rhythmic structure?

The successive durations of visual units alone have no accents through which a rhythmic relation can be established. These accents are to be found in the *content of the frame* and are closely related to another aspect of film that Mitry proclaimed as the most important for establishing film rhythm. This is *the intensity of a shot*:

> Rhythm [in film] has more to do with relationships of intensity [than duration] – but relationships of intensity contained within relationships of duration [...]. The intensity of a shot depends on the amount of movement (physical, dramatic or psychological) contained in it and on the length of time it lasts.[6]

Bearing all Mitry's observations in mind, film rhythm could be redefined as the relationship between the intensity of a frame's content and the duration of its visual units. However, this definition does not make it very clear that film is an audio-visual form and that the content of the frame is aural as well as visual, so that both components are responsible for its intensity. In general, most theoreticians who resist the comparison between film and music rhythm, and whose favourite argument is that the eye is the organ of space and the ear of time, somehow manage to overlook the fact that sound and music are as much part of film form as image is, so that its sonic and temporal aspects are as significant for the general perception of rhythm as are its visual aspects. Moreover, when aural and visual elements act together, as they do in film, they open a whole new perceptual dimension that belongs almost exclusively to this medium. Sergei Eisenstein was among the first to focus on this potential of sound film defining it as its 'fourth dimension': the area where for 'overtones' of aural and visual perception the new common formula 'I feel' is established.[7]

The involvement of aural and visual elements in the establishment of film rhythm inspired Michael Chion's thesis on 'transsensorial perception'. According to this, rhythm belongs to the elements of film vocabulary that are neither specifically auditory nor visual and which become decoded in the brain as rhythm *after* passing a certain sensory path of the eye or ear. Chion argues that the senses, when perceiving an artwork, act as 'channels, highways more than territories or domain'. 'When kinetic sensations organized into art are transmitted through a single sensory channel', he continues, 'they convey all the other senses at once'.[8]

6 Mitry, *Semiotics*, 222. 7 Sergei Eisenstein, 'The fourth dimension in the kino' in Dusan Stojanovic, *Teorija filma*, Beograd: Nolit, 1978: 189. 8 Michael Chion, *Audio-vision*, New York:

It is obvious that the crucial aural input in the process of establishing film rhythm comes from music itself. Aside from all its other functions in film, music by 'just being there' gives film its sense of temporality. As Mitry noticed, silent film was incapable of making the spectator experience a real feeling of duration, because what was missing 'was a sort of beat which could internally mark the psychological time of the drama in relation to the primary sensation of real time' and 'this beat, this "temporal content", was provided by music'.[9] The strength of music's ability to provide kinetic force to film even on its own is convincingly shown in Ingmar Bergman's *Persona* (1966), in the scene showing the face of Liv Ullmann lying on a bed. This totally static, and at the same time extremely engrossing, close-up lasts for several minutes, while the only movement is provided by the musical accompaniment of a baroque violin concerto and the gradual darkening of the image in its last seconds.

Apart from obvious kinetic and rhythmic values inherent to any music, which act as a cohesive and metronomic underscore to film, music also influences the creation of film rhythm through its relationship with psychological time. Since music plays a prominent role in creating a picture's general affective tone and, consequently, influences the intensity of the content of a certain scene, music inevitably forms a functional relationship with psychological time. Owing to the character of the music and the general mood it generates, the passage of time within a certain take can be experienced as accelerated, slowed-down, or completely frozen. It is obvious that through this relationship with psychological time music indirectly influences the creation of film rhythm. Michael Chion suggests that notions of temporality and its rhythmic and affective inflections can be imprinted in film through sound in general, be they the noises of nature (the sound of water can be particularly striking, as Tarkovsky's films have shown), the intonation and cadences of human speech, or noises of industrial surroundings, as used recently in David Cronenberg's *Spider* (2002) with unsettling effect. Moreover, accents made in sound have an immediate effect on our auditory receptors. Directly or indirectly, through accentuation, duration, movement or mood, it is clear that sound, especially music, has an important role in creating film's rhythm together with its visual elements.

RHYTHM OF THE SHOT AND THE CUT

However, the question still remains: how do we define, establish and analyse rhythm in film? For most filmmakers the answer to this question depends on whether they belong to one of two groups: those who believe that film rhythm is created in the editing room or those who prefer to feel time passing in unin-

Columbia University Press, 1994: 136–7. 9 Mitry, *Esthetique et psychologie du cinema*, 118–19.

terrupted shots and think that rhythm is established through the complex orchestration of the mise-en-scène, its composition, light and movement.

The opposing views of the 'shot versus the cut' aesthetics articulated in the theoretical and practical work of Sergei Eisenstein and the writings of André Bazin were blended in the Hollywood machine to form a new, *continuity* style. As Robert Kolker indicates, on the level of ideology, this style emerged as a 'capitalist version of Eisensteinian montage and a secular version of Bazin's deep-focus, long-take style'.[10] On the structural level, this style of classical Hollywood, as well as its contemporary, post-modern version influenced by MTV aesthetics, might not follow Eisenstein's aesthetic and ideological principles of montage fully, but it certainly relies more heavily on editing than mise-en-scène with regard to the establishing of rhythm and the principles of storytelling.

Unlike Eisenstein, who believed that drawing attention to the relationship between shots was important for creating a dialectical synthesis of idea, emotion and perception, classical Hollywood style was more concerned with telling a story while covering all traces of its formal and technical devices, which included opting for a short length of shot. Even though the American contemporary style of film-making is not so concerned with keeping its devices invisible – on the contrary, young directors are quite fond of showy camera work and visual pyrotechnics – the length of shots is still kept short while the rhythm of editing is often influenced by either the aesthetics of music videos or popular music styles. This is the case with Darren Aronofsky's film *Requiem for a Dream* (2000). The audio-visual pattern that depicts drug consumption in this film represents a striking part of its structure and invests the film with a powerful dramaturgical and emotional effect. As one critic observed, it also gives the film a 'certain precision musicality [...] a rhythmic pulse which echoes his protagonists' relentless decline. In a recurrent motif he [Aronofsky] strips down the mechanics of drug use to their fundamentals: a needle is filled; a bank note rolled; a television switched on. Blood vessels expand, pupils dilate. Cut, after cut, after cut'.[11]

The longer version of this pattern is based on what Aronfosky calls 'hip-hop editing': a style inspired by hip-hop music and its techniques which, translated to film, means that images and sounds are treated as samples. The 'hip-hop montage sequence' combines shots of very short duration with slightly longer ones, thus establishing diversity within a pattern, which allows the process of *grouping* to take place. The techno music acts as the 'scaffold' for the sequence not only rhythmically but also aesthetically. The doubling of musical and visual accents has an almost visceral effect on the viewer like the techno music itself and at the same time it clearly evokes the drug-induced rush which some of the shots illustrate. The repetition of single shots of drug

10 Robert P. Kolker, 'The film text and film form' in John Hill and Pamela Church Gibson, (eds), *The Oxford guide to film studies*, Oxford: Oxford University Press, 1998: 18. 11 Danny Leigh, 'Feeling needled', *Sight and Sound*, December 2000: 28.

consumption within a pattern emphasizes the addictive nature of the habit, while the repetition of the whole pattern in slightly varied manifestations, and its strategic positioning in the overall structure, gives it an important dramaturgical function. By connecting all the characters in their addictive habits this miniature montage sequence conveys one of the main ideas of the film, according to which the nature and tragic consequences of all addictions are equalised, be they drug habits or obsession with trash TV and the distorted image of life it advocates. For the fact is, their addictions are – as any addiction by definition is – anaesthetics for some deeper pain or craving: a renunciation of reality that can have catastrophic consequences. On the other hand, the repetition of the pattern and its rhythmic character imply how much these characters are overpowered by their habits.

Supporters of long takes and elaborate mise-en-scène propose an essentially different approach to the problem of film rhythm. Andrei Tarkovsky, who believed that rhythm was both the most important expressive and formative element of cinema, articulated the essence of this aesthetic by saying that 'the distinctive time running through the shots creates the rhythm of the picture; and rhythm is determined not by the length of the edited pieces, but by the pressure of the time that runs through them'.[12]

If we compare any Tarkovsky film with the analysed sequence from *Requiem for a Dream*, the prolonged length of single shots in Tarkovsky's film emerges first as the most obvious difference between the two. It is within these long shots that Tarkovsky finds the source for his 'time-sculptures' and through which he establishes the rhythm of his films. In the dream sequence from the film *Mirror* (1974), for instance, its peculiar rhythm and oneiric quality is created through the orchestration of the most prominent kinetic elements in the mise-en-scène: the elegant movement of the camera with slow panning across the room or gradual widening of frame, the movement of an actress in slow motion, water dripping from her wet hair and water and pieces of ceiling dripping from above as if it is raining inside the house. The fact that the actress who is playing Tarkovsky's mother in this sequence also plays his wife in the rest of the movie (both are women separated from or deserted by their husbands) points to more than one personal ghost that obviously haunted Tarkovsky into making *Mirror*, while this particular dream-sequence reveals most vividly feelings of buried grief that the breakdown of both families brought to Tarkovsky as a child, and later in his adult life.

The sonic dimension of this sequence is as vital as the visual one, extending our perception beyond the lines of actual visual frames through the subtle presence of non-diegetic sounds. Its unsettling content is created by the sound of trickling water, electronic sounds mixed with the muffled sound of a male choir and the noises of nature where the hooting of an owl is employed as a

12 Andrei Tarkovsky, *Sculpting in time*, London: Bodley Head, 1986: 117.

mild sonic accent. Unlike in *Requiem for a Dream*, where sound is used mostly as an accent, which corresponds to the film's rapid cutting, in Tarkovsky's film the sound is more sustained, stretching in vast sheets, emphasizing the aspects of duration and the unequal rhythms of mobile framing and slow-motion movement more than anything else.

Shortly after entering the world of Tarkovsky's films it becomes clear that their director is not very concerned with establishing consistent rhythmic patterns, either visual or sonic, at least not on the more perceptible micro-level. Although recurring audio-visual motifs, like the image and sound of water, represent one of his trademarks, the pulse of Tarkovsky's films is irregular, resembling the rhythm of non-Western music free from metre and a stable beat. Incidentally, this could explain why Western audiences brought up on firmly patterned musical forms, either classical or popular, sometimes find this kind of rhythm difficult to connect to. The same applies to other non-Hollywood films created by directors who share a similar perception of time that favours free rhythm. This includes a substantial number of Asian directors and many European ones too.

Because of their fixation with the passing of time and their distinctive rhythmic quality Tarkovsky's films can also be compared to certain works of contemporary Western music, like those of Morton Feldman. Curiously, Feldman was not particularly interested in working with time directly and his idea was more to let time be, than to treat it as a compositional element. Also, very much unlike Tarkovsky, Feldman was fascinated by patterns. He realized that the abstract essence of combined patterns applied in music could actually accommodate his main concern – the use of musical colour. However, although his piece *Why patterns?* for flute, glockenspiel and piano consists of a large variety of patterns, they are assigned to each instrument separately and never precisely synchronized. The time signatures are different for each instrument, changing constantly throughout the piece. As a result, Feldman's music, with its long time spans, the sense of metre completely deleted and an emphasized feeling of the passing of time, closely resembles Tarkovsky's films in spite of the very different approaches and processes these artists employ.

By confronting the two opposing aesthetic approaches and understandings of film rhythm – 'the shot versus the cut' – manifested in the examples of Aronofsky's and Tarkovsky's films, it is obvious that in both cases rhythm is created by the interaction of visual and sonic components. Furthermore, both approaches deal with important issues and can accomplish effective rhythmic structures so the only possible conclusion is that we have here two different kinds of rhythm existing in parallel and in interaction. These two types of rhythm were actually identified by Léon Moussinac as internal and external rhythm, where the former includes both diegetic action and the way the camera records it, while the latter is created by the way film is timed and cut.[13]

13 Léon Moussinac, 'Naissance du cinéma' in Stojanovic, *Teorija filma*, 94–9.

The coexistence and interaction of these two types of rhythm are strikingly similar to the relationship between chronometric and integral time that embody metric and rhythmic levels of musical existence.[14] These two levels of architectonic musical structure, identified by David Epstein as two modes of temporal structure, exist as structural entities separate in terms of their hierarchical organization, yet their interaction, as is the case with the two types of film rhythm, is implanted at the core of the overall experience of the medium.

In his book *Shaping Time*, Epstein develops the argument for viewing metre and rhythm as architectonically parallel systems that are also perceptively and cognitively processed as parallel. However, this processing, as Epstein says, involves a 'morphologically unified parameter – the temporal stream of music'.[15] The aspect of parallel coexistence of internal and external rhythm in film is even more obvious than the parallelism between metre and rhythm in music to the extent that certain directors make conscious decisions to focus on one of them, whereas in music this division is of an analytical nature with the result that neither composers nor listeners have to be aware of it. However, in the same way that the conjunction and opposition of metre and rhythm in music unfold through continuous tension and adjustment to each other, so do external and internal rhythm in film interrelate, dealing with different temporal aspects and still being dependent on each other for the creation of a 'morphologically unified parameter – a single temporal stream'.

Ultimately, whether consciously recognized as separate, and whatever the processes of their perception are, the two levels of structural hierarchy either in music or film cannot fulfil their function on their own. The interaction with the other structural level is necessary to create a meaningful, completed form. Moreover, the underlying tension between rhythm and metre in music or, on the other hand, the orchestrated relationship between internal and external rhythm in film, act as a source of the basic structural and affective powers inherent to each medium.

If one looks at external and internal rhythm in film from a different perspective – a perspective that emphasizes their individual characteristics more than the relationship between them – it could be said that internal rhythm in

14 Western understanding of rhythm in music is associated with the existence of a regular pulse with more or less regularly recurring accents, which is one possible definition of metre. Like other aspects of musical organization, metre is architectonic in nature so that metrical arrangement not only divides temporal flux into equal units but collects those units into small groups which we call measures. The architectonical level on which this process of grouping takes place was defined by David Epstein in temporal terms as 'chronometric time'. Parallel with metrical grouping, on the higher architectonical plane, another level of rhythmical grouping takes place, which Epstein defines as 'integral time'. Rhythmical grouping is the process of organizing separate sounds mentally into structural patterns while being influenced by the various aspects of music which beside duration include pitch, intensity, timbre, texture and harmony, although rarely all at the same time. See David Epstein, *Shaping time*, New York: Schirmer, 1995: 40–2.

15 Ibid.

film corresponds loosely to music rhythm free of metre, while external rhythm in film bears some characteristics of metric rhythm in music. From the examples presented earlier it could be concluded that choosing to focus on internal or external rhythm implies a preference for a particular aesthetic approach. Those directors who base their rhythmic structure on editing also tend to focus on external rhythm and think more in terms of grouping and rhythmical patterns. On the other hand, internal rhythm has more of the characteristics of musical free rhythm; it is not underlined by patterns which correspond to the stable metrical beat of Western music and is usually a point of focus for directors who prefer long takes and the aesthetics of 'the shot'.

Although justified by common practice, this generalization might prove to be limiting after all, not least because there are directors who, like Tarkovsky, tend to concentrate on internal rhythm but still 'think in patterns', like Jim Jarmusch. The pulse of his movies may be as slow as in Tarkovsky's but it is involved in the creation of 'groups' which work on the macro-level, thus establishing distinctive macro-rhythms. The macro-rhythmical structure of certain Jarmusch films – *Dead Man* (1995) particularly – is so sophisticated that it resembles a model of musical structure or, as some critics have argued, a poetic one.

The organisation of macro-rhythmical structure is an important aspect in creating any art form, not only film. In each form elements on the micro-level engage in certain dynamic relationships that are hierarchical in character, similar to the structure of a musical work. It has already been mentioned how the repetition and structural positioning of a short rhythmic pattern in Aronofsky's film takes on an important dramaturgical function. In the case of Jarmusch's *Dead Man*, the reflection of the beginning of the film in its ending and the recurrence of distinctive narrative and musical motifs led Kent Jones to compare the structure of *Dead Man* to 'an epic film poem with rhyming figures and refrains'.[16] Alternatively, it could be argued that it closely resembles the musical ternary ABA1 form, where even the introduction and coda mirror each other. However, the subtlety of the form here is not an end in itself, even though our primary response to its structure might happen only on the subconscious level. By following the rhythm of macro-patterns, their relationships and inner dynamics, the deeper meaning of the structure emerges, revealing its intrinsic connection to some of the film's main ideas, particularly the idea of 'passing through the mirror' mentioned by the Indian character. By the end of the movie it has become clear that he was referring to the mirror of water that, according to Indian beliefs, will send its protagonist from timeless purgatory back to the spirit world.

Another approach to defining film rhythm has been suggested by Claudia Widgery who focuses on the elements of film kinesis as the strongest means of expressing rhythm. Having in mind all kinetic aspects of film – movement

16 Kent Jones, 'Dead Man'. *Cineaste*, 22: 2, 1996: 45–46.

within a shot, movement of the camera, movement of editing and the general feeling of temporality established by it – Claudia Widgery proposes to define film rhythm as the 'interaction of a shot's kinetic content with timing of its cutting and the dynamics of the individual shots that precede and follow it'.[17]

Although Widgery's definition addresses only visual aspects of kinesis in film, she later concludes that music represents film's 'ultimate extra-diegetic source of kinesis' since music rhythm, 'particularly that with a steady pulse, arguably has a more immediate and visceral kinetic impact than the rhythm of cutting itself'.[18] It could be added that, even though the influence of the music in this context is indisputable, it was shown in the examples of Tarkovsky's and particularly Aronfsky's films, that even sound itself, especially if employed as a rhythmic accent, can bring the same immediacy and visceral effect to film kinesis.

Since various parameters of music rhythm ('surface' rhythm, harmonic rhythm, tonal or formal rhythm) relate to different aspects of visual kinesis, Nicholas Cook suggests that the 'process of analysis, then, might be expected to have the effect of breaking down global categories such as "music" and "pictures" through the discovery of component parameters that contribute independently to the multimedia experience'.[19] This coincides with the argument of Gestalt psychology that the rhythmic identity of a film work is built on even more complex relationships between film *dominants* where movement is only one dimension of it. As Dusan Stojanovic claims in his book *Film as a Means of Overcoming Language*, the dominants of a picture, which include shape, line, volume and colour as well as the dominants of movement, space-time and sound, are all involved in what Gestalt psychology calls the *laws of organization in perceptual forms*. All these elements create certain dynamics in form and its perception, which is crucial for our apprehension of film rhythm in its totality.[20]

With this in mind I will suggest yet another definition according to which film rhythm is established through the interaction of external and internal dominants of aural, visual and kinetic content, in which the role of accents responsible for the mental grouping of film's constituents into rhythm can be played by any sonic or visual element of a frame's content. Because of the complexity of film's audio-visual structure and all the parameters involved a complete analysis of film rhythm may be impossible, let alone full control of all its constituents, but one can at least try to be aware of them.

17 Claudia Widgery, 'The kinetic and temporal interaction of music and film: Three documentaries of 1930s America', unpublished PhD thesis, University of Maryland College Park, UMI, 1990: 133. **18** Ibid., 143. **19** Nicholas Cook, *Analysing musical multimedia*, Oxford: Clarendon Press, 1998: 143. **20** Dusan Stojanovic, *Film kao prevazilazenje jezika* [*Film as a means of overcoming language*], Beograd: Institut za film, 1984: 165–6.

Cultural ventriloquism: the voice-over in film adaptations of contemporary Irish and Scottish literature

SARAH NEELY

When I delivered this paper in April 2003, I was in the process of polishing up my thesis for submission. My thesis, like this article, situates itself in relation to a body of work comparatively studying Scottish and Irish culture.[1] As with all comparative study, the danger of its application is that connections are forced that don't really exist. My apprehension on this score was further compounded when, the day after I presented my paper, I attended a debate on contemporary Irish cinema that included a discussion of the new 'Irish' film in circulation, *The Magdalene Sisters* (Peter Mullan, 2002). Enthusiasm for the film was, however, dampened by the Irish director Jim Sheridan who pointed out that it had, after all, been made by 'some Scottish guy'.[2]

1 For comparative literary criticism see: Patricia Horton, 'Bagpipe music: some intersections in Scottish and Irish writing', *Scotlands*, 4:2, 1997: 66–80; Ellen-Raïssa Jackson, 'Cultural identity in contemporary Scottish and Irish writing', unpublished PhD thesis, University of Glasgow, 1999; Ellen-Raïssa Jackson and Willy Maley, 'Celtic connections: colonialism and culture in Irish-Scottish modernism', *Interventions: The International Journal of Postcolonial Studies*, 4:1, 2002, special issue on Postcolonial Studies and Transnational Resistance, edited by Elleke Boehmer and Bart Moore-Gilbert: 67–78; Willy Maley, 'Ireland, verses, Scotland: crossing the (English) language barrier', in Glenda Norquay and Gerry Smyth (eds), *Across the margins: cultural identity and change in the Atlantic archipelago*, Manchester and New York: Manchester University Press, 2002: 13–30; Glenda Norquay and Gerry Smyth, 'Waking up in a different place: contemporary Irish and Scottish fiction', in Glenda Norquay and Gerry Smyth (eds), *Across the margins*, 154–70; Marilyn Reizbaum, 'Canonical double cross: Scottish and Irish Women's writing', in Karen R. Lawrence (ed.), *Decolonizing tradition: new views of twentieth-century 'British' literary canons*, Urbana and Chicago: University of Illinois Press, 1992: 165–90; Marilyn Reizbaum, 'Not a crying game: the feminist appeal: nationalism, feminism and the contemporary literatures of Scotland and Ireland', *Scotlands*, 1:1, 1994: 24–31; Ray Ryan, *Ireland and Scotland: literature and culture, state and nation, 1966–2000*, Oxford: Oxford University Press, 2002. For a similar analysis in film criticism see Ellen-Raïssa Jackson, 'Dislocating the nation: political devolution and cultural identity on stage and screen', *Edinburgh Review*, 110, 2002: 120–31 and Martin McLoone, 'Internal decolonisation? British cinema in the Celtic fringe', in Robert Murphy (ed.), *The British cinema book*, London: BFI, 2001, 2nd edition: 184–90. 2 Although I do not have a recording of tbe event and cannot be certain of his exact words, this is the response I have recorded in my notes of the event. 'New Irish cinema – day of debate', *The Irish Film Board – 10th anniversary*, Saturday, 12 April 2003, Irish Film Centre, Dublin.

While such a response is evidence of a more general resistance – on the part of critics as well as practitioners – to acknowledge the links and connections forged by filmmakers, it is also a common practice to consider Scottish and Irish texts in relation to their *English* counterparts. Expressing his irritation at this practice in studies dealing with Scottish literature, Robert Crawford indicates that texts are either 'constantly absorbed into English Literature or else exiled from it for special attention in a specialist area'.[3] In response to these tendencies, several critics have seen Irish and Scottish comparative studies as a way of compensating for the limitations of other studies. In many ways the formation of the Irish-Scottish Academic Initiative in 1995 aimed to offset the 'Anglocentricity' of studies that either expelled Scottish literature to the margins or overlooked it entirely. Similar issues are also evident in cinema studies. While debates circulate as to whether or not Ireland or Scotland have had, or ever really will have, a sustainable film industry, critical overviews continue to tack on Ireland and Scotland and Wales to volumes devoted to British cinema (or else ignore them altogether).[4] The purpose of this paper – like Irish-Scottish studies in general – is to adopt an alternative approach that addresses texts comparatively (while still considering their relationship to British cinema more generally). More specifically, this piece aims to examine the prevalent use of the voice-over in Irish and Scottish cinema as a mode through which marginalized cultures may subvert the dominant forms of Hollywood.

THE VOICE IN IRISH AND SCOTTISH LITERATURE

The influence of fiction written in the first person, expressing a singular voice independently of an intrusive narrator, has been felt in both Irish and Scottish cinema.[5] In common with other adaptations of first-person novels,[6] the use of

3 Robert Crawford, *Devolving English literature*, Oxford: Clarendon Press, 1992: 305. 4 Andrew Higson, in his recent exploration of heritage cinema, is representative of this general critical practice. Although in the opening of his new book, he claims to recognize the importance of addressing Scottish, Irish, and Welsh heritage films, Higson avoids taking the task on himself by arguing that the scope of his book would not allow for it. Andrew Higson, *English heritage, English cinema: costume drama since 1980*, Oxford: Oxford University Press, 2003: 4. 5 In 'Ireland, verses, Scotland', Willy Maley draws a distinction between styles of narration in Scotland and Ireland. He claims that whereas Scottish writers like James Kelman and Welsh abandon the tradition of containing the unruly language of their characters within a formal, standardized narration, Irish writers like Seamus Deane, 'wearing the clothes-pegs of dialogue', avoid this option (p. 19). He does, however, admit that Roddy Doyle and Patrick McCabe are exceptions to this (p. 21). In the same book, Glenda Norquay and Gerry Smyth argue, in 'Waking up in a different place', for a comparison between Welsh and Doyle in terms of their tendency to 'dispense with what Joyce called "perverted" commas, those scriptive markers of different voice-zones by means of which the textual world is orchestrated in line with established discourses of power'

the voice-over in Irish and Scottish cinema has been a recurring characteristic. This is largely due to the wealth of literature offering new and innovative voices and the fear felt by adaptors of losing the texts' distinctiveness. Much of what is at risk of being lost in the process of adaptation is the manner in which these voices challenge the conventions of 'official' language through various modes of parody. One of the best examples of this, in Scottish literature, is Tom Leonard's poem 'The 6 O' Clock News' which, as the title suggests, interrogates the BBC register and reveals what might be lurking behind the notion of 'official' language.[7] Roddy Doyle's *The Commitments* also deals with issues of accent and authenticity in its portrait of a band's adoption of black American soul music as their own. Irvine Welsh often adopts a similar approach. For instance, in his short story, chewing over the world of international celebrity, 'Where the Debris Meets the Sea',[8] Welsh depicts Kim Basinger, Kylie Minogue, Madonna and Victoria Principal in a California beach house passionately debating the contents of various magazines (*Wide-o*, *Scheme Scene* and *Bevvy Merchants*) in a broad Edinburgh accent while wistfully contemplating the possibility of a holiday in Leith. Apart from the humorous effects that this generates, such cultural crossovers not only suggest the ways in which a culture adopts the forms of another culture but also questions the power relationships between the two.

In cinema, this questioning is relayed through film language as well as speech and dialogue. Just as the use of the vernacular exposes the hidden hierarchies of the English language, these texts also aim to tackle the dominant forms of Hollywood cinema. In *When Brendan Met Trudy* (Kieron Walsh, 2000), for example, the narrative sets up a play between various communicative modes. The opening sequence, parodying *Sunset Boulevard* (Billy Wilder, 1950), establishes the central character as another Joe Gillis, narrating from beyond the grave. A similar technique is evident in Neil Jordan's adaptation of Patrick McCabe's *The Butcher Boy* (Neil Jordan, 1997) in the way in which it employs techniques of the Western, Sci-Fi films, cartoons and comic books.[9] It is important to note that these imitative devices almost always seem to be led by the imaginative musings of the film's (and novel's) central character Francie Brady. Francie's distinct voice serves as a way of dealing with the outside world. Trying on different voices, Francie acts out scenarios from his thriving fantasy world. For instance, in the novel, when he first enters the industrial school he declares it to be '*The Incredible School for Pigs!* ... in [his] telly voice'. In the film, this is a voice that we hear as his own, but in a way

(p. 161). 6 For an in-depth discussion of this, see Sarah Kozloff, *Invisible storytellers: voice-over narration in American fiction film*, Berkeley, Los Angeles, and London: University of California Press, 1988: 72. 7 Tom Leonard, 'The 6 o'clock News', from 'Unrelated incidents', in *Intimate voices: selected work, 1965–1983*, Newcastle upon Tyne: Galloping Dog Press, 1984: 88. 8 Irvine Welsh, 'Where the debris meets the sea', *The Acid House*, London: Vintage, 1995: 87–92. 9 Patrick McCabe, *The Butcher Boy*, London: Picador, 1993.

that mimics the television quality of the voice-over. This mix of the individual voice and play with film language is also evident in the adaptation of other writers' work such as Irvine Welsh, William McIlvanney and, to a certain extent, Roddy Doyle. It might even be argued that the lukewarm reception of the much anticipated adaptation of Alan Warner's *Morvern Callar* (Lynne Ramsay, 2002) was down to its silencing of the distinctive voice of its central character and a subsequent loss of the 'local'.[10]

ADAPTATION AND THE VOICE-OVER

Generally speaking, the employment of the voice-over has been identified as detrimental to the development of a distinct visual aesthetic in cinema. A disdain towards bringing the spoken word into film may be traced back to a general aversion to the sound film or 'talkie' when it first made an appearance in the late 1920s. In the prologue to *The Voice in Cinema,* Michel Chion argues that resistance to sound derived from a fear of becoming too realistic at the expense of the imaginary; Chion also points out that the use of voice-over has been seen as one of the least realistic uses of sound.[11] The turn of film away from its ties with literature may also explain its apprehension towards excessive wordiness. The use of voice-over in the cinema has been a particular point of contention. Having once served as a useful story-telling device, it was seen, after years of clichéd use, to have become little more than a narrative crutch devoid of artistic merit. The consensus then became that it was better to provide the information contained in the voice-over through action, or at least through dialogue within the action. Therefore, the employment of a voice-over in the adaptation of a novel has been routinely condemned for its perceived failure to translate the literary into cinematic terms.

Others, convinced of the device's merits, have argued for its use. Sarah Kozloff has remarked upon its ability to relate effectively feelings of intimacy and irony.[12] Michel Chion praises the device for communicating a degree of suspense particularly through the mystery generated by a narrator who remains unseen (the 'disembodied voice'). For Chion, the 'acousmêtre', as he refers to it, possesses magical powers deriving from the unseen voice. Virtually every film employing a voice-over retains at least some degree of this mystery, even if it is very brief, since voice-overs are generally introduced without the corresponding image of a physical body. It is at the juncture when the body is revealed – what Chion refers to as the 'deflowering' – that 'the voice loses its virginal-acousmatic powers, and re-enters the realm of human beings'.[13] Viewed

10 Alan Warner, *Morvern Callar,* London: Vintage, 1996. **11** Michel Chion, *The voice in cinema,* trans. Claudia Gorbman, New York: Columbia University Press, 1999. **12** Kozloff, *Invisible storytellers*, 2. **13** Chion, *The voice in cinema*, 23.

in this light, it can be important that the unveiling of the voice is delayed as long as possible. This is certainly so of *The Butcher Boy* where the connection of the voice-over to an older Francie Brady (in a mental institution) would be bound to affect the spectator's acceptance of the commentary. As some critics suggested, the technique even angered those spectators who felt tricked into identifying with someone later revealed to be mentally disturbed.

Other critics have been less supportive of the device. Seymour Chatman concludes that 'since films *show* everything, off-screen voices in general have come to be thought obtrusive and inartistic, and those speaking in truncated syntax and free-associative patterns particularly so'.[14] This appears to imply that the more the speech is psychologically representative and natural, the less necessary it is to rely on the use of voice-over. This conclusion may be linked with Kaja Silverman's view that it is the narrative image's association with regional accent that may bring the narrator too close for any large degree of authority.[15] This is an interesting point. Although recent films have witnessed a rise in the popularity of the device, there remains a significant degree of inflexibility surrounding the types of voice-overs deemed to be acceptable. The voice-overs frequently encountered in contemporary cinema arise from a particular form of adaptation, namely the literary classic or period drama. In these films, the narration adheres to classical conventions and is delivered in a formal and measured fashion. Rarely is the reliability of the narration questioned. Within this context, the voice-overs employed in recent Scottish and Irish suggest an unconventional use of the device that challenges existing modes. In the terms of Gilles Deleuze they may be seen 'to stutter', or 'invent a minor use of the major language'.[16] Thus, just as various literary movements attempted to subvert dominant literary models by working within their own idioms and traditions, so the use of unorthodox filmic devices within mainstream cinema holds out the possibility of destabilizing it. This could describe the literature upon which the films are based, but also the films' process of negotiation with the language of mainstream cinemas, manipulating existing forms to accommodate some of their own.

THE VOICE-OVER IN CONTEMPORARY IRISH AND SCOTTISH CINEMA

In contrast to the use of the voice-over in British/English heritage cinema, in which an articulate voice reinforces the detail of the camera in a self-assured

14 Seymour Chatman, *Story and discourse,* New York: Cornell University Press, 1978: 194. 15 Kaja Silverman, *The acoustic mirror,* Bloomington and Indianapolis: Indiana University Press, 1988: 49. 16 Gilles Deleuze, *Essays critical and clinical,* Minneapolis: University of Minnesota Press, 1997: 107–108.

fashion, the voice-over in several of the films looked at here is marked by fragmentation and an often discordant relationship to the image. The voice, divided between cultural discourses, alternates between modes of articulation (often, English, but more often American). Andrew Higson describes the voice-over in the heritage film as serving to 'foreground the authenticity of the "original"' and celebrate 'the purity of the word'.[17] Although the adaptations of the contemporary writers discussed here might also be said to confirm the links of the films to their literary predecessors, the employment of the voice-over is less concerned to validate the 'authenticity' of the revered text than the authenticity of character. The existence of a sometimes-obtrusive voice-over, that avoids the transparent use of the device in heritage cinema, is further evidence of this commitment.

Films such as *Trainspotting* (Danny Boyle, 1996), *The Commitments* (Alan Parker, 1991), *The Snapper* (Stephen Frears, 1993), *The Butcher Boy,* and *Dreaming* (Mike Alexander, 1990) draw upon the voice-over in an effort to retain vestiges of the 'local' evident in their literary counterparts. *Trainspotting* amalgamates the first-person vignettes of several characters from Welsh's novel into Renton's solo narration.[18] Working from a more conventional narration, *The Snapper* and *The Commitments* maintain the intimate feel of Doyle's narration (delivered in the third person) through their use of the voice-over.[19] Like the consolidation of voices in *Trainspotting*, the effect of the voice-over in these adaptations is to encourage identification and further submerge the spectator into the world of the characters. The voice-over in *The Butcher Boy* and the adaptation of William McIlvanney's short story 'Dreaming' is similar. When coupled with the film's general engagement with various modes of communication in contemporary culture, the device also serves as a means of exposing some of the hollow restraints placed upon the convention. For instance, in *Dreaming*, a story of an unemployed, disenchanted youth trying to carve a niche for himself in the midst of Thatcherite Britain, Sammy's fantasy world, involving television presenters, French cinema, and Billy Connolly, is literally enacted on-screen.[20] In one scene parodying the French new wave, Sammy delivers a comic French voice-over as the camera pans around the restaurant before resting on an older couple ('Sartre' and 'de Beauvoir') who the narrator reveals 'discuss the existential nature of human relationships'. In *The Butcher Boy*, Neil Jordan accomplishes this play across discourses by filling the role of the Virgin Mary with a well-known rock star (with strong views

17 Higson, *English heritage, English cinema*, 42. 18 Irvine Welsh, *Trainspotting,* London: Martin Secker and Warburg, 1993. However, the abandoned attempts to create voice-overs for Begbie and Tommy may also reveal the filmmakers' pull towards smoothing out the collusion of voices rather than featuring them outright. 19 Roddy Doyle, *The Snapper* and *The Commitments* in *The Barrytown trilogy,* London: Vintage, 1998. 20 William McIlvanney, 'Dreaming' in *Walking wounded,* London: Sceptre, 1990: 163–75.

on the Catholic Church), speaking in a regionalized accent, peppered with contemporary swear words. In many ways, the film engages with the very neuroses Silverman exposes – that the regional lacks authority – by playing on preconceptions concerning the authority of image and voice and the contrast between what is seen and what is heard.

These acts of parody form a central component in the transgressive workings of these narratives. While Sammy's imitative imaginings and performances are often in homage, humour almost always results from the assumed incompatibility of different discourses (either west-coast Scots, with west-coast Hollywood, or Kilmarnock café culture compared to that of existential Paris). Likewise, the comical effects produced by Sinead O'Connor playing the Virgin Mary are sharpened and undercut by a questioning of voice and authority. A similar questioning is broached in *The Commitments* by the band's deliberation over whether they should sing in their own accents. In the end they decide not to, but opt to alter the lyrics to reflect their Dublin environment instead. Interestingly, the band are not allowed this concession in the film version.

In *The Butcher Boy* the voice-over provides Francie with a mode of escape from his oppressive surroundings while, paradoxically, the voice-over renders Francie a mouthpiece for the articulation of various cultural texts. The articulation, generated from the fantasy space Francie has created, is channelled through the discourse of popular culture. John Scaggs has described this as an occurrence where 'a subject [is] presented with the status of object by his own de-culturing manoeuvres' and his/her control is usurped by the language he/she speaks. Scaggs crystallises this notion through his reiteration of Lacan's postulation that he does not *speak*, but is *spoken*.[21] Although Scagg's analysis is succinct, Francie's appropriation of different voices affords him an outlet for expressing emotions that are often curtailed. Within the frame of the film, when Francie Brady is unable to articulate his feelings, the voice-over steps in, speaking through the words and devices of various media and allowing his voice to reach its fullest articulation. Only, we must remind ourselves, it is not the Francie we see on screen, but an adult voice (an older Francie of the future) imposed onto a child (his younger self).

In the film adaptation of McIlvanney's short story, Sammy's relationship with language is equally complex. In a sequence unique to the film version, Sammy visits Pauline where she is babysitting, and a scenario parodying art cinema ensues. The depiction of an awkward teen rumble is replaced with a much more sophisticated scenario. A title, 'L'Amant', commences the sequence, replete with boudoir lounge music. Both Pauline's and Sammy's voices are then dubbed with the much older voices of a man and woman speaking in French. The film is then impulsively subtitled in the characters' Scots dialect. This

21 John Scaggs, 'Who is Francie Pig? Self-identity and narrative reliability in *The Butcher Boy*', *Irish University Review*, 30:1, 2000: 51–8.

moment – like the film's instances of film-noir-styled voice-over, or Francie Brady's comic-book-style narration – highlights the layering of languages and produces a form of self-conscious mimicry that exposes the powerful workings of language. A similar effect is achieved in *When Brendan Met Trudy* in a sequence where the two characters act out Jean-Luc Godard's *À Bout de Souffle* (1960). However, their conversations in French are quickly interrupted by contemporary Dublin, before their returned English speech is then curiously subtitled in Irish, pointing to ideas around power and language in contemporary Ireland. This playful use of subtitling, like the uses of voice-over that I have discussed, achieve their impact through their reworking of classical narrative conventions.

In some ways the acts of ventriloquism, or throwing voice, in *The Butcher Boy* and other films may be taken to illustrate the filmmaker's own feelings towards the film industry. Like Francie's manipulation of various discourses, Jordan appears adept at melding various media, especially in the case of *The Butcher Boy,* a film which has served as a key example in recent studies of Irish cinema of successful negotiation of the constraints of mainstream cinema production.[22] Even though Jordan claimed it would have been difficult 'to think of a film more non-mainstream', it was, after all, a mainstream film produced on a ten-million-dollar budget and backed by Warner Brothers. While this film was clearly a success in Jordan's opinion and proved his ability to get his own story through the web of the film industry, he has more recently expressed pessimistic feelings towards the constraints of the industry that have led him more in the direction of novel writing.[23]

CONCLUSION: THE PARTICULAR IN THE MAINSTREAM

Although the films discussed here involve various reflections on identity (not only Irishness and Scottishness but also British and European identities more generally), their self-conscious subversion of the devices of mainstream cinema links to a growing concern amongst filmmakers regarding the production and distribution practices of Hollywood. Various critics in both Ireland and Scotland have examined the effects of Hollywood funding on the cultural representation within the films. Colin McArthur has argued the case for a 'poor cinema' which would reclaim its independence from outside funding sources – namely Hollywood.[24] More recently, Martin McLoone has suggested the rel-

22 See Martin McLoone's *Irish film: the emergence of a contemporary cinema,* London: BFI, 2000 and Lance Pettit, *Screening Ireland: film and television representation*, Manchester and New York: Manchester University Press, 2000. 23 Sylvia Patterson, 'Interview with Neil Jordan', *Sunday Herald Magazine,* 2 March 2003: 20–25. 24 Colin McArthur, 'In praise of a poor cinema', *Sight and Sound*, August 1993: 30–2.

evance of the debates surrounding Third cinema[25] to the development of a national cinema in Ireland. But the reality is, as McLoone is quick to point out in his analysis, that if national cinemas are defined in terms of entirely self-funded production 'then there is little "national" cinema to be found anywhere in the world, other than in Hollywood'.[26] This reality no doubt results from issues around funding and distribution, but it is also the product of the increasingly collaborative nature of filmmaking. Furthermore, the idea that a cinema can exist independently not only through finance and production but also ideologically seems a continual point of contention amongst critics. In her essay on women's 'guerrilla' cinema in 1990, Teresa De Lauretis argued that no longer could the alternative and the mainstream be so easily distinguished from one another. She wrote:

> if it is difficult today to think of a System that one may oppose directly, from the outside, from a position of ideological purity and without complicity, is "alternative" rather meant in a less stringent, or *weak sense*: as another option, perhaps, for either grassroot or emergent forms of the social imaginary, an option which would not replace but would coexist more or less peacefully with other, mainstream forms [...].[27]

This is a reality for filmmakers that can also prove a virtue. Some critics may view the filmmaker's binds to Hollywood, or sometimes European cinemas, in the same light as Francie Brady's appropriation of various cultural texts, as restricting. In effect, films become the 'mere mouth pieces' for articulation, a cinema that 'does not *speak*, but is *spoken*'. Others, however, will read the films as innovative texts which adeptly manoeuvre around and subvert existing forms. When confronted with this debate, it is difficult not to think of the debates in Ireland and Scotland surrounding the use of the English language in literature. While Edwin Muir praised Ireland's promotion of the English language across the fronts of a national literature and hoped for similar developments in Scotland, writers in Ireland looked in admiration to writers such as Hugh MacDiarmid in Scotland for his use of the vernacular.[28] Muir's main reason for promoting English boiled down to a fear that dialect could only represent Scotland in 'bits and patches' whereas the deployment of English across the board would hopefully result in a literature which represented the whole.[29] Although writers such as Irvine Welsh seemingly write against such proposals, and a look at the success of *Trainspotting* across a global

25 Specifically, the debates McLoone refers to are around the proposal developed by Fernando Solanas and Octavio Getino in 'Toward a third cinema', *Cineaste*, 4:3, 1970–1: 4. 26 McLoone, *Irish film*, 119. 27 Teresa De Lauretis, 'Guerrilla in the midst: women's cinema in the 80s', *Screen*, 31:1, Spring 1990: 6–25. 28 Willy Maley discusses this at great length in 'Ireland, verses, Scotland'. 29 Edwin Muir, *Scott and Scotland*, London: Routledge, 1936: 112.

market confirms the universal is to be found in the particular, I cannot help thinking of the new questions around modes of articulation that several of the texts often at the heart of this debate must face when adapted to film. Maybe the choice between 'English' and dialect is never an altogether clear distinction for a writer to make, but the added influences and pressures of the established forms of mainstream cinema further complicates matters. This not only involves the matter of language and subtitling, but also the comprehension of a global market of local issues.[30] However, although we may find the English language debates applicable because of the similar responses elicited from their critics, the two diverge in very important ways. Whereas Muir's promotion of English language was solely independent from the use of dialect, what a number of contemporary Irish and Scottish films have illustrated, including several mentioned throughout this essay, is the possibility of a sort of double articulation, representing the 'bits and patches' within a framework as stringent and homogenizing as Hollywood.

30 Roddy Doyle, also a panelist at the 'New Irish Cinema – Day of Debate', 2003, expressed the view that he felt the publishing industry had proven much more encouraging towards the use of local dialect and particularities. In film, especially at the distribution stages, Doyle explained, changes are frequently suggested and made.

A formalist analysis of contemporary Irish film: *Disco Pigs* and *Accelerator*

DIÓG O'CONNELL

This paper seeks to explore the narrative style adopted in two recent Irish films, *Accelerator* (Vinny Murphy, 1999) and *Disco Pigs* (Kirsten Sheridan, 2001). It is an exercise in formal analysis in an attempt to reveal how characters in film function at different levels. By closely examining, at the level of structure, what is at work in these narratives, further light can be shed on other aspects of the story, notably the modes of address. Formal analysis can uncover aspects of style and craft that indicate the type of story world created. By attempting such 'structural' analysis, I propose to appropriate a methodological device from the field of film narratology, and the writings of David Bordwell and Edward Branigan[1] in particular. Cognizant of the well-documented shortcomings of the formalist approach,[2] this method still has the potential to offer a starting point for the re-analysis, in filmic terms, of story and in turn to reveal what is achieved by telling stories in particular ways.

Although Irish film has rarely been examined in this way I argue that it is timely to re-visit and appropriate the approach that was first advanced by Bordwell and others in 1985. Far from being outdated, the focus on story appears to be re-emerging in the field of Film Studies[3] and in Irish Studies.[4] Given that the debate around national identity is contributing less to an understanding of contemporary Irish cinema than it did to its predecessor, the first wave,[5] the discourse of narratology offers the potential for new insights. The

1 See David Bordwell, *Film art: an introduction*, New York: 1990 and Edward Branigan, *Narrative comprehension and film*, London: Routledge, 1998. 2 These have been explored in the key debates of *Screen* in the late 1970s and 1980s. See, for example, Rosalind Coward, 'Class, "culture" and the social formation', *Screen*, 18: 1, Spring 1977; Iain Chambers et al., 'Marxism and culture', *Screen*, 18: 4, Winter 1977/78; Rosalind Coward, 'Response', *Screen* 18: 4; Paul Willemen, 'Notes on subjectivity – on reading "Subjectivity under siege"', *Screen* 19: 1, Spring 1978, 45; Colin McCabe, 'The discursive and ideological in film – notes on the conditions of political intervention', *Screen* 19: 4, Winter 1978/79. 3 See Thomas Elsaesser and Warren Buckland, *Studying contemporary American film: a guide to movie analysis*, London: Arnold, 2002 and Kristin Thompson, *Storytelling in the new Hollywood*, Cambridge: Harvard University Press, 1999. 4 See Richard Kearney, *On stories*, London and New York: Routledge, 2002 and Roy Foster, *The Irish story: telling tales and making it up in Ireland*, London: Penguin, 2001. 5 This term refers to films from Bob Quinn's *Caoineadh Airt O Laoghaire* (1975) to Joe Comerford's *Reefer and the Model* (1988) and includes directors such as Cathal Black, Pat Murphy, Kieran Hickey, Thaddeus

first wave has been documented and categorized as experimental at the level of form and content and investigative and interrogative at the level of the social and political and has provided ample material for discourse within the field of Irish cinema. However, an emphasis upon the narrative and stylistic approach that is seen to interrogate aspects of the national psyche may ignore the 'universal' in storytelling. Although not popular since the emergence of post-structuralism, the notion that stories can cross borders and speak to the 'human condition' is what has contributed to the dominance of Hollywood in Europe and America since the development of the studio system. While the notion of cultural imperialism as a negative offshoot of this phenomenon is not to be ignored, the positive impact of Hollywood on world cinema has largely been neglected as an area of enquiry. The potential, therefore, for theoretical analysis of the second wave[6] lies not within the national identity debate alone but in a discourse that embraces the notion of the global within the concept of national cinemas.[7]

Bordwell's controversial claim that a film does not position anyone but rather cues the spectator to execute a definable variety of positions[8] is befitting of a post-national world.[9] In support of this claim, he describes normalized principles of composition, which can be identified as stages of plot development that progress from introducing the setting and characters to exploring and resolving the conflict. In comprehending a film, one schema in particular guides our hypothesis, the one that represents the canonical story format. Bordwell says that 'nearly all story-comprehension researchers agree that the most common template structure can be articulated as a "canonical" story format, something like this: introduction of setting and characters – explanation of a state of affairs – complicating action – ensuing events – outcome – ending'.[10] More recently Warren Buckland has adopted this position through his analysis of comprehensibility, of seeing how a story can be comprehended on the basic level of story structure and in terms of how the film's narration conveys the story to its spectators. Bordwell argues that if the film does not correspond to the canonic story, 'the spectator must adjust his or her

O'Sullivan as well as Quinn and Comerford. Many of these directors came from an art college background and would have been influenced by a wider avant-garde and Third Cinema movement. 6 This term refers generally to films produced with the support of Bord Scannan na hÉireann since 1993. 7 For a current discussion on this discourse, see Alan Williams (ed.), *Film and nationalism*, NJ: Rutgers, 2002. 8 See David Bordwell, *Narration in the fiction film*, London: Methuen, 1985:30. 9 The relationship between global and local is taking precedence over the national, suggesting a post-national state. The position Ireland finds itself in in the new millennium is no different to any other European nation/state; although, for Ireland, the changes have come about much later. While Ireland (or any country for that matter) could not define itself exclusively in national terms due to the proliferation of external influences for many decades, its effect on Ireland is much more recent. It is within this context that the search for a new discourse on Irish cinema takes place. 10 Bordwell, *Narration in the fiction film*, 35.

expectations and posit, however tentatively, new explanations for what is presented'.[11] The first step, therefore, in this type of analysis is to examine 'the set of formal correspondences between fabula and syuzhet'.[12] This will reveal the extent to which the unfolding syuzhet corresponds to the logical, temporal, and spatial nature of the fabula constructed. The fabula is defined in terms of events that unfold in cause – effect relationship and is seen as the raw material that makes up the story. The syuzhet is the artistic organization of these events, the reshaping of the fabula into a story and story world.[13] In comprehending a film, this schema (representing the canonical story format) in particular guides the spectator's hypotheses.

Despite the conventionality of structure across different narratives, films still work at many levels by engaging the audience at various emotional depths and by encouraging diverse emotional responses. According to Elsaesser and Buckland,[14] this engagement happens at the level of 'knowledgeability'. Knowledgeability functions at more than one level whereby the character may only be given access to fabula or plot events, called restricted narration, or whereby the audience is given access to details beyond those of character knowledgeability, called omniscient narration. While knowledgeability as defined here works at one level, 'story breadth', it also works at the level of 'story depth'. This can range from deep knowledge, which delves into the character's mental life, or knowledge which remains on the surface, simply showing the characters' behaviour.[15] What this type of breakdown suggests is that characters function on different narrative levels, some characters 'say and do' while other characters 'see and hear'. This approach clearly has implications for the type of story world created, not just at the level of form, but also content. Therefore, this methodology offers the potential for deeper penetration of narrative understanding. By using Edward Branigan's theory of focalization, this paper will delineate the different approaches to narrative and character that distinguish *Accelerator* and *Disco Pigs*.

In terms of narrative structure, *Disco Pigs* and *Accelerator* adhere to Bordwell's canonical story format. Yet, in the spectrum of narrative construction, they place polar levels of emphasis on plot and character. It is at the level of objective and subjective narrative that the key differences in story construction and design emerge. Key to the analysis of subjective and objective narrative is focalization. Focalization is the means whereby the analyst isolates where a character actually experiences something through 'seeing and hearing'. According to Branigan, it is not about surface acting or narrating but can extend to the character that thinks, remembers, fears or wonders. It is the character that plunges to greater emotional depths of experience through desire, belief or thought that 'sees and hears'.

11 Ibid., 36. 12 Ibid., 54. 13 Ibid., 275. 14 Elsaesser and Buckland, *Studying contemporary American film*. 15 Ibid., 172.

Branigan goes on to distinguish two types of focalization, each representing a different level of a character's experience. External focalization is the character's 'visual and aural awareness of narrative events' and internal focalization is the representation of the character's private and subjective experiences, ranging from simple perception (optical vantage point) to deeper thoughts (dreams, hallucinations, memories).[16] While Bordwell's approach facilitates a linear reading, Branigan's methodology develops a horizontal and vertical reading, which can be used to reveal the complexity of an individual shot or scene.[17] What makes this approach significant at this juncture in Irish cinema studies is the potential it allows for reclaiming the 'story' as a focus of analysis. Not only can it lead to an analysis of content through form, it can shed some light on recent Irish cinema and what sets it apart from its predecessor.

'ACCELERATOR'

Accelerator opens in the wasteland of an urban ghetto where 'joy-riding' is considered a way of life. Johnny T, the main protagonist is on the run from paramilitary vigilantes because of his 'anti-social behavior'. As Bordwell indicates, a film's beginning is crucial because the spectator's hypothesis needs to be established. From the outset Johnny T is introduced as a character on the cusp of change. Having stood up before his community admitting he was a joy-rider before going on yet another spree, he needs to escape, heading to Barcelona, stopping off in Dublin en route. It is here that he meets Whacker, his antagonist, who challenges him to a race, from Belfast to the Papal Cross in the Phoenix Park. The prize of the 'girl', in the form of Whacker's girlfriend Louise, and the £200 prize money convinces him after his initial reluctance to rise to this challenge before finally hanging up his 'hot-wires' for the last time.

The structure of *Accelerator* is unusual, yet arguably characteristic of the second wave (*About Adam*, Gerry Stembridge, 2000; *Intermission*, John Crowley, 2003; *Goldfish Memory*, Liz Gill, 2003) in the way that it shifts focus from the main protagonist and antagonist to introduce a series of other characters in what Syd Field would call the 'second act' or Kristin Thompson would describe as the 'set-up' and 'development' phase. The episodic nature of the narrative allows a whole range of characters to be introduced and explored by taking the focus off the main characters. What the narrative of *Accelerator* achieves through this approach is similar to the 'smart' movies of the 1990s,[18] albeit without the trope of irony. *Accelerator* displays a propensity to continue along the path of the first wave that clearly positions the story within an

16 Edward Branigan, *Narrative comprehension and film*, 103. 17 Ibid., 193. 18 Jeoffrey Sconce, 'Irony, nihilism and the new American "smart" film', *Screen* 43:4, Winter 2002.

ideological framework, despite the apparent intentions of the director.[19] This approach to film-making seeks to contextualize film in its wider societal environment. Rather than confining extra-textual relations to the world of cinema, *Accelerator*, like many first wave films (*Maeve*, Pat Murphy, 1981; *Pigs*, Cathal Black, 1984; *December Bride*, Thaddeus O'Sullivan, 1990) uses its narrative beyond the function of story world creation to comment on a wider context in ideological (in this case, social-realist) terms. What *Accelerator* combines is a generic road-movie structure with a 'social commentary' that speaks specifically of a time and place through its characterization and mise-en-scène. Although episodic narratives are not necessarily pre-determined to explore characterization at the level of 'restricted narrative', in *Accelerator* the generic device of the race is what takes priority over internally focalized characters.

Johnny T as the main protagonist in *Accelerator* is positioned objectively in relation to the narrative. The opening sequence is structured around what he 'says and does'. Through the phone call he makes to his cousin in Dublin (objective point of view), the audience learns of his desire to go to Barcelona to escape his fate. His encounter with Whacker, his antagonist, is direct and head on; an example of 'objective narrative,' or in Branigan's words, 'external focalization'. The spectator sees what the character sees, but not from the character's position in the narrative. External focalization allows for the spectator to share the understanding or attention of the character but not their experience. In terms of 'plunging into the psychological state of the character', external focalization or objective narrative is confined largely to the surface. This is what structures the narrative of *Accelerator*. As a consequence of the restricted points of view given to the viewer, insight into how Johnny T is feeling and thinking is largely absent. Whacker's character is affirmed by what others say about him: his mother is absent and his father is in prison. *Accelerator* gives access to fabula events (restricted narration) and is therefore primarily action-driven.

The distinction between internal and external focalization is useful in representing the different levels of character experience. External focalization is what distinguishes the approach of *Accelerator* and is common to 'high concept' films that characterize much of Hollywood's output since the 1980s. Similarly, films that position the character as motivated by external factors, such as race, gender, nationality, and socio-economic position, often remain

19 Vinny Murphy, like other directors of the second wave (including Gerry Stembridge, *About Adam*), was reacting to the perceived notions of what Irish film is, a preoccupation with the 1950s, the Catholic Church and the Northern Ireland 'Troubles'. In an interview in the *Sunday Independent*, 4 July 1999, Vinny Murphy says '*Accelerator* doesn't sound like an Irish film, but is actually more Irish than anything.' In an interview with Ted Sheehy in *Film Ireland*, 75, April/May 2000, Murphy said that what drove him in making this film was 'kicking against other Irish films. The 1950s thing? … I'm not a fan. All that sexual guilt, it doesn't exist in that form any more' (p. 19).

externally focalized at the level of narrative construction. The narrative in *Accelerator* presents the events to the audience through what the characters 'say and do'. The interiority or deeper thoughts of the characters are largely absent from the story and plot.[20] The audience, by the end of the film, has neither been presented with (through the plot) nor has gleaned (from the story) the deeper thoughts or motivations of the characters.

Unlike the narrative of *Disco Pigs*, Whacker is presented as a victim of circumstance as opposed to fate. He is the way he is because of the cards dealt to him in life. He restores himself at the end by refusing the 'blood money' but there is no character redemption and therefore he must die. Therefore, both characters, acting as protagonist and antagonist, it can be argued are cyphers. Their role is at the level of social justification to drive or validate the narrative. Cast in the generic mould of the road movie, this film adopts the Aristotelian or Proppian structure whereby plot is paramount. While the characters are 'consistent and life-like', they serve only as 'agents of action' or cyphers, simply pushing the plot forward. As cyphers, they represent something outside of themselves, providing social commentary and thus positioning the film in a world beyond its function as story-teller, a function of film that more recent Irish productions appear to be rejecting (*Dead Bodies*, Robert Quinn, 2003; *Intermission*, John Crowley, 2003).

While *Accelerator* lends itself to analysis along the lines of national identity because the narrative is speaking of a time and a place that relates extratextually to a wider societal context, later second wave films resist such an analysis. More recent films such as *Dead Bodies*, *Intermission*, *Goldfish Memory* and *Timbuktu* (Alan Gilsenan, 2004) appear to emerge from a specifically cinematic context and use these 'worlds' rather than the 'nation-state' as their reference points. *Dead Bodies* plays with structure by employing many of the conventions of the 'thriller' genre while *Intermission* functions as a 'themed' film that explores a concept, in this case 'love', common to an array of characters. This narratorial device reflects what has been happening in America during the 1990s, a type of film that Jeffrey Sconce calls 'smart' film, 'an American school of filmmaking that survives (and at times thrives) at the symbolic and material intersection of "Hollywood", the "indie" scene and the vestiges of what cinephiles used to call "art" films'.[21] It is difficult to situate either *Dead Bodies* or *Intermission* within the 'national identity' debate, thus marking a distinction between first and second wave films.

20 There are many examples of 'social realism' films that display characters who are externally mobilised but also display an emotional depth or interiority; for example, the British social realism of the 1950s and 1960s, and the Italian neorealism of the 1940s and 1950s. While films of these movements can explore characters at the level of internal focalization, their motivations are often explained as outside of their own control. **21** Sconce, 'Irony, nihilism and the new American "smart" film'.

Because the episodic exploration of the other characters in *Accelerator* and their relationships and what happens to them is connected to the main narrative thread but without clear cause or motivation, what is absent from this narrative is Bordwell's 'hermetically sealed world', that is a design that adheres to the rules of construction whereby the removal of one element would cause the structure to collapse. While this approach to film (the construction of a 'hermetically sealed world') devised by Hollywood in the early part of the twentieth century has been criticized, particularly by *Screen* theorists, for serving to mask any points of tension, it is useful in assessing narrative structure and shedding light on the story constructed. Consequently, this approach can reveal, in a film like *Accelerator*, an absence of a deep emotional experience for the audience. While the audience may be satisfied at another level, that of entertainment and spectacle and/or through the reception of an ideological message that comments on the disenfranchisement of the urban, male youth, *Accelerator* points to a common problem in contemporary Irish film, and one that has been identified by many writers and critics,[22] namely, the absence of characters that present us with a depth of perception, feeling and thought, even at the level of irony.

A key scene in the film is when the two cars (occupied by Johnny T and Whacker) encounter the checkpoint. Analysing this scene along the lines of subjective and objective narrative reveals core narrative tensions. The audience is presented with two subjective positions, firstly when the checkpoint is revealed from Johnny T's point of view and, secondly, when the soldiers are seen from Whacker's point of view. When Whacker shoots at the soldiers, the camera shots are presented in an objective way as Whacker utters the words 'Shoot to Kill Mother Fuckers'. Continuing the trend of fatalism attached to characters in films about Northern Ireland, the explanation for Whacker's actions appear to remain outside of the story. It doesn't fit the narrative setup either as a sociological statement or as a way of progressing the character and plot. Furthermore, this type of scene reveals generic tensions within the film. Influenced by the ubiquitous American road movie through its notions of rootlessness and aimlessness and its exploration of male existential angst, this film simultaneously evokes and defies the generic traits. While the road movie is seen as a simplification of all life, it generally has a restorative and recuperative function. According to Baudrillard the thrill of travelling to different places does not lie in the experience of learning about other places or discovering local customs but in realizing that the place you are travelling in is immortal. Travelling, by freeing you from the social, puts you on a different plane, thus evoking a spiritual dimension that is evidently absent in *Accelerator*. The narrative approach, therefore, suggested by the relationship of fabula to

22 For example, Hugh Linehan, 'Myth, mammon and mediocrity: the trouble with recent Irish cinema', *Cineaste*, 24: 2–3, 1999: 46–50.

syuzhet would suggest that in the absence of a 'deep emotional experience' the audience would be elevated to a different plane, either one of political or sociological statement or insight. While the visual style through mise-en-scène suggests such a course at the opening of the film, particularly through the representation of the urban environment, the romantic closure (which is genre-defying), both narratively and aesthetically, disavows any political reading and negates the emotional experience.

'DISCO PIGS'

The main obstacle to analysis of contemporary Irish cinematic storytelling is the monolithic predisposition towards mainstream Hollywood narrative structure. When 'Hollywood' as a tool of categorization is mentioned, it is commonly assumed to embrace one clearly defined structure. When *Disco Pigs* is described as 'simply another variant on the age-old "couple on the run" formula',[23] Harvey O'Brien is echoing a widely-held antipathy to what is deemed 'Hollywood cinema'. However, the success of Hollywood cinema is due not just to its universal appeal that crosses cultural borders quite easily, but its ability to re-invent and change. Hollywood in the silent era used pictures to tell stories to a multi-cultural and multi-lingual audience of immigrants in the growing urban centres of the United States, thus constructing a narrative that targeted a multi-cultural and consequently a global audience as the Hollywood narrative structure developed further with the coming of sound. In *Alternative Scriptwriting* Ken Dancyger and Jeff Rush explore the restorative three-act structure and its features but also look to alternatives which have emerged from what is broadly deemed Hollywood.[24] More recently, Dancyger's *Global Scriptwriting*[25] charts the narratological changes and developments of the last decade. What is evident from these scriptwriting manuals is the fluidity of mainstream narrative and the blurring of boundaries between 'mainstream' and 'alternative' cinema in more recent times. While the parameters for analysis of the first wave were more demarcated with the polarization of mainstream and avant–garde or Third cinema, it is less so now. Probing contemporary Irish cinema suggests that the conception of narrative frameworks and styles can be less clearly categorized. It is within this context that my analysis of the canonic story of *Disco Pigs* occurs.

Disco Pigs opens at the moment of birth, when Pig and Runt are born on the same day and in the same hospital. They are placed side by side in the

23 http://indigo.ie/~obrienh/acc.htm 24 They explore other structures such as ironic three-act structure (*Chinatown*, Roman Polanski); two-act structure (*She's Gotta Have It*, Spike Lee); one-act structure (*Mean Streets*, Martin Scorsese; *Working Girls*, Lizzie Borden). 25 Ken Dancyger, *Global scriptwriting*, Boston: Focal Press, 2001.

nursery and reach out, moments old, to hold hands, a literary motif that will recur throughout the narrative.[26] The events advance forward to age sixteen: Pig and Runt are inseparable, living next door to each other and excluding the world from themselves. They envisage themselves as king and queen and co-exist in their imaginations. The 'explanation of the state of affairs' is the playing out of the unique friendship these two characters have with each other, which is at odds with the conventions of their outside world. A sequence of scenes, incorporating real time and flashback, demonstrates the dysfunctional nature of this friendship. The scene in the off-license when Pig and Runt bully the boy behind the counter and the scene in the disco where Pig and Runt play out a game of seduction and attack are examples of this disturbing world they have created and inhabit. The 'complicating action' is Pig's growing sexual awakening towards Runt, first signaled in the key scene in Shandon church tower and further reinforced when he tries to kiss her. The 'ensuing events' explore Pig's growing violence and Runt's attempts to move away when she begins to be attracted to Markey. The growing gap is further 'plotted' when Runt is sent away to a reform school. Bordwell's 'outcome' is the sequence when the relationship finally breaks down on Pig and Runt's seventeenth birthdays and the 'ending' is the death scene, when Runt kills Pig and Pig allows Runt to kill him. In reading the structure along general canonic lines, *Disco Pigs* appears quite conventional in form. Kristin Thompson's methodology of breaking the narrative into four parts (set-up, complicating action, development and epilogue) is equally applicable. What these approaches illustrate, therefore, is an appropriation, at face value, of a conventional narrative structure along the lines of 'classical narrative'.

However, when the narrative style of *Disco Pigs* is scrutinized further, it is revealed from the opening sequence that the audience is plunged into the 'subjective levels' of characterization. This contrasts with the narrative of *Accelerator* which focuses its exploration in an 'objective' or 'externally focalized' way. The device central to the approach in *Disco Pigs* is the use of voice-over. In analyzing the use of voice-over, narrative theory has its part to play. Although early narrative theory proclaimed the 'autonomy of narrative structure',[27] more recently the field of narratology has recognized that fiction film demonstrates how the medium can have a complicating effect on the narrative text. Examining voice-over in particular, Seymour Chatman argues that film, in theory, could offer a means of expression that is much more complex and narratively rich than commercial cinema often exploits.[28] While the voice-over is a device developed in Hollywood, in *film noir* of the 1940s in particular, European cinema is credited with its more complex use. In an Irish con-

26 This is clearly a reference to Heathcliffe and Cathy in *Great Expectations*. 27 Seymour Chatman, 'New directions in voice-narrated cinema', in David Herman (ed.), *Narratologies*, Ohio: Ohio State University Press, 1999. 28 Ibid., 315.

text, Neil Jordan's *The Butcher Boy* (1997) employs the voice-over to articulate the older Francie's words and, as Martin McLoone argues, 'the visuals and voiceover […] works as a parallel discourse to what we see, opening out a complex world of fevered imagination laced with humorously inappropriate speculation and exploration'.[29]

In *Disco Pigs*, the voice-over along with the visuals provides an entry point to the world of Pig and Runt where they reign as king and queen in their imagined kingdom. In the opening sequence, the voice-over of Runt is internally focalized. 'Once upon a time before there was blue' is heard over visuals of the baby Runt just before and during the moment of birth. Conveying her inner thoughts and feelings from the moment of birth, she says in voice-over, 'I want for something different and that's when I hear him […] at that moment we become one and we need no one else. Nobody.' This sequence establishes the subjective narrative style, one that will explore 'simple perception' and 'deeper thoughts' as it works through the inner turmoil of its characters, and articulated through image and voice. From the outset the poetic, allegorical style is in contrast to the social-realist style adopted by *Accelerator*.

Disco Pigs uses a wider range of narrational devices in contrast to the restricted focus of *Accelerator*, thus creating narrative layers that demand more processing by the audience. This is not to place a hierarchical order on these two films; rather the terms of narratology as defined by Bordwell and Branigan delineate a schema, stating that the more complicated the schema to be hypothesized, the more processing time required by the audience. Thus, dealing with the interiority of characters through the medium of film requires different narrational devices. *Disco Pigs* achieves this through point-of-view shots. A key illustrative scene occurs as Pig surveys Cork city from the top of Shandon church. Runt calls Pig to come and look at the skirt she made. From the top of the church, the camera cuts to a long shot of Runt: 'What do you think?' she asks as she holds out her skirt. In an externally focalized shot, the camera cuts to Pig and then zooms in; the spectator shares the character's attention rather than his experience.[30] The camera then cuts to Runt from Pig's point of view (internally focalized). A series of soft-focus, close-up shots follow as Pig describes how Runt looks, 'like some model you see off the telly'. The audience now shares the character's experience, rather than attention. Runt breaks this internal focalization and the two head off.

This sequence is characteristic of the style of the film. Much of the narrative is internally focalized, either from Pig or Runt's point of view. While this film clearly appropriates mainstream cinematic devices, it is less conventional in its narrative structure than *Accelerator*. It can be argued that in being less conventional, it is more complex in story terms, by embracing the

29 Martin McLoone, *Irish film: the emergence of a contemporary cinema*, London: BFI, 2000: 215.
30 Branigan, *Narrative comprehension and film*.

depths of narrative that cinema allows and thus telling a story that is more multi-layered.

This internal focalization or subjective narrative is repeated throughout the film. After Pig kisses Runt, through his voice-over he verbalizes his fantasy. In terms of story design, once he starts on this trajectory, he is heading in one direction, towards his downfall. When Runt goes to Donegal the presence of Pig is felt throughout even though he is not with her on screen. Adopting a catatonic state, spatially the two are held together in the narrative. Runt senses his approach when she says, 'He's close', while Pig jumps off the bus as it passes the big austere building that is the reform school.

Focalization is a tool that can reveal the potential of the cinematic narrative form and the extent to which the writer and director exploit it in telling a particular story. Not all stories attempt to evoke an emotional experience but all function to arouse some kind of state (through, for example, spectacle, comedy, irony), and so position the audience. Focalization, in this case, reveals the limitations of the narrative of *Accelerator* which neither evokes a deep emotional experience nor engages its subject matter in an ironic way. What it does instead, which may account for its popularity among certain audiences,[31] is to invoke the genre of road movie, mainly through its iconography and milieu. On the other hand, it is unclear what is its ultimate aim in invoking the genre. It neither challenges the status quo nor reinforces it but instead manages to present fatalistically and romantically a solution and narrative closure (contra-generic) for its protagonist and antagonist.

Unlike *Accelerator*, much of what is happening in the story in *Disco Pigs* happens at a different narrative level, in the thoughts of the characters. Although not obviously appropriating the genre, *Disco Pigs* hinges on many themes that are seen as characteristic of the 'road movie' or 'buddy movie'. The rebellion, insecurity, alienation and general angst of the typical road movie character is reflected in *Disco Pigs*. The road movie as a rite of passage for oedipally-driven young males could explain what is happening to Pig. *Disco Pigs* takes some of the conventions of the road movie but interestingly turns them on their head. Through internal focalization, the narrative plunges the audience towards the interior struggle of the character thus pointing out a key narrative difference between the two texts. While *Disco Pigs* constantly plunges the audience to greater character depth through internal focalization and subjective narrative, *Accelerator* hardly ever does. In terms of drama and emotional engagement, *Disco Pigs* allows for the spectator to engage emotionally

31 *Disco Pigs* took less than £50,000 at the Irish box office. *Accelerator* took £177,485 and was particularly successful in the west Dublin suburb of Tallaght. This could be due to the fact that the writer/director was well-known in the area having been involved in youth theatre workshops. Tallaght's reputation as a location for 'joy-riding' in the 1980s in particular may also account for the disproportionate interest in this film in this area.

whereas in *Accelerator*, the audience is kept at arms length. However, *Accelerator*'s purpose is not one of Brechtian distanciation but signals a trend emerging in contemporary Irish film, one that it can be said has its basis in American independent film of the 1990s. Focalization, therefore reveals the relationship and distinction between fabula/plot and syuzhet/story in both films, pointing out the narrative tools used to tell quite different stories. It is through formal analysis that such differences are revealed.

WHITHER SECOND WAVE?

In conclusion, it remains to re-state the case for the formalist approach as one step in defining a new discourse that will enhance our understanding of recent Irish film. As mentioned earlier, the formalist approach has not been widely accepted as an end in itself within the *academe*, in particular since the emergence of post-structuralism. This position has been to the detriment of any advance of the study of the craft of scriptwriting, storytelling, narrative and filmmaking in general. In other art forms, such as music and architecture, the art of practice is an integral part of the study of the discipline, whether engaging as a practitioner or theoretician. The formalist approach to film analysis can contribute to the pedagogy of scriptwriting and advance such studies beyond the traditional position that asserts creativity as inherent and 'god-given' and which cannot be learned. Furthermore, formalist approaches to narrative can narrow the space between theory and practice which contemporary film studies has failed to do in recent times.

In the context of this paper, what formal analysis reveals are the different approaches to story world and story design adopted by the writers and directors of these two films. The appropriation of narratological tools of analysis can have the effect of revealing similarities and differences. While the approach to story design in *Accelerator* and *Disco Pigs* is quite different and therefore interesting from the perspective of scriptwriting, the similarities between the films are possibly more revealing. As already mentioned the national identity debate has not served the second wave of Irish cinema well by imposing an out-dated model on this body of work. More useful is to explore film in terms of a post-national discourse where the emphasis is placed on the relationship between the global and the local, thus offering a space to determine and explore the tensions that apply to contemporary cinema.

What the formalist approach facilitates is the identification of the local and the global, the national and the international, the universal and the specific. Far from being contradictory terms, as often asserted in the national identity debate, this template of opposites facilitates the opening up of readings that account for the unusual 'mid-Atlantic' position Ireland finds itself in. Both *Accelerator* and *Disco Pigs* display structural similarities to the new American 'smart' film.[32] In coining this term, Jeoffrey Sconce appropriates Bordwell's narratological analysis of classical Hollywood and European art cinema to delineate what he sees as characteristic of American 'smart' films which made notable impact on American cinema in the 1990s. He writes:

> Perhaps the most significant change in narrative causality involves the increasing prevalence of multi-protagonist stories and episodic story structure. Although certainly not true of all contemporary smart cinema, many of these films (especially the 'dramas') do favour a rotating series of interlocking episodes, centring not on a central unifying character's dynamic action (as in classical Hollywood cinema) nor on a relatively passive observations (as in previous art cinema), but rather on a series of seemingly random events befalling a loosely related set of characters.[33]

This formal shift away from both classical Hollywood and European art cinema, Sconce argues, suggests a postmodern exploration of the *condition humaine*. When he defines the favoured narrative structure of these films as one which embodies 'a range of characters subjected to increasing despair and/or humiliation captured in a rotating series of interlocking scenes in which some endure while others are crushed'[34] he could quite easily be referring to *Accelerator* and to a lesser degree *Disco Pigs*.[35] While cause and effect play a dominant role in *Disco Pigs*, chance is *Accelerator*'s underpinning motivation. Similarly *Dead Bodies*, *Goldfish Memory* and *Intermission* rely on a series of chance encounters to motivate the action and justify the consequences in these narratives. Formal analysis therefore identifies in these films 'characters trapped by annihilating fate and narrational strategies that seem without empathy'.[36]

Applying a formalist analysis to these two films is useful in revealing stories that resonate at many levels, particularly the local and the global. Parallels between *Accelerator* and American 'smart' films are evident in the nihilistic approach towards characterization, yet this film has a strong, clear local resonance as evidenced in its aesthetics of the urban milieu in which the characters inhabit. The foregrounding of urban, working-class youth culture echoes the ideological project of many first wave films. *Disco Pigs*, on the other hand, while suggesting the nihilistic tendencies of its main characters adopts a more redemptive outcome by the close of the film. Less local in its resonance, it draws on the traditions of storytelling from drama and literature in its exposition.

Finally, as a preliminary study this approach reveals the complexities embedded in contemporary Irish cinema, particularly in relation to their modes

32 See Sconce, 'Irony, nihilism and the new American "smart" film', 349–61. 33 Ibid., 362. 34 Ibid. 35 According to these definitions, *Disco Pigs* could be seen as more traditional in structure and more closely aligned to classical narrative. 36 Sconce, 'Irony, nihilism and the new American "smart" film', 364.

of address. Irish cinema is finding a new identity, asserting its voice from many directions. While it could be argued that *Accelerator* displays influences from British social realism and the road movie genre and *Disco Pigs* is closely aligned to classical Hollywood, both films exhibit tensions between the local and the global. Rather than using this as a stick with which to beat the second wave, these oppositional and parallel influences may offer the key to revealing what is at work in the evolution of contemporary Irish cinema.

Far from cultivating a marginal film culture, Irish cinema remains in a tug of war between American and European influences. The project of the second wave of Irish cinema, it can be argued, while less concerned with national issues and themes than the *condition humaine*, is the playing out of dual influences through its formalist address. What formal analysis therefore can highlight is the aesthetic style and structural influences that are shaping the 'new wave' and thus give some account of what has been happening in Irish cinema over the past ten years.

Convents or cowboys? Millennial Scottish and Irish film industries and imaginaries in *The Magdalene Sisters*

JONATHAN MURRAY

This essay begins with two quotations. The first emanates from Scottish film culture in 1993, the second from its Irish counterpart seven years later:

> The homogeneity of the [Scottish Film Production] Fund's cultural choices does suggest that it is most comfortable institutionally with 'quality'/art house projects [...] the new generation of Scottish film-makers show little sign of being interested in art-house fare. Their sights are set on making the equivalents of *El Mariachi*, *Just Another Girl on the I.R.T.* and *Reservoir Dogs* [...] and getting them into the multi-plexes.[1]

> I was afraid there might be the last lingering cobwebs of a misunderstanding, that the Irish Film Board was only interested in art house work, middle class audiences, utilising films in rural settings from 1953.[2]

The juxtaposition of territorially, temporally and taxonomically neighbouring arguments about the textual and industrial characteristics of two emergent 'Celtic' cinemas has been widely urged during the last decade or so. This is telling and starts to explicate two important stories. The first concerns the reasons for the parallel industrial expansion of the Scottish and Irish cinemas in the 1990s; the second is concerned with the structuring terms of influential academic and critical accounts of these processes.

Irish, and more especially Scottish, feature production between the mid-1980s and early 1990s was fragmentary in the extreme. Some years saw no domestic projects made in one or both countries. What little local activity *did* take place tended by necessity to conform to a restricted range of budgetary and aesthetic types. With a few prominent Irish exceptions – *The Field* (Jim Sheridan, 1990), *The Commitments* (Alan Parker, 1991) – significant proportions of both contemporary cinemas were financed through very low levels of indige-

1 John Brown, 'Poor Scots', Letter, *Sight and Sound*, 3:10, October 1993: 64. My insert. 2 Irish Film Board Chief Executive Officer Rod Stoneman quoted in Gerry McCarthy, 'Interview with Rod Stoneman', *Film West*, 41, Autumn 2000: 33.

nous public subsidy. Funders such as the British Film Institute Production Board (Scotland) and Channel Four (Ireland) were particularly important patrons in this period. The contemporary 'Celtic' films that emerged through this kind of institutional support often took the form of experimental and/or politically radical art cinema. Representative examples from Scotland include *Silent Scream* (David Hayman, 1990) and *Blue Black Permanent* (Margaret Tait, 1993) and from Ireland *Reefer and the Model* (Joe Comerford, 1988) and *Hush-a-Bye Baby* (Margo Harkin, 1989). Unfortunately, films such as these tended at best to achieve fleeting specialist theatrical distribution at home and festival screenings abroad, a niggardly prelude to terrestrial television broadcast. As late as the mid-1990s, Scotland and Ireland were justifiably regarded as 'dark corners' of both or either Anglophone and European cinemas.[3]

Yet since that time, both Scottish and Irish cinemas have grown to a degree both remarkable and unforeseen. As a result of public and private investment, both cinemas have achieved an unprecedented continuity of domestic production. It is indeed 'hard to imagine from the vantage point of 2003 how complete the transformation of the institutional and cultural landscapes for film in Ireland [and, comparably, Scotland] has been'.[4] Between 1993 and 2003, Scotland and Ireland produced a far greater number of indigenous features (27 and 76 respectively) than at any other time in their respective cinematic histories.[5] A significant, if still minor, proportion of the titles in question – such as *Trainspotting* (Danny Boyle, 1996) and *Ratcatcher* (Lynne Ramsay, 1999) – enjoyed a far wider degree of domestic and international distribution and critical notice than previously experienced within either nation. These achievements, as the earlier quotes suggest, have also been identified in terms of a collective journey from 'art house' to 'multiplex' that has swept away the 'cobwebs' associated with the long-term paucity and invisibility of domestic production.

Paradoxically, however, these developments have also generated an often-uneasy academic and/or critical response. While the 1990s may have witnessed an unprecedented increase in the volume of Scottish and Irish features, influential observers of the Atlantic Archipelago as a whole have expressed concern that the formal, narrative and cultural diversity of British cinema more generally has been narrowing.[6] This, in turn, has been seen to have occurred

3 See, for example, John Hill, 'Introduction', in John Hill, Martin McLoone and Paul Hainsworth (eds), *Border crossing: film in Ireland, Britain and Europe*, London/Belfast: Institute of Irish Studies/University of Ulster/BFI, 1994: 3. 4 Kevin Rockett, 'Introduction', in Kevin Rockett, *Ten years after: the Irish Film Board, 1993–2003*, Galway: Irish Film Board, 2003: viii. My insert. 5 For details on the Irish figure, see Rockett, *Ten years after*; the total for Scotland is largely derived from data contained in Duncan Petrie, *Screening Scotland*, London: BFI, 2000: 227–8 but also includes a number of features not supported by any of the institutions whose funding activities Petrie summarizes, or which have been produced since the publication of his work. 6 John Hill, 'The rise and fall of British art cinema: a short history of the 1980s and 1990s', *Aura Film Studies Journal*, 4:3, 2000: 30. This perception is – to the present author's mind at least –

because of the way in which British and Irish filmmakers and funders have typically sacrificed cultural objectives in favour of increased commercialism and international mainstream distribution. A local film financier like the Glasgow Film Fund may be seen to represent this shift. An inward investment initiative established in 1993, the GFF made an immediate industrial impact through its part-funding of *Shallow Grave* (Danny Boyle, 1995). Buoyed by that film's international success, one of the institution's officers asserted in crude, bullish terms, that were to resonate throughout the rest of the decade, the determination of the organisation to leave behind the known territory of 'beautifully shot films for art-house cinemas' and aim instead for 'films that would be commercially successful [...] and [...] cater to an international market'.[7]

This pursuit of an 'international market' has also been seen to carry consequences for the way in which Scottish and Irish cinemas may explore, articulate and preserve the specificity and diversity of local identities. Commercialism is identified with American cinematic influence and the risk that emergent Celtic film cultures end up offering 'a type of Hollywood regionalism'.[8] Consequently stern warnings about 'the futility of applying [...] Californian templates [...] without modification to local cultures'[9] have become a central element of Scottish and Irish academic debates alike. The oft-aired anxiety is that 'mart' cinema is replacing, or has already overtaken, its 'art' equivalent as a disproportionately privileged mode of both countries' feature output at the start of a new century.

This essay seeks to complicate these received critical perspectives through a textual analysis of the first *bona fide* Scottish/Irish feature co-production, *The Magdalene Sisters* (Peter Mullan, 2001). This film has proved something of a watershed for local film production, combining commercial and critical success.[10] In commercial terms, the film passed the €1 million mark at the Irish box office by the end of November 2002, and became the highest-earning domestic film of the year; the film had also taken £1.84 million at the British box office by the end of March 2003, after but a few weeks on theatrical release.[11] The intense degree of cross-cultural audience and distributor

both more urgent and salient to the circumstances of the United Kingdom than those of the Irish Republic. 7 Kevin Kane quoted in Karen McVeigh, 'Starring Glasgow, a character actor of many parts', *The Independent*, Metro, 19 April 1995: 20. 8 Kevin Rockett, 'Irish cinema: the national in the international', *Cineaste*, 24:2–3, 1999: 25. 9 Luke Gibbons, 'The Esperanto of the Eye?', *Film Ireland*, 55, October/November 1996: 20; for a Scottish parallel, see Jonathan Murray, 'Sundance in Scotland?', *Vertigo*, 2:2, Spring 2002: 18–19. 10 For a detailed account of the film's co-production history, see Jonathan Murray, 'Sibling rivalry? Contemporary Scottish and Irish cinemas', in Liam McIlvanney and Ray Ryan (eds), *Ireland and Scotland: culture and society, 1707–2000*, Dublin, Four Courts Press, forthcoming. 11 UK Box office returns quoted www.filmcouncil.org.uk/filmindustry/?p=UKBOstats (6/4/03); Irish returns quoted in Ted Sheehy, '*The Magdalene Sisters* makes a deep impression', www.Screendaily.com (28/11/02).

interest in the film was in turn largely provoked by its status as an international critical *succès d'estime* and winner of the Golden Lion award for Best Film at the 2002 Venice Film Festival.

The Magdalene Sisters is of particular interest here because, contrary to much of the anxiety about the 'Americanization' of millennial Scottish and Irish cinemas, transatlantic cinematic influences and reference points structure this local text in ways that have proved commercially and critically productive in international terms. More importantly, these transatlantic elements also enable *The Magdalene Sisters* to perform a politically progressive role in domestic arenas. This suggests that the most extreme critical fulminations against the homogenizing power of American filmmaking over what are perceived as defenceless, infant Celtic cinemas – 'young film-makers overwhelmed by the Hollywood orthodoxy to conform to action-genre conventions and MTV-style editing'[12] – are too simplistic in their cultural sweep and pessimism. By contrast, *The Magdalene Sisters* suggests that the more appropriate way to conceive recent Scottish and Irish cinemas is in terms of 'trying to work through difference critically – trying to live with Hollywood rather than trying to mimic it'.[13] Such arguments could, of course, be applied to almost any national film culture on the face of the planet. They are, however, particularly apposite to these two historically peripheral Anglophone examples. Both have been moulded by successive generations of local filmmakers and audiences' remarkably high degree of exposure to external cinematic traditions, particularly those of Hollywood and the British metropolis. *The Magdalene Sisters,* therefore, illustrates very effectively the progressive potential in the 'working through of difference' that marks out this area of modern Scottish and Irish cultural production and experience.

Shot on location in southwest Scotland utilizing a disused Benedictine convent in the town of Dumfries, *The Magdalene Sisters*' narrative is set in County Dublin between 1964 and 1968. The film explores a traumatic aspect of modern Irish history, the incarceration of women deemed 'morally lax' by their families and/or wider communities in laundries run by female religious orders within the Roman Catholic Church. Unmarried mothers, sexually active single women and rape victims among others were effectively imprisoned for their 'crimes'. These unfortunates were exploited as unpaid labour, physically and psychically brutalized for the duration of a sentence the length of which was deliberately unspecified, on occasion ending only with the victim's death. Widely quoted estimates state that some 30,000 women passed through the Magdalene laundry system before the last asylum closed its doors in 1996.[14]

12 Debbie Ging, 'Screening the green: cinema under the Celtic Tiger', in Peadar Kirby, Luke Gibbons and Michael Cronin (eds), *Reinventing Ireland: culture, society and the global economy*, London: Pluto Press, 2002: 183. 13 Martin McLoone, *Irish film: the emergence of a contemporary cinema*, London: BFI, 2000: 200. 14 For a succinct journalistic overview of the Magdalene asylums, see Fintan O'Toole, 'The sisters of no mercy', *The Observer*, Review, 16 February 2003: 6.

The Magdalene Sisters was initially inspired by, and subsequently based closely upon, extensive video testimonies recorded for a range of television documentaries on the subject of the laundry system. The film's writer/director Peter Mullan structured his script around the representative original 'crimes' and subsequent imprisonment of four actual victims of the Magdalene asylums. These he transposed to a central quartet of fictional teenage characters in the finished film.[15] The opening sequences of *The Magdalene Sisters* provide short back-stories for three of the main characters' respective incarcerations. Margaret's family, acting on the advice of their priest, send her away after she is raped by a cousin during a family wedding; Rose is ostracized by her parents after giving birth to a child outside of wedlock; Bernadette is expelled from the orphanage where she lives simply for being 'too pretty', and therefore a temptation to local men. The trio are for four years trapped in a laundry run by the sadistic Sister Bridget, exploited as unpaid labour and physically and psychologically maltreated throughout. Eventually, Margaret's brother secures his sister's release; Bernadette and Rose make a forcible and successful escape. End titles sketch the basic trajectories of the characters' subsequent lives.

A recurrent feature of the near-universally rapturous critical notices of the film in Britain involved the assertion that the film throws into relief the artistic and cultural bankruptcy of much American cinema and demonstrates the innate superiority of European national alternatives that remain largely unsullied by transatlantic influence. This led to claims that *The Magdalene Sisters* 'has an emotional complexity and lasting impact that knocks spots off your average Hollywood production' and that it 'points Scottish cinema in an inspiring new direction that owes more to popular European cinema than to [...] America'.[16] Although these viewpoints echo more general critical anxieties about the direction of Scottish and/or Irish cinemas outlined above, they are, nonetheless, misguided. First, *The Magdalene Sisters* is notable for its judicious use, not ostentatious rejection, of a number of American cinematic influences and reference points. Second, these borrowings indicate neither the film's wholesale submission to American popular culture influences nor an indigenous critique of them. Rather, *The Magdalene Sisters*' Hollywood intertext works in ways that are not only commercially astute in an international arena but also politically radical in a domestic context.

In the first instance, Hollywood cinematic influences and reference points grant both the text, and the highly specific historical and cultural milieu it depicts, a degree of cross-cultural legibility, and therefore marketability. In

15 See the director's comments in Robert McMillen, 'A life of misery', *Irish News*, 3 January 2003: 21; Steve Pratt, 'Scrubbing away the sin of single motherhood', *Northern Echo*, 18 February 2003: 11. 16 Allan Hunter, 'Church of the poisoned mind', *Daily Express*, 21 February 2003: 41; Hannah McGill, 'The bigger picture', *Glasgow Herald*, 8 March 2003: 18.

the second case, these references are used to highlight the mutually supportive existence and influence of parallel oppressive idealizations of Catholic feminine identities within the Irish and American national spheres. This creates a complex acknowledgement and exploration of a range of historical-cultural reasons for, and the degree of domestic complicity in, the existence of the Magdalene asylums. The laundries and the associated discourses of gender and denominational identity from which they drew social legitimation are therefore neither mystified nor reified into an inexplicably exclusive and essentialized Irish national neurosis.

The Magdalene Sisters engages with the pragmatic challenge of commodifying its locally specific and traumatic subject-matter for international markets through the adoption of a sub-generic narrative framework derived from classical Hollywood practice. Contrary to the crudely anti-American effusions the film's commercial and critical success provoked, its most perceptive contemporary reviewers pointed out that 'what we're really watching here is a prison movie'.[17] In interview, Mullan stressed the openness and consciousness of this creative decision: 'It's in the tradition of [*One Flew over the*] *Cuckoo's Nest* (Milos Forman, 1975) and [*The*] *Shawshank* [*Redemption*] (Frank Darabont, 1994) – an old-fashioned drama'.[18] While the text's narrative events and character experiences are drawn from documentary testimony, many of these are narratively and generically codified, particularly in the film's early stages. The laundry is partly constructed as a local variant upon the more universal narrative trope of the corrupt prison and/or political regime's centre of detention. Its inmates abruptly disappear or are summarily removed from their former homes in unmarked cars at break of dawn; Sister Bridget is initially presented as the sadistic Head Warden, taunting the central trio with the punitive terms of their sentence; victims are institutionally stripped of their given names and personal histories (Rose becomes not a number, but 'Patricia'); minor characters quickly instigate the prison movie's standard generic subplots, themes and character types, such as the difficulty but necessity of escape (Oona O'Connor) and the decrepit or psychically broken collaborator (Kate and Oona respectively).

Yet in the industrially and culturally vulnerable contexts of highly localized national production, such commodifying strategies should not only be assessed with reference to the criteria of technical execution and commercial success. Texts may satisfy the latter and yet still constitute reactionary, or at best apolitical, interventions within local political and cultural contexts. The danger is that aspirant commercialism entails the dilution of national and regional representations to the point of banality or trivialization for either

17 Anthony Quinn, 'The Sisters Grimm', *The Independent*, 21 February 2003: 8. 18 Quoted in Cameron Simpson, 'Mullan welcomes "humble" Catholic opinion', *Glasgow Herald*, 17 February 2003: 2.

domestic or international audiences. From this viewpoint, there is a risk that the depiction and assessment of historically specific individual and national trauma is sidelined and becomes little more than a 'testimony to the way the human spirit can survive even the most appalling hardships'.[19] Fintan O'Toole, for example, sees this as an unavoidable drawback to *The Magdalene Sisters.* For him, the film's success ultimately does no more than illustrate the outermost, but stubbornly impenetrable, boundaries that constrain the bittersweet Celtic cinematic phenomenon that is 'Hollywood regionalism':

> [It] worked so well in Ireland [because ...] it does belong in a familiar genre: the Hollywood prison drama [...]. Particularly in a small and relatively intimate society... the conventions of a familiar genre dull the pain a little.[20]

In contrast, it is my contention here that it is precisely the text's accomplished engagement with Hollywood cinematic precedents and reference points that facilitates its radical and complex intervention within local histories for domestic audiences, rather than, as O'Toole implies, compromising this valuable project.

One key sequence in the film indicates how the film invites a complex reading of Scottish/Irish and American national cultural and cinematic exchanges. Towards the film's end, the laundry inmates are given a brief respite from their backbreaking labours on Christmas Day. Before the assembled internees and a smattering of local religious and business dignitaries, Sr Bridget confesses 'a secret love [...] since I have been 13 years old, I have been in love with the films'. This is a prelude to an unaccustomed 'treat', the screening of a surprise movie. The film in question has been chosen by an attending prelate, and is the saccharine Hollywood film *The Bells of St Mary's* (Leo McCarey, 1945). In this film, Bing Crosby and Ingrid Bergman play a worldly priest and devout nun at loggerheads over the running of a parochial school threatened by closure, but not so preoccupied that they cannot save the dilapidated premises and vulnerable young souls housed within. The bitterly ironic contrast between beatific American fiction of Catholic institutional charity and the horrific Irish experience of the same phenomenon is obvious to fictionalized inmates and cinema audiences alike. Oblivious to the cultural incongruity and personal hypocrisy involved, Bridget weeps at Sr Benedict/Bergman's onscreen plea to God to 'help me see Thy Holy Will in all things'. The intercut reaction shots of Rose, Margaret and Bernadette reveal their despairing alienation from both their local persecutors and external popular culture.

19 Allan Hunter, 'A cry from the heart', *Scotland on Sunday*, Review, 16 February 2003: 9. **20** O'Toole, 'Sisters of no mercy', 6. My insert.

At first viewing, it does indeed seem that American cinema has ensured that even if the laundry's physical torture has momentarily ceased, its psychological equivalent proceeds unabated, underscoring the ideological importance of 'Hollywood collu[sion] in the promotion of the inviolate sanctity of priests and nuns'[21] within mid-twentieth century Irish society. Bridget's position of power, and her abuse of it through acquiescence in authoritarian discourses bolstered by hypocritical claims of denominational sanctity and sexual purity, is both emphasized and ridiculed through its incongruous equation with a contemporary American analogue. The latter might in turn be seen as contributing to, and legitimating, her status as a willing and energetic tool of local institutionalized oppression. Indeed, Bridget confesses in her introduction to *Bells of St Mary's* that she does not 'love' just any kind of film, but that Hollywood genre *par excellence*, the Western, above all. As she recalls 'the look on my dear mother's face the day I told her that if I didn't get into the convent and give my life to God, then I'd be a cowboy instead'. It is difficult to resist the too-easy inference that the popular cultural and ideological milieu she left behind (American cinema) is by definition as compromised as, and somehow forms a facilitating precursor to, that which she subsequently embraced (Irish institutional Catholicism). Such a reading invites the construction of an opposition between regressive American cinematic interventions into local societies and an emergent, politically legitimate Celtic film culture (embodied in a film like *The Magdalene Sisters*). In this over-simplistic reading, the latter simply aims to provide an ideological corrective to the heinous consequences of traditional national and popular cultural oppression imposed from across the Atlantic.

Yet the *Bells of St Mary's* sequence is open to a more dialectical reading of the troubled historical interchanges between American and Irish cultures depicted in *The Magdalene Sisters*. A more nuanced understanding of the thematic workings of both this scene and its pivotal function within the ideological structures of the text as a whole allows for a re-examination of some of the key terms of contemporary Scottish and Irish debates on the industrial and national-cultural consequences of contemporary Hollywood cinematic influence.

The conservative local impact of the *Bells of St Mary's*, and that of the wider classical Hollywood Catholic cycle of which it is a synecdoche, is not simply the product of intrinsically reactionary textual features or of the national culture and film industry that produced them. It also derives from its selective appropriation within a particular socio-historical context. *Bells* is specifi-

21 Alexander Walker, 'Lost in schmaltzy limbo', *London Evening Standard*, 20 February 2003: 46. It is perhaps worth noting that this particular critic's position on the film may also be seen in the light of his persistent criticisms of British and American cinematic representations of Ireland (and particularly Northern Ireland) past and present which, he argues, systematically idealize Republican identities, histories and cultures and denigrate their Unionist counterparts.

cally chosen and approved by the local archbishop and screened on projection equipment donated, as Sister Bridget informs the girls, by 'Mr Laneghan, one of Dublin's most respected businessmen'. Thus, the repressive exercise of material and cultural authority by representatives of native institutional and economic capital legitimates the inmates' incarceration and demonization *in tandem* with the cinematic discourses of Catholic femininity that in national-cultural terms are imported from without.

There are, therefore, severe limitations to readings of *The Magdalene Sisters* that would place exclusive or predominant emphasis upon the problematic fact of mid-twentieth-century Irish (or for that matter, Scottish)[22] popular cultural 'colonization' at the hands of a commercially and industrially dominant Hollywood cinema. This is so whether such analyses are mainly concerned to uncover the recent contours of Scottish and Irish cultural and social histories, or to employ *The Magdalene Sisters* as a standard-bearer for contemporary Celtic national cinemas that disavow creative or institutional recourse to transatlantic filmic influences and precedents. Such approaches run the risk of fostering a reductive binarism in the identity politics at work within modern Scottish and/or Irish filmic and wider national spheres. In contrast, *The Magdalene Sisters*' dual engagement with Irish history, US cinema and the material interactions between the two is more complex. It simultaneously acknowledges, yet also seeks to harness for progressive ends, the enduring centrality of Hollywood cinema as a refractive lens through which shared identity and experience on both sides of the Irish Sea have often been conceptualized. Through *The Magdalene Sisters*' careful foregrounding of the interlocking hegemonies of institutional Catholicism and American popular culture at work in the laundries, a multifaceted reading of subaltern local histories and identities emerges. This reading is one structured by the vital understanding that the differential allocation of political, economic and cultural capital inside colonized societies is administered *within*, as well as across, national borders.

Therefore, the textual prominence accorded to *The Bells of St Mary's*' reactionary, desexualized discourse of Catholic femininity does not connote Irish culture's repressive subjugation by a more powerful American Other. Rather, the sequence in question creates a deliberate formal and thematic parallel with the equally disturbing spectacle of the repressive role of indigenous and pre-cinematic popular cultural traditions as presented in *The Magdalene Sisters*' much remarked upon opening scene. Here, a priest sings the traditional ballad 'The Well Below the Valley' at the family wedding during the course of which Margaret is 'disgraced' by her rape. 'Well' is one of the texts (no. 21) collect-

22 Peter Mullan has persistently noted in interviews the ubiquity and contemporary influence of classical Hollywood representations of Catholicism within the 1960s and 1970s Scottish Catholic community in which he grew up. For a representative example, see the director's comments in James Mottram, 'The asylum seeker', *Scotland on Sunday*, Review, 8 September 2002: 1.

ed in the seminal foundational work of British Ballad Studies, F.J. Child's edited collection *The English and Scottish Popular Ballads* (5 volumes, 1882–98). It is a folk re-telling of the story of Christ and the Woman of Samaria (*John* 4:1–42). The text in all its variants narrates the meeting between a male stranger and a woman at a well, of whom the former begs a drink. It engages with precisely the issues of patriarchially-sanctioned sexual and/or familial abuse of women that are about to disrupt Margaret's life within the film. These include incest ('For six young children you had born/...There's two of them by your Uncle Dan') and infanticide ('There's two buried 'neath the stable door').[23] The imaginary male stranger's pitiless reaction to, and prediction of, the woman's blameless damnation ('You'll be seven years a-ringing the bell/You'll be seven more burning in hell') structures and anticipates those of the material male authority figure performing the ballad. It is the priest who both advises Margaret's family that she should be removed to the Laundry and transports her there himself. Finally, the woman at the well's combative response to the stranger ('I'll be seven years a-ringing the bell/But the lord above may save my soul/From burning in hell') is equally significant. It articulates the logic of female salvation through traumatic penitence for the 'sin' of falling victim to male abuse. This is precisely the native cultural discourse that legitimates the barbarism of Margaret's immediate ostracization and incarceration and the silent communal acquiescence in this. The explanatory historical analysis *The Magdalene Sisters* offers for the existence of the laundry system in Ireland is, therefore, one that stresses the material effects within local society of a range of prescriptive models of femininity, whether these are given a specifically denominational coding or not. Vitally, such models are presented as independently generated within distinctive Irish and American national cultures at different historical periods and across a range of creative media.

Read in this manner, *The Magdalene Sisters* becomes an important film for Scottish and Irish cinema studies for two reasons. Its complex interrogation of a troubled and until recently taboo aspect of local histories is, of course, to be welcomed in and of itself; yet the terms in which that interrogation is conducted also seem suggestive of more productive approaches to the issue of the American influence so often privileged and bemoaned within millennial local film criticism. In *The Magdalene Sisters*' historical diegesis, as within the contemporary local film-industrial nexus from which it sprang, the key problem that should preoccupy us is not the spectre of local cultures succumbing to waves of ideological colonization from without (specifically, American film). Rather, the phenomenon to be contested is that of local cultures whose public representatives

23 Indeed, these two subjects provide central and recurrent themes for the traditional ballad corpus of the British Isles. See, for example, Deborah Symonds, *Weep not for me: women, ballads and infanticide in early modern Scotland*, University Park, Penn.: Pennsylvania State University Press, 1997.

conceptualize the domestic impact of external cultural influences upon local cultural identities and traditions in simplistic and reductive terms. This can quickly degenerate into a policing of the construction of idealized and increasingly mono-accentual models of national film cultures and identities.

After all, Bridget's compromised status is signalled in the text not through her subordination to an essentially reactionary American cinematic apparatus, but rather by her active desire to engage with this particular form of cultural difference (and, indeed, with all others) in Manichean terms, deified, as in *The Bells of St Mary's*, or demonized, as with every Western produced since the advent of sound, 'gone the way of the devil like so much of the modern world'. Nothing is left in-between. Critical approaches to ongoing Scottish and Irish industrial consolidation and cultural diversification should avoid constructing a methodological analogue of Bridget's binaristic world-view. There is limited mileage in proposing an unavoidable and definitive choice between 'convent' and 'cowboys', European indigeneity and American ubiquity, for either or both national cinemas. Identifying the most commercially productive and culturally progressive national filmmaking models, local adaptations of which will further nurture both Scottish and Irish film cultures, is too important and complex a task for such analytical indulgences. Scottish and Irish cinemas are national cultural phenomena that in their increasing maturity cannot, as *The Magdalene Sisters* illustrates, be necessarily, entirely or ideally reduced to a set of self-consciously corrective local responses against traditional and/or contemporary transatlantic cinematic influences active in the domestic sphere.

Key in this respect are the secondary characters of Father Fitzroy, the priest who supposedly ministers to the spiritual needs of the asylum but systematically rapes Crispina, a mentally handicapped internee, and Srs Jude and Clementine, the nuns who sexually humiliate their defenceless charges. The pathetically and destructively stunted nature of this trio's identities and actions (particularly in their sexual aspects) is constructed, as with the character of Bridget, as representative of wider historical institutional and national pathologies. Significantly, however, the explanation offered for the existence of the latter here proceeds not, as in Bridget's case, through a diagnosis of native exposure to, and active fashioning of, an ideological contagion extracted from popular American film. By contrast, Fitzroy, Jude and Clementine are deployed in order to flag a contemporary local inability to competently, let alone progressively, appropriate and/or innovate film production technologies and creative approaches *of any kind*. Thus, Fitzroy brings a new 8mm camera to the asylum in order to document a rare moment of respite, the inmates' sports day. The *naïveté* of the technology involved, his incompetence in deploying it (audience point-of-view is briefly confined to the priest's shaky footage) and the nuns' painful gaucherie in front of what is, in local historical terms, the unfamiliar presence of the recording elements of the cinematic apparatus ('try to act natural' Fitzroy exhorts, in a moment of black comedy) are made clearly apparent.

Ultimately, then, *The Magdalene Sisters* allows audiences to understand a previous moment in Irish history and culture as both externally oppressed and internally oppressive not simply because of the remarkable local domination and/or misappropriation of Hollywood cinema (Bridget), or because of that cinema's symbiotic ideological relationships with indigenous cultural formations ('The Well below the Valley'). Equally telling is the contemporary material absence and/or practical impossibility of any sort of distinctive indigenous audiovisual culture (Fitzroy, Jude, Clementine), let alone one structured by a carefully exclusive hierarchy of admissible industrial and formal influences garnered from other national film cultures. *The Magdalene Sisters* itself powerfully illustrates the progressive local political impact that the Celtic cinemas which emerged in the wake of the historical period this film depicts can at their best make. The radical terms of this film's interventions within vexed debates about national history and identity mirror, and give credence to, those employed by the most voluble supporters of a range of national cinema projects within the Atlantic Archipelago.[24]

Given the film's potentially talismanic status for Scottish and Irish film cultures and criticisms, it seems important to acknowledge that *The Magdalene Sisters*' impressive international commercial and national cultural achievements largely spring from its simultaneously entrepreneurial and critical engagement with a range of American filmmaking precedents and traditions. If *The Magdalene Sisters* offers encouraging material illustration of an area of critical consensus, namely the progressive potential of emergent Scottish and Irish cinemas, then it also creates an equally heartening complication of a hotly contested one, the rightful place (if any) of American influences in the successful completion of those cross-cultural projects. The film foregrounds perhaps the most urgent challenge facing millennial Scottish and Irish filmmakers and academic critics alike. In the face of persistent disdain and complaint, it stubbornly remains the case that at present, 'contemporary Irish film [like its Scottish counterpart] is imbued with, yet gives localised inflection to, US film genres'.[25] *The Magdalene Sisters* shows both the necessity and virtue of ongoing local explorations and reformations of, but not definitive alienation from, these kinds of national film cultural landscapes. Their topography will never be adequately navigated with a critical compass whose fixed points reproduce the damaging illusion of definitive Scottish and Irish choices to be made between monolithic poles of 'mart' and 'art', 'Hollywood' and 'Europe'.

24 See, for example, John Hill, 'British cinema as national cinema: production, audience and representation', in Robert Murphy (ed.), *The British cinema book*, London: BFI, 1996: 244–54. 25 Lance Pettitt, *Screening Ireland: film and television representation*, Manchester: Manchester University Press, 2000: 276. My insert.

Notes on contributors

DENIS CONDON received a BA in English and German at St Patrick's College, Maynooth. His MA research for the School of Applied Languages and Intercultural Studies, Dublin City University, focused on cinematic portrayals of youth rebellion as a way of expressing dissent in East Germany. He is currently working on a PhD at the Centre for Media Studies at the National University of Ireland, Maynooth, on early film and the cinema in Ireland before the foundation of the state. The essay in this volume is taken from this work, showing how key Irish-produced films drew on a variety of representational strategies in constructing an Irish national identity.

MAEVE CONNOLLY graduated from the National College of Art and Design with a BA in Fine Art (Sculpture) in 1992. She has exhibited video and photographic work at the City Arts Centre and Project, Dublin, the Context Gallery in Derry, and other venues. She also developed site-specific work for exhibitions such as EV+A in Limerick. In 1998, she completed an MA in Film and Television Studies at Dublin City University. Her research interests encompass national cinemas, televisual culture, avant-garde film and contemporary arts policy. She was awarded a PhD in 2004 for a study of Irish film and the avant-garde at the School of Communications, Dublin City University, research which was supported by a Government of Ireland Scholarship from the Irish Research Council for the Humanities and Social Sciences. Previous publications include *The glass eye: artists and television* (2000), co-edited with Orla Ryan, as well as reviews and articles for journals such as *Circa* and *Variant*. She has lectured on film and arts practice at Dublin City University, Dundalk Institute of Technology, and currently teaches film studies, specializing in animation, at Dun Laoghaire Institute of Art, Design and Technology.

TOM GUNNING is Edwin A. and Betty L. Bergman Distinguished Service Professor in the Art History Department at the University of Chicago. Author of *D.W. Griffith and the origins of American narrative film* (1991) and the *The films of Fritz Lang: allegories of modernity and vision* (2000), he has written numerous essays on early and international silent cinema, and on American cinema, including Hollywood genres and directors as well as avant-garde film. He has lectured around the world and his works have been published in a dozen languages. His recent work has centred on the role that film and photography play in the rethinking of the body and perception in the modern era, especially the turn of the nineteenth to the twentieth century, exploring the way that film and photography allowed new representations of space, time and the body which were triggered by the major technological and sociological changes of that era.

JOHN HILL is Professor of Media Studies at the University of Ulster. He is the author, co-author or co-editor of a number of books, including *Sex, class and realism: British cinema, 1956–63* (1986), *Cinema and Ireland* (1987), *Border crossing: film in Ireland, Britain and Europe* (1994), *The Oxford guide to film studies* (1998) and *British cinema in the 1980s* (1999). His history of the cinema and Northern Ireland is due to appear in 2005.

DANIJELA KULEZIC-WILSON attained a BA in musicology at the University of Belgrade. She worked as an editor at Radio-Television of Serbia, wrote music and film music reviews for newspapers and magazines, is a member of the editorial board of the magazine *Musical Wave* in Belgrade and occasionally writes for the *Journal of Music in Ireland*. She is currently a post-graduate student at the University of Ulster working on a thesis on screen musicality, examining the relationship of film and music. It explores the common parameters between these two arts – time, rhythm and movement – and also applies musical criteria to film in order to examine how certain characteristics typical of music can be found in film on the structural, expressive, and affective levels. The article in this volume is drawn from this research.

DERVILA LAYDEN received a BA (Modular) degree at University College Dublin, and an MA (Narrative and Modernity) at NUI, Maynooth. She is currently working on a PhD at the Centre for Film Studies, UCD, which involves the examination of stories told in both written and filmed literature in Ireland between the years 1991 and 2001. The research is particularly concerned with identifying how stories have mobilized and reflected change over the decade and what story types have been prevalent in this change. The paper in this volume is an excerpt from the research, dealing with two specifically Northern Ireland films analyzing the ways in which they document cultural and political change in Northern Ireland, and also how they provide a space for negotiating this process of change.

BARRY MONAHAN received a BA in Drama Studies (Trinity College Dublin), an MA in Film Studies (University College Dublin) and his PhD (TCD) for a study focusing primarily on the relationship between the Abbey Theatre and Ardmore Studios (2004).

JOSEPH MOSER received a BA in Fine Arts in Creative Writing and Literature from Emerson College, Boston. His fiction has appeared in *The Emerson Review* literary magazine, and in a creative writing textbook, *Where the stories come from: beginning to write fiction*. In 2003, he was awarded an MA degree in English from the University of Texas at Austin, and is currently pursuing a PhD and teaching a course in rhetoric and composition at UT-Austin. His article in this volume is drawn from his Master's thesis and he plans to expand his discussion of Jim Sheridan's films as part of a dissertation that will also include analysis of Irish drama.

JONATHAN MURRAY teaches in the Centre for Visual and Cultural Studies at Edinburgh College of Art. He is currently completing a PhD thesis on 1990s Scottish cinema at the University of Glasgow, and has published a number of scholarly articles, radio documentaries and comment pieces on various aspects of Scottish film culture past and present.

SARAH NEELY completed a BA in Communications and English Literature at the University of Iowa in 1996, and received an MPhil from the University of Glasgow in Creative Writing. She has recently completed a PhD in the Department of Theatre, Film and Television and the Department of English Literature at the University of Glasgow, researching the adaptation of contemporary Scottish and Irish literature and film. She has also written on a number of other areas of film adaptation including the teen film and Shakespeare. Her thesis focused on the adapted works of several writers, including Bernard MacLaverty, Patrick McCabe, Christy Brown, Roddy Doyle, Irvine Welsh, Christopher Rush, Alan Warner, and William McIlvanney. The subject of the paper in this volume draws together the various issues surrounding the voice-over reoccurring throughout the thesis. She is currently a Lecturer in Media Studies at the University of Paisley, Scotland where she teaches courses on adaptation, British cinema, and scriptwriting.

DIÓG O'CONNELL received a BA at University College Dublin and a MA at Dublin City University. From 1993 to 1999 she was Lecturer and Course Leader of Media and Communications Studies at Mary Immaculate College, University of Limerick. In 2000 she was appointed Lecturer in Film and Media Studies at Dún Laoghaire Institute of Art, Design and Technology. Her teaching and research is informed by her practical work in film and television drama. The article in this collection is based on research being carried out in the pursuit of a PhD at DCU, part of a thesis concerned with an analysis of contemporary Irish film (1993–2003), focusing especially on those films that have been supported by the Irish Film Board.

MARGARET O'NEILL received a BA in Media Studies from the University of Ulster in 1995, having written a dissertation on the representation of women in the films of Ingmar Bergman, and received an MA in Film and Television from the University of Warwick in 1998, with a thesis on the ethnographic documentaries of Trinh T. Minh-ha. She is presently researching issues of memory and trauma in both documentary and fiction film for a PhD in the Department of Radio/Television/Film at Northwestern University, Chicago, and is a teaching assistant in the School of Communication at Northwestern.

EMILIE PINE received a BA in English from Trinity College Dublin, after which she spent a year studying film at postgraduate level at the University of California, Berkeley. She is currently completing her PhD thesis at Trinity College on a study of Irish film and theatre in the 1930s. The project seeks to put film and drama of this decade into context by looking at the cultural, social and economic factors that influenced production and consumption during this period.

KEVIN ROCKETT is a Lecturer in Film Studies and Fellow at Trinity College Dublin. He is the author, co-author or editor of a number of books, including *Cinema and Ireland* (1987), *Still Irish: a century of the Irish in film* (1995), *The Irish filmography: fiction films 1896–1996* (1996), *The companion to British and Irish cinema* (1996), *Neil Jordan: exploring boundaries* (2003), *Ten years after: the Irish Film Board, 1993–2003* (2003), and *The Los Angelesation of Ireland: film censorship, culture and society* (2004).

ELLEN E. SWEENEY received a BA in English from Bryn Mawr College and an MA from New York University's John W. Draper Program in the Humanities and Social Thought where she concentrated on the representations of trauma in literature and film. The article in this collection is adapted from her Master's thesis, and is the first step in her doctoral project in the Film Studies Program at the University of Iowa: a comparative analysis of cinematic representations of trauma and their relationship to national history in Irish and Hindi (popular) cinema.

Index

Compiled by Julitta Clancy, Registered Indexer